THE NEW HIGH-YIELD DEBT MARKET
A Handbook for Portfolio Managers and Analysts

The New High-Yield Debt Market

A Handbook for Portfolio Managers and Analysts

Edited by
Frank J. Fabozzi

Associate Editor
Rayner Cheung

HarperBusiness
A Division of HarperCollins*Publishers*

International Standard Book Number: 0–88730–430–3

Library of Congress Catalog Card Number: 90–43694

Printed in the United States of America

Library of Congress Cataloging-in-Publication Data

The new high-yield debt market : a handbook for portfolio managers and
  analysts / [edited] by Frank J. Fabozzi : associate editor, Rayner
  Cheung.
    p.   cm.
  Includes index.
ISBN 0-88730-430-3
  1. Bonds. 2. Portfolio management. I. Fabozzi, Frank J.
II. Cheung, Rayner, 1964-
HG4651.N37   1990
332.63'23 — dc20   90-43694
                                                            CIP

90 91 92 93 MM/HC 9 8 7 6 5 4 3 2 1

CONTENTS

v

PREFACE

As a source of capital for small- and medium-sized growth companies, high-yield bonds have proven to be an important financial innovation. By mitigating what had been inefficient and highly illiquid market conditions, the development of the high-yield market into a $200+ billion financial institution has provided both issuers and investors with many opportunities. Prior to the introduction of original issue high-yield bonds, growth companies with no credit history depended almost exclusively on restrictive bank financing to fund their growth. Equity markets were accessible only to firms in the few industries deemed fashionable by Wall Street pundits — computers, cellular telephones, and biotechnology being the most obvious examples. A few firms did manage to raise mezzanine capital through private placements with insurance companies and high net worth investors, but illiquidity raised financing costs to levels that were prohibitive for all but a fraction of the companies eligible for this type of financing. However, the existence of a healthy private placement market for mezzanine debt did illustrate one essential feature of this type of security: in the long run, investors who held diversified portfolios of this low-rated debt earned returns that were unambiguously superior to returns on less risky debt instruments such as government bonds and high-grade corporates. This fundamental fact has not changed.

The growth of the public high-yield bond market coincided with the longest postwar economic expansion in the United States. Economic stability provided the ideal environment in which to test-market high-yield securities. Investors who participated in the high-yield market during its early years (1977–1983) were well rewarded by excess returns and, surprisingly, relatively stable prices and market liquidity.

These excess returns, in turn, attracted increasingly larger amounts of capital into high-yield bonds, and for a while there was too much money chasing too few issuers. Although yield spreads did narrow, the principal effect of the supply–demand imbalance was to drive deal quality to the point where yield spreads no longer compensated for the implied risks. This process was brought about, in part, by Wall Street firms competing for market share in what had become a highly lucrative segment of the investment banking industry. As their enthusiasm for underwriting spreads grew, the bankers' competence for due diligence became compromised. Many marginal deals were completed purely for the fees and the prestige they would bring to their underwriters. Most were sold under highly untenable assumptions — for instance, that earnings would indefinitely continue to grow ("hockey stick projections") or that escalating asset values would permit the owners to refinance on much more attractive terms. Optimism was the rule, and while many sound financings were underwritten, the proportion of poorly structured deals increased dramatically. By late 1988, the supply–demand imbalance had been reversed, and to keep investor interest from waning, many issuers were forced to offer higher-yield spreads.

The troubles experienced in recent years in the high-yield market, and the well-publicized case of Michael Milken, have made some influential federal and state lawmakers and regulators question the economic role and viability of this market. However, as a May 1, 1990 *New York Times* editorial ("The Perils of Bashing Junk Bonds") noted:

> Michael Milken is a convicted felon. But he is also a financial genius who transformed high-risk bonds — junk bonds — into a lifeline of credit for hundreds of emerging companies. Snubbed by the banks, these businesses would otherwise have shriveled.
>
> In other words, the Milken case presents issues far more important than one person's slide from the financial pinnacle. There is no condoning Mr. Milken's criminality. But if overzealous Government regulators overreact by indiscriminately dismantling his junk bond legacy, they will wind up crushing the most dynamic parts of the economy....
>
> What's needed is not vindictive junk bond bashing; it's prudent financial regulation. For example, it makes sense to outlaw greenmail. It makes sense to help regulatory authorities by requiring that pension funds, insurance companies and banks provide updated figures for the market value of their junk bonds and other assets.

But a frenzied attack on all junk bonds makes no sense. If that continues, the nation will wind up transforming Michael Milken's downfall into an economic catastrophe.

Unfortunately, this warning may have come too late. With the benefit of hindsight, it can now be said that the one single event that sealed the fate of the high-yield bond market was the passage in August 1989 of the Financial Institutions Reform, Recovery, and Enforcement Act (FIRREA), the savings and loan bailout bill, which forced all thrift institutions to divest their holdings of high-yield bonds by August 1994. Although Congress was legitimately concerned about the use of federally insured monies to invest in highly speculative debt instruments, at the time of FIRREA's passage no thrift had actually failed because of imprudent investments in junk bonds. In fact, empirical evidence did not support the strong anti–high-yield bond position taken by Congress. One study found that, of all the investments available to savings institutions in the United States, high-yield bonds were second only to credit cards in terms of historical return performance. In another study, Professor Lawrence White of New York University, once a member of the former Federal Home Loan Bank Board, found that the losses experienced by S&Ls attributable to their investment in high-yield bonds were small. Nevertheless, under tremendous political pressure to dampen the wave of junk-financed takeovers and buyouts, Congress opted to ban S&Ls from further investments in non–investment grade instruments. This effectively removed 10 percent of the new issuance buying power from the market.

By itself, preventing new investments in high-yield bonds would not have caused this market to collapse; new deals would have been held back until sufficient numbers of new buyers could be found to replace the S&Ls. However, when Congress further required these institutions to divest all their junk bonds within five years, 7 percent of all high-yield holdings were effectively dumped onto the market, and liquidity vanished. Within a month of FIRREA's passage, the high-yield market began to decline dramatically. As of this writing, the yield spread of the "average" high-yield bond has widened from a historical average of 450 basis points off Treasuries to between 800 and 900 basis points. Prices have fallen an average of 20–25 percent as new buyers have failed to emerge in sufficient numbers to meet the distressed sellers.

In one sense, Congress' concern about federally insured monies funding low-rated credits was justified; several S&Ls have become insolvent after they were forced by FIRREA to mark their high-yield bonds to market. The fact that Congress bootstrapped itself into this crisis is also obvious: to justify an 850-basis-point yield spread, the expected annual default rate must exceed 8.7 percent (assuming an average recovery rate of 15 cents per dollar), and no one seriously believes that $17 billion of junk bonds will default every year.

Heightened perceptions of default risk did not cause the high yield market to collapse. Rather, it was the federally mandated S&L divestiture, together with the resulting disappearance of market liquidity, which brought about its demise. Put another way, if Congress were to force seven homeowners out of every hundred to sell their homes within five years, would not home prices decline 20 percent, 30 percent, 50 percent? And what would be the effect on the other 93 if they had to mark their financial statements to market at that moment?

At the time of this writing, there are proposed federal and state regulations that would either have pension funds and insurance companies divest their holdings of high-yield bonds, severely limit the amount they hold, or impose requirements that will make holding these securities less attractive. For example, the National Association of Insurance Commissioners is planning to propose rules that would increase the reserves on high-yield bonds held by insurance companies. This will limit the participation of these companies, which as a group hold about one-third of outstanding issues, presently making them the largest investor group.

Given the troubles facing the high-yield bond market, it would seem that a book on how to invest in this market is ill-advised. We don't think that this is the case at all. In a market sector where sellers are forced because of regulation and/or marked-to-market constraints to dispose of their holdings, attractive investment opportunities arise. Although liquidity concerns are justified, there are some investors, such as pension funds, that do not have this concern. Further concerns over liquidity and interim price volatility eventually prove ephemeral because they have no actual bearing on the payment of principal and interest.

However, those who plan to take advantage of the investment opportunities that arise must have the skills to identify mispriced securities and a strategy for managing a diversified portfolio of these securities. The purpose of this book is to provide state-of-the-art strategies for capitalizing on the opportunities in this market.

To be effective, a book of this nature should offer a broad perspective. The experiences of a wide range of experts are more informative than those of a single expert, particularly because of the diversity of opinion on some issues.

Frank J. Fabozzi, Editor
Rayner Cheung, Associate Editor

SECTION I

Background

1

High-Yield Bonds, Corporate Control, and Innovation

John D. Paulus
Managing Director and
Chief Economist
Morgan Stanley & Co. Incorporated

Stephen R. Waite
Economist
Morgan Stanley & Co. Incorporated

The development of the high-yield bond market in the 1980s may constitute the most important financial innovation in the United States since the creation of a national securities market during World War I, when Liberty Bonds were sold on a widespread basis to American households. There are two reasons for advancing this admittedly ambitious claim. First, high-yield securities have been instrumental in the development of an active market for corporate control, where large blocks of capital can be mobilized to gain control of undervalued corporate assets. The restructured business units, in which incentives are dramatically altered by providing senior management and directors with meaningful equity stakes, have generally enjoyed impressive improvements in operating cash flow and worker productivity. Second, these securities have provided an important source of finance for many new companies in high-growth, innovative industries, often operating on the frontiers of technology. Without the high-yield market, many of these companies, which are now offering products and services undreamed of by the public little more than a decade ago, would have been stymied in their attempts to expand.

3

In the first section of this chapter, we offer a complete classification of the $187 billion of high-yield bonds that has been issued since 1983 according to the functional use of the proceeds — funding leveraged buyouts and recapitalizations; financing rapidly growing, innovative industries; aiding fallen angels, and so on. In the second section, we examine the contribution of high-yield bonds to the market for corporate control and analyze their effect on efficiency in American business. In the third section, we describe the role of high-yield bonds in nurturing rapidly growing, mostly new industries that produce either highly innovative products or goods and services that enhance the quality of life in America. In the fourth and final section, we offer a few observations on the likely future course of the high-yield bond market.

Who Uses High-Yield Bonds and Why

Since 1983, $187 billion of high-yield bonds has been issued to the public, with annual issuance reaching a peak of $41.8 billion in 1986, as shown in Exhibit 1. New issue volume has tended to decrease slightly since then, with the calendar falling to $37.5 billion and $34.7 billion in 1987 and 1988, respectively. Through the first nine months of 1989, new high-yield bond issuance totaled $24.6 billion. Still, even while decelerating, the rate of expansion of the outstanding volume of high-yield bonds will exceed 15 percent in 1989.

The shaded portion of each bar in the figure represents the volume of high-yield bonds that was devoted to financing corporate control activity associated with free cash flow — mainly leveraged buyouts (LBOs) — and the figure above each bar is the percentage of total high-yield proceeds used each year for that purpose. Notice that in the last three years the share averaged just under 50 percent; before 1987 it averaged around 15 percent, indicating that, at least in recent years, a larger portion of new issue bonds has been devoted to financing the market for corporate control. For reasons to be discussed in the final section, this trend is likely to be reversed in coming years.

It is important to distinguish between transactions associated with corporate control activity motivated by free cash flow considerations and those related to other takeover activity — that is, mergers and

EXHIBIT 1 *Recent Trends in Use of High-Yield Bonds*

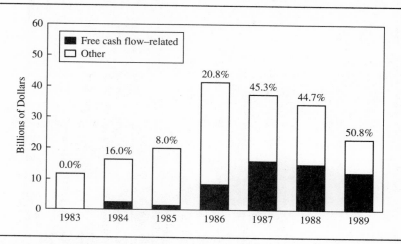

Notes: Issuance includes convertible and nonconvertible debt. Data for 1989 are through September 30, 1989. Free cash flow–related debt includes issuance associated with leveraged buyouts, leveraged recapitalizations, and share repurchases. Numbers at tops of bars represent corporate control/free cash flow–related share of total.
Source: Security Data Corporation and Morgan Stanley & Co. Incorporated.

strategic acquisitions by one corporation of another — because proceeds used to finance the former have a fundamentally different purpose from those used to make strategic acquisitions. In corporate control transactions related to free cash flow, the funds are used to gain control of undervalued assets in industries characterized by large but slowly growing cash flows and limited internal investment opportunities (tobacco is a prime example). Companies in such industries typically have large amounts of free cash flow — that is, cash flow that cannot be invested profitably in internal projects and that should be, but often is not, paid out to the shareholders. The purpose in gaining control of these companies is to ensure that such free cash flow is in fact paid out to suppliers of capital. In contrast, strategic acquisitions occurring in high-growth industries provide an entrepreneur, usually a corporate CEO, with an opportunity to integrate into the acquiring company's mainline business a rapidly expanding product in the same or a similar industry.

EXHIBIT 2   *Schematic of High-Yield Issuance*

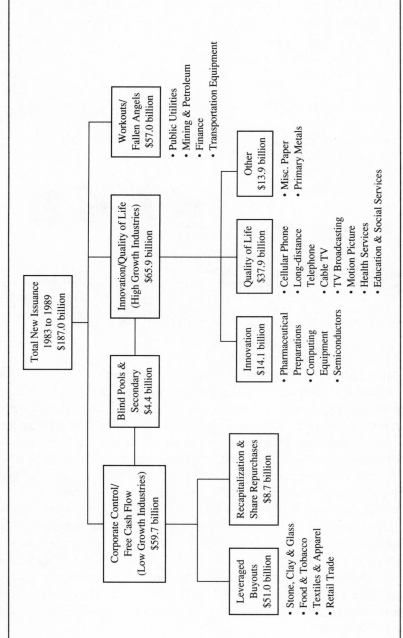

Source: Security Data Corporation and Morgan Stanley & Co. Incorporated.

A detailed classification of high-yield financings is displayed in Exhibit 2. The use of high-yield proceeds is broken down into three major categories: (1) financing acquisitions of assets in corporate control/free cash flow–related transactions, (2) funding expansion (including acquisition-related) in high-growth companies, mostly in innovation or quality-of-life industries, and (3) financing adjustment in so-called fallen angels, that is, companies that have been downgraded to below investment grade.

As shown in Exhibit 2, out of the $187 billion of total new issues, $59.7 billion (about 32%) was used to finance corporate control/free cash flow activity. Of that amount, $51.0 billion funded leveraged buyouts; $7.9 billion was used for recapitalizations, which were adopted by existing management to facilitate the payout of free cash flow in order to avoid losing control; and $0.8 billion was devoted to share repurchases. Most of these activities were associated with companies in mature, slow-growth industries, such as food, tobacco, textiles, apparel, paper, retail trade, and stone, clay, and glass.

On the other hand, high-yield proceeds used to finance investments in the high-growth, primarily innovative, or quality-of-life industries totaled $65.9 billion, slightly larger than the amount associated with corporate control. For the most part, these industries are relatively new and have limited access to other sources of finance. The main users of high-yield bonds in the innovative subcategory (innovative in the sense that a large portion of the expenditures in these industries is on research and development) have been companies in pharmaceuticals preparations, computing equipment, semiconductors, instruments, and miscellaneous electrical industries. Most of the proceeds of high-yield bond sales for these industries were used to finance non-acquisition-related expansion. Additionally, a substantial proportion of these bonds were convertible into equity.

The main users in the quality-of-life subcategory are companies involved with motion pictures, cellular phones, long-distance communication, cable television, TV broadcasting, health care, and education services. These high-growth industries have been intensive users of high-yield bonds, issuing $37.9 billion since 1983. A significant portion of these proceeds, it might be added, was used for strategic acquisition–related expansion.

The third subcategory in the high-growth grouping, imaginatively labeled "other," includes many companies that are in mature industries but have been able to exploit the high-yield market to pursue strategic policies of rapid growth. Examples are Stone Container and Gaylord Container in the otherwise slow-growing paper industry and Triangle Industries in primary metals. Again, much of the proceeds of these bond issues was used for acquisitions.

The third major category consists of workouts and fallen angels, where companies that have been downgraded to below investment grade have issued bonds in an effort to address whatever problems had caused their poor rating. Examples would include Consumers Power, BankAmerica, and Harley-Davidson. Some $57 billion of high-yield bonds issued since 1983, which accounted for about 30 percent of the total market, fall into this category.[1] Thus, of the total value of high-yield bonds issued since 1983, over two-thirds represents bonds sold by companies seeking either to unlock shareholder value by paying out free cash flow to the suppliers of capital (corporate control transactions) or to expand operations (primarily innovative/quality-of-life companies).

High-Yield Bonds, Corporate Control, and Economic Performance

Why has there been a need for corporate control transactions? As the twentieth century progressed, the public corporation — that is, a large enterprise owned by many public shareholders with small stakes and, therefore, effectively controlled by senior management — came to be the dominant and, until the 1980s, unchallenged form of business organization in the United States. Because of its size, the public corporation was able to access the capital markets and to raise vast amounts of funds when necessary, a characteristic that proved to be a great

---

1. There is also a fourth, but relatively minor, category in Exhibit 2, consisting predominantly of transactions involving a blind pool of funds. Such proceeds are raised for a generally defined, rather than specifically stated, objective, such as "to make an acquisition." For example, Pantry Pride used a blind pool in the acquisition of Revlon, the purpose of which was to wrest control from the existing management. Thus, although not an LBO, this transaction was driven by corporate control considerations. Alternatively, blind pools have been used to make strategic acquisitions in rapidly growing industries. Thus, in Exhibit 2 we show them connecting with both the corporate control/free cash flow and high-growth, innovative/quality-of-life boxes.

virtue in certain industries where profitable investment opportunities outstripped internally generated cash flow.

But the effective divorce of ownership from control, which is the essence of the public corporation, can prove to be a problem in slower growing industries that generate substantial free cash flow, which, as noted earlier, is cash flow that cannot be invested profitably in internal projects. Most studies have shown that senior management in public corporations tends to be compensated more on the basis of sales growth than on increased rate of return on assets.[2] This raises the potential for conflict between the incentives of management personnel, who may wish to maximize sales growth, and the many fragmented owners, who prefer that management maximize shareholder value.

When free cash flow is invested internally at, by definition, below-market rates of return, the market valuation of assets in the affected corporation necessarily will be depressed. It is the existence of such undervalued corporate assets that has motivated the development of the market for corporate control, for in this market, entrepreneurs seek to gain control of these assets and to remove the impediment to their full valuation, namely, the misuse of free cash flow.[3]

The financial vehicle that has been utilized in this process of restoring asset values is the leveraged buyout, which ensures that free cash flow is paid out to the suppliers of capital and not invested internally in unprofitable projects. In an LBO the entrepreneur finances his purchase largely with debt and then restructures the company by selling off subsidiaries that do not fit with strategic objectives, cutting nonessential costs and, importantly, providing large equity stakes for management. In this process, the conflict between management's

---

2. See Kevin Murphy, "Corporate Performance and Management Remuneration: An Empirical Analysis," *Journal of Accounting and Economics* 7, 1985, pp. 11–42, and Michael Jensen and Kevin Murphy, "Performance Pay and Top Management Incentives," *Harvard Business School Working Paper 89-059*, March 1989 (unpublished).

3. For a detailed discussion on the theory of free cash flow and its role in the market for corporate control, see Michael C. Jensen, "The Free Cash Flow Theory of Takeovers: A Financial Perspective on Mergers and Acquisitions and the Economy," in *The Merger Boom*, edited by Lynn E. Browne and Eric S. Rosengren (Federal Reserve Bank of Boston, Conference Series 31, 1987, pp. 102–143), and "Eclipse of the Public Corporation," *Harvard Business Review*, September–October 1989.

EXHIBIT 3   *The Role of High-Yield Financing in LBOs*

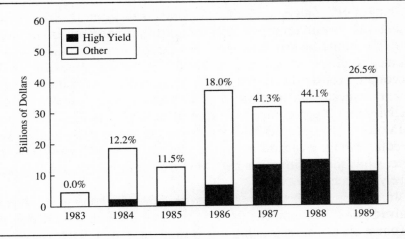

Notes: High-yield issuance includes convertible and nonconvertible debt. LBO volumes represent completed transactions only and include deals of $35 million or more. Data for 1989 are through September 30, 1989. Numbers at tops of bars represent high-yield share of LBO financing.
Source: Security Data Corporation and Morgan Stanley & Co. Incorporated.

objectives and those of the owners is resolved, and free cash flow is paid out to the suppliers of capital to the LBO, principally the holders of high-yield bonds and commercial banks or other institutional lenders. The recipients of these payments, in turn, have the opportunity to invest them in profitable ventures of their choosing.

The high-yield bond market has played a pivotal role in financing the market for corporate control. As seen in Exhibit 3, the dollar value of LBO transactions accelerated dramatically after 1985, when a high-yield blind pool played a key role in the takeover of Revlon by Pantry Pride. This event demonstrated that a so-called unfriendly suitor could succeed in forcing a buyout — in this case *not* an LBO — provided the financing was available. Since then, LBO activity has averaged a little over $35 billion per year. Of this, slightly over 30 percent of the financing (31.2% to be exact) has been supplied by the high-yield market.[4]

---

4. The rule of thumb has been that high-yield bonds tend to finance 30%, bank loans (senior debt financing) 60%, and equity 10% of the typical LBO.

Contrary to the popular belief that leveraged buyouts have been indiscriminately applied to virtually every segment of the U.S. economy, a disproportionate share of LBOs has taken place in slow-growing industries, as the theory of corporate control predicts. In investigating this point, we first calculated an "LBO Intensity Measure" for all domestic industries, equal to the ratio of the share of all LBO activity accounted for by the industry to its share of U.S. output. For example, if a specific industry were to account for, say, 5 percent of LBO activity and 2 percent of U.S. output, its LBO Intensity Measure—LIM for short—would be 2.5. Obviously, industries with LIMs exceeding 1 have engaged in above-average LBO activity, given their size, while those with measures below 1 have not been involved intensively in such activity.

In Exhibit 4, we list the industries with high LIMs that were involved in a large number of LBO transactions (with the exception of "Tobacco," which reflects just one transaction, the RJR deal). We also show their average rate of growth for sales from 1970 to 1979 relative to that of both the manufacturing sector and the overall U.S. economy during the same period. Negative signs indicate that the industry

EXHIBIT 4   *Selected LBO-Intensive Industries*

Industry	LBO Intensity Measure	Relative Sales Growth	
		Manu-facturing	U.S. Economy
Stone, Clay, & Glass	9.5	0.0	1.2
Food	3.3	−1.6	−0.4
Tobacco	32.6	−3.9	−2.7
Textiles	4.9	−3.8	−2.6
Paper	2.8	−0.5	0.7
Apparel	4.2	−4.9	−3.7
Rubber & Plastic	1.4	1.3	2.5
Retail Trade	1.6	N.M.	−2.6

Notes: Growth rates are annual averages over the period 1970 to 1979 with the exception of retail trade, which is for 1974 to 1979. Growth rates are based on data expressed in current dollars. N.M. stands for "not meaningful." Sales growth is shown in percentage points.

Source: Morgan Stanley & Co. Incorporated, S&P Compustat, and the U.S. Department of Commerce.

expanded more slowly than the average growth rate in the relevant benchmark (either the manufacturing sector or the total economy). As is evident by the preponderance of such signs, the industries with the highest intensity of leveraged buyouts generally grew more slowly than either the manufacturing sector as a whole or the total U.S. economy in the 1970s.

Looking at the LBO-intensive industries alone, our evidence demonstrates that the use of high-yield bonds to finance LBO activity tended to be heaviest in the slower growing segments of such industries. This can be seen by first calculating the intensity of the use of high-yield bonds for LBO transactions for individual segments of the slow-growth industries displayed in Exhibit 4. This measure is equal to the ratio of the share of LBO-related high-yield bond use in a specific industry by an industry segment to the segment's share of output within that same industry. For example, gypsum products accounted for 64 percent of the high-yield bond proceeds used in LBOs within the stone, clay, and glass industry ($2.1 billion out of $3.3 billion), while producing just 3.1 percent of the output in that industry, giving it an extraordinarily high intensity measure of 20.5 (64 divided by 3.1). We then calculated growth rates of these segments relative to their own (generally) slow-growing industry. As seen in Exhibit 5, in most cases, the segments that accounted for disproportionately large shares of LBO-related high-yield bond use generally were underperformers in terms of sales growth within their respective industries.

The companies that have been most intensively involved in LBOs, then, in most cases have come from mature industries plagued by slow growth and, therefore, poor internal investment prospects. As noted earlier, the large volume of free cash flow usually found in such industries often causes a conflict between managers, who sometimes are inclined to invest it in order to expand operations, and fragmented owners who seek maximum share values. This conflict can be resolved through an LBO, which causes the incentives of managers to coincide with those of the new, no longer fragmented owners by giving the managers significant equity stakes in the leveraged buyout — that is, by making them owners.

That the LBO promotes more active ownership can be seen in Exhibit 6, which summarizes research by Kaplan on management equity stakes before and after the buyout of 76 companies between 1980 and

EXHIBIT 5 *Relative Sales Growth within Slow-Growing LBO-Intensive Industries*

Industry	Intra-Industry High-Yield (LBO) Intensity Measure	Relative Within-Industry Growth	Memo: LBO-Related High-Yield Issuance ($ Billions)
Stone, Clay, & Glass			$3.3
Gypsum Products	20.5	3.9	2.1
Plumbing Fixtures	22.2	−1.2	1.1
Food			3.9
Dairy & Related Products	13.1	−2.9	2.5
Bottled & Canned Soft Drinks	4.5	1.5	1.3
Sugar & Confectionery Products	12.5	−4.1	0.3
Textiles			2.0
Weaving Mills, Cotton	8.7	−0.8	1.7
Apparel			2.6
Women's Undergarments	38.5	−7.2	1.5
Paper			2.9
Paper Mills, except Building	2.2	1.2	1.7
Corrugated & Solid Fiber Boxes	2.2	−0.4	0.7
Rubber & Plastic			2.1
Fabricated Rubber	1.4	−7.2	0.4
Retail Trade			12.7
Grocery Stores	2.4	0.0	7.1

Note: Growth rates are based on data expressed in current dollars and are annual averages over the period 1970–1979, with the exception of grocery stores, which is for 1974 to 1979.
Source: Security Data Corporation, S&P Compustat, U.S. Department of Commerce.

1986.[5] For all insiders, the stakes increased by a factor of 6 percent to 22 percent of total equity. Through such substantially increased equity stakes, the LBO changes the incentives of managers, who be-

5. The data in Exhibit 6 represent management buyouts. Hence, since not all LBOs are management buyouts (although most are), the data in the exhibit may overstate management ownership associated with leveraged buyouts in general. Nevertheless, equity stakes of managers tend to be substantially higher after completion of a non-management LBO. See Steven Kaplan, "The Effects of Management Buyouts on Operating Performance and Value," *Journal of Financial Economics* (1989).

EXHIBIT 6 *Pre- and Post-Buyout Equity Ownership*

	Equity Ownership of Management Median Percentage of Total Shares Held
Pre-Buyout	
Chief Executive Officer	1.1%
Two Top Managers	1.5
All Other Managers	1.2
All Post-Buyout Managers	3.5
Post-Buyout	
Chief Executive Officer	6.4%
Two Top Managers	7.5
All Other Managers	10.9
All Post-Buyout Managers	22.6

Note: Median percentage has been used because the mean is affected by extremes in values.
Source: Steven Kaplan, "The Effects of Management Buyouts on Operating Performance and Value," *Journal of Financial Economics* (1989).

have more as entrepreneurs, ensuring that post-buyout decisions will be based more on rate of return considerations than on sales growth.

One result of emphasizing efficiency and profitability is improved worker productivity, and in this regard the performance of LBOs has been impressive. Research by Lichtenberg and Siegel of over 1,100 plants involved in 131 public and private leveraged buyouts between 1981 and 1986 indicates, as shown in Exhibit 7, that productivity tended to rise sharply relative to industry trends in the year that the buyout took place and in the next year as well.

Other work by Lichtenberg and Siegel has shown that a major source of productivity gains when industrial plants change hands is the slimmed-down bureaucracies under the new owners.[6] Like LBOs, these ownership changes therefore address a stubborn problem affect-

6. See Frank Lichtenberg and Donald Siegel, "The Effects of Takeovers on the Employment and Wages of Central Office and Other Personnel," *National Bureau of Economic Research Working Paper* No. 2895.

EXHIBIT 7 *LBO Productivity Relative to Industry Trends*

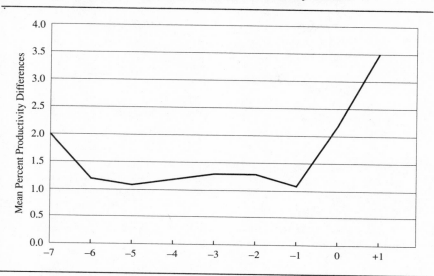

Note: The *x* axis represents years prior to, during, and after the buyout (e.g., "0" is the buyout year, and "+1" means one year after the buyout).
Source: Frank Lichtenberg and Donald Siegel, "The Effects of Leveraged Buyouts on Productivity and Related Aspects of Firm Behavior," *National Bureau of Economic Research Working Paper* No. 3022.

ing American competitiveness, namely, the steady rise in the ratio of white- to blue-collar workers in industrial companies. Although blue-collar productivity has advanced at an impressive pace in recent years, white-collar output per hour seems to have stagnated. Since the white-collar work force accounts for 40 percent of all workers in American manufacturing companies, finding ways to raise productivity of such job holders clearly is of great importance in solving this nation's competitiveness problem.[7]

The focus on efficiency and profitability also improves cash-flow performance. Kaplan investigated management buyouts before and after the transaction and found that for a sample of 48 management

---

7. See Stephen S. Roach, "White-Collar Productivity: A Glimmer of Hope?" *Special Economic Study,* Morgan Stanley, September 16, 1988.

EXHIBIT 8 *Evidence on Post-Buyout Performance*

Performance Measure	Median Change (Absolute)		Median Change (Relative to Industry)	
	−1 to +1	−1 to +2	−1 to +1	−1 to +2
Operating Income to Assets	13.7%	20.1%	16.6%	36.1%
Operating Income to Sales	7.1	11.9	12.4	23.3

Notes: Performance measures are based on data from 48 management buyouts completed over the period 1980 to 1986. The notation "−1" refers to the year before the buyout took place, "+1" is the year following the buyout, and so on. "Absolute" median change refers to total firm performance as opposed to that relative to industry.
Source: Steven Kaplan, "The Effects of Management Buyouts on Operating Performance and Value," *Journal of Financial Economics* (1989).

LBOs over the 1980 to 1986 period, operating income — earnings before depreciation (which is a noncash charge), interest expenses (which are a payment to suppliers of capital), and taxes — moved sharply upward following the transaction. As shown in Exhibit 8, the rate of return on assets, found by dividing operating income by assets, rose almost 14 percent from the year prior to the buyout to the first year after the transaction and 20 percent by the second year after the LBO. Moreover, the improvement in the rate of return was even more impressive relative to the specific industry average for each of the firms involved in the transaction, as indicated in the right panel of Exhibit 8.

Other studies corroborate the work of Kaplan. Smith, for example, employing a different sample of LBOs, found significant gains in pre- and after-tax returns on operating assets, both adjusted and unadjusted for industry trends, in the year immediately following the buyout. In addition, she was able to estimate an equation to test these findings and discovered a positive and significant relationship between changes in operating performance and changes in corporate ownership structure (i.e., increased ownership among senior management).[8]

---

8. See Abbie Smith, "Corporate Ownership Structure and Performance: The Case of Management Buyouts," University of Chicago, January 1989 (unpublished manuscript).

EXHIBIT 9   *Additional Evidence on Post-Buyout Performance (in Percentage Points)*

Performance Measure	Median Change (Absolute)		Median Change (Relative to Industry)	
	0 to +1	0 to +2	0 to +1	0 to +2
Pretax Return on Operating Assets	6.6	5.6	2.6	1.4
After-tax Return on Operating Assets	6.2	7.1	4.5	8.4

Note: Returns are calculated using earnings before interest and depreciation, with and without taxes.
Source: S&P Compustat, Morgan Stanley & Co. Incorporated.

In a further attempt to ascertain the post-buyout performance of recently completed transactions, we studied cash flows from a sample of 11 companies involved in leveraged and management buyouts between 1984 and 1986. The pretax and after-tax improvements in rates of return on assets for these companies for the first and second years following the buyout are displayed in Exhibit 9. We found that after the buyout these companies enjoyed modest pretax and somewhat larger after-tax improvements in rates of return relative to industry averages.

These "real" constructive changes, and not mere "paper shuffling" as some critics contend, are what underpin the extraordinary premiums paid to shareholders of companies that have been bought out with the aid of high-yield bonds. These premiums, as shown in Exhibit 10, ranged between 40 percent and 56 percent according to several recent studies. Thus, since there has been $190 billion in LBOs completed since 1983, shareholders of these companies realized premiums of between $76 billion and $106 billion (assuming a premium of between 40% and 56%).

It must be emphasized, moreover, that beyond the benefits accruing to shareholders alone, LBOs enhance the efficiency and competitiveness of the macroeconomy in other ways. In addition to boosting productivity and cash flows in companies involved in LBOs, leveraged buyouts indirectly improved resource allocation in the overall economy by forcing some corporations threatened by a buyout to adopt

EXHIBIT 10   *Equity Premiums Associated with*
LBO Transactions

Average Equity Premium Offered in LBO Transactions

Study	Premium	Number of Transactions in Sample
DeAngelo, DeAngelo, & Rice	56.3%	72
Lowenstein	56.0	28
Lehn & Poulsen	40.0	89
Easterwood, Hsieh, & Singer	48.6	110
Kaplan	45.9	75
Amihud	42.9	15
Mean	48.3	65

Source: Yakov Amihud, "Leveraged Management Buyouts and Share-holders' Wealth," in *Leveraged Management Buyouts: Causes and Consequences,* edited by Yakov Amihud (Dow Jones-Irwin, 1989), pp. 3–34.

strategies to maximize shareholder value. Sometimes this has been encouraged by corporate boards that have increasingly tied executive compensation to stock market performance. For example, according to a survey by Towers, Perrin, Sibson, and Co., long-term incentives, usually in the form of stock options and restricted stock, accounted for 42 percent of total corporate executive compensation in 1988, up sharply from just 15 percent 10 years earlier. Towers, Perrin reports that the median number of shares reserved for option plans for senior managers at the top 100 companies was 4.8 percent of shares outstanding in 1988, up from 2.5 percent in 1975.

In addition, irritation over such actions as the adoption of "poison pills" has encouraged institutional investors to seek a louder voice in corporate decision making. In 1987, pension funds, mostly from the public sector, launched 55 anti–poison pill resolutions at the annual meetings of American corporations, gaining 29 percent of the votes cast. In 1988, 19 more selective proposals were introduced that garnered 38 percent of the vote, with one case winning 61 percent of the votes on the resolution, which was not binding on management. Recently, Fidelity Investments, a large mutual fund manager based in Boston, announced that it intends to take a more active role in influencing decisions in companies in which it owns large blocks of stock.

Clearly, institutional investors, prodded in part by the emergence of LBOs, have begun to stir in an effort to become more active owners of American capital.

High-Yield Bonds in the Innovation/Quality-of-Life Industries

In addition to their role in financing the market for corporate control in mainly mature, slow-growing industries, high-yield bonds have been instrumental in funding the expansion of many dynamic industries offering a wide array of new products. Such industries, in contrast to those involved intensively in the market for corporate control, have been growing rapidly, reflecting the sharply rising demands for these new products.[9] Prime examples of such products are developments in cellular phone networks and fiber-optic communication, advances that have fundamentally altered where and how information flows. Other prominent examples include the proliferation of cable television and the development of innovative programming in television broadcasting, which have given U.S. households the greatest variety in television of any country in the world.

From a corporate finance perspective, firms in fast-growing industries typically require external sources of capital. The reason for this is that these firms are unable to generate sufficient cash internally to exploit all profitable investment opportunities, whether in the form of new outlays for plant and equipment or the acquisition of existing assets. Thus, the various markets for external capital, both domestic and international, can be viewed as enlarging the supply of funds available to these high-growth corporations for investment in highly profitable projects. Seen in this manner, external capital is the fuel used to propel value-creating corporate growth in these industries.

High-yield bonds have become an important financing tool for these industries, often substituting for more traditional forms of external capital, such as bank loans and equity. Unlike the large, mature industries that dominate the corporate control segment of the high-yield bond market, these high-growth industries are typically small and pro-

---

9. We have omitted for study the category "other" in the innovation/quality-of-life sector.

EXHIBIT 11   *The Major Corporate Universe: Noninvestment- and Investment-Grade Firms*

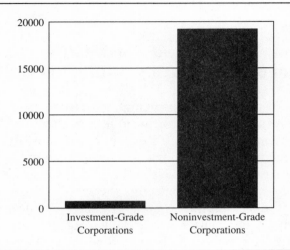

Notes: The major corporate universe includes those firms having sales in excess of $25.0 million. Figures are for the early 1980's.
Source: Internal Revenue Service, Standard and Poor's.

duce goods and services less established in the marketplace. As a result, operating risk for corporations within these industries is often high, and when viewed from a perspective of credit quality, such firms are necessarily classified as noninvestment or speculative grade. Nevertheless, these corporations, as shown in Exhibit 11, are the rule, not the exception. Prior to the proliferation of new issuance in the high-yield market, the public bond markets were accessible by only some 800 investment-grade firms, or roughly 4 percent of the major corporate universe.

Though noninvestment-grade firms dominate the corporate landscape, the macroeconomic contribution of these corporations varies. For instance, despite having the same speculative credit rating as that of, say, a public utility or a savings and loan (i.e., industries found in the workout/fallen angel sector), companies in the personal computer or cellular phone industry face a range of investment opportunities very different from that available to downgraded companies in those other industries. Thus, we will attempt to provide a more detailed assessment of the attributes of firms within the innovation/quality-of-life category that are intensive users of the high-yield bond market.

In order to derive a selected list of intensive users of high-yield bonds, we first separated the innovation from the quality-of-life industries. To do this, we computed research and development's share of total operating expenses for all industries in the innovation and quality-of-life categories. This percentage was then used as a proxy for degree of innovation, with industries having high R&D shares classified as innovative. We then calculated issuance intensity measures for a number of industries, akin to those described in the previous section. Among the innovation industries found to be relatively major issuers of high-yield debt were pharmaceutical preparations in the chemicals industry, computing equipment in nonelectrical machinery, and semiconductors in the electrical machinery industry, with respective intensity measures of 1.4, 2.5, and 1.3 (see upper section of Exhibit 12).[10] Not included in the exhibit because of low intensity ratios are various machinery, nonelectrical machinery, and miscellaneous manufacturing industries. In the quality-of-life industries shown in the bottom panel of Exhibit 12, we found high intensity ratios in industries ranging from cellular phones (37.6) to education and social services (1.7). Industries characterized by relatively low-issuance intensity not shown in the table include radio broadcasting, general medical facilities, and miscellaneous services.

To gain further insight into the more intensive users of high-yield bonds, we computed over designated periods average annual growth rates of shipments and capital expenditures for innovation industries and average annual growth rates of sales and capital expenditures for quality-of-life industries.[11] We then compared the results to similar calculations for three different benchmarks. Exhibit 13 shows these relative growth rates — that is, the difference between the growth rates for the industries and those for the respective benchmarks. In the exhibit, the numbers in the first and fourth columns reflect intra-industry comparisons (e.g., pharmaceutical preparations relative to the bench-

---

10. The intensity measure for pharmaceutical preparations is an adjusted figure reflecting the exclusion of a single zero-coupon security totaling $1.3 billion. Otherwise, this industry would have received a disproportionately large weight relative to all nonfree cash-flow–related issuance.

11. It should be noted that the periods for which average annual growth rates were calculated vary by industry because of data availability.

EXHIBIT 12   *High-Yield Issuance in Innovation/*
Quality-of-Life Industries

Industry	Total Issuance (Billions)	Share of Total Industry Issuance	Intra-Industry Intensity Measure	Research and Development Share of Total Operating Expenses
Innovation				
Chemicals	$3.3			
Pharmaceutical Preps.	0.9	27.3%	1.4	19.5%
Nonelectrical Machinery	5.9			
Computing Equipment	3.2	54.2	2.5	16.8
Electrical Machinery	3.1			
Semiconductors	0.4	12.9	1.3	38.8
Quality-of-Life				
Communication	12.4			
Cellular Phone	1.4	11.3	37.6	N.A.
Long-Distance Telephone	2.0	16.1	4.6	N.A.
Cable Television	4.4	35.5	16.1	N.A.
Television Broadcasting	3.8	30.6	38.3	N.A.
Services	14.9			
Motion Picture	3.9	26.2	3.8	N.A.
Skilled Nursing Care Facilities	1.0	6.7	2.4	N.A.
Education & Social Services	0.2	1.3	1.7	N.A.

Notes: The industry intensity measure is defined as the subindustry share of total industry high-yield issuance divided by that industry's share of total industry GNP. Innovation industry GNP shares are derived from U.S. Census Bureau industry GNP statistics over the period 1983 to 1986. The respective shares for the communication and service industries are derived from Compustat sales data over the period 1986 to 1988. Research and development expense shares are averages over the 1983 to 1988 period. N.A. means not applicable.
Source: Security Data Corporation, U.S. Department of Commerce, S&P Compustat, and Morgan Stanley and Co. Incorporated.

mark industry), the second and fifth compare these subindustries with overall manufacturing, and the third and sixth columns contrast the subindustries with the private nonfarm economy.[12]

---

12. For comparative purposes, the benchmark "private nonfarm economy" for quality-of-life industries is defined as the S&P Industrials—a group composed of 2,350 corporations from the Compustat database.

EXHIBIT 13   *Relative Shipments/Sales and Capital Spending Growth in Innovation/Quality-of-Life Industries*

| | Relative Performance Measures (in Percentage Points) | | | | | |
| | Shipments/Sales | | | Capital Expenditures | | |
	Industry	Overall Manu-facturing Activity	Private Nonfarm Economy	Industry	Overall Manu-facturing Activity	Private Nonfarm Economy
Innovation						
Chemicals						
Pharmaceutical Preps.[a]	7.0	6.9	2.3	9.5	3.7	2.8
Nonelectrical Machinery						
Computing Equipment[b]	12.2	12.4	7.8	11.8	8.9	8.0
Electrical Machinery						
Semiconductors[b]	0.9	6.0	1.4	1.0	8.1	7.2
Quality-of-Life						
Communication						
Cellular Radiotelephone[d]	47.1	N.A.	46.4	63.9	N.A.	68.6
Long-Distance Phone[c,f]	14.4	N.A.	13.9	0.3	N.A.	1.6
Cable Television[d]	33.2	N.A.	32.5	2.6	N.A.	7.3
T.V. Broadcasting[c]	2.1	N.A.	1.6	10.4	N.A.	11.7

EXHIBIT 13 *Continued*

	Relative Performance Measures (in Percentage Points)					
	Shipments/Sales			Capital Expenditures		
	Industry	Overall Manu-facturing Activity	Private Nonfarm Economy	Industry	Overall Manu-facturing Activity	Private Nonfarm Economy
Services						
Motion Picture[e]	5.1	N.A.	15.7	6.6	N.A.	15.4
Education & Social Services[c]	5.4	N.A.	16.2	5.6	N.A.	10.1

Note: Growth rates are based on data expressed in current dollars. N.A. means not applicable.

a. Relative performance measures based on average annual growth rates over the period 1980 to 1986.
b. Relative performance measures based on average annual growth rates over the period 1980 to 1985.
c. Relative performance measures based on average annual growth rates over the period 1983 to 1988.
d. Relative performance measures based on average annual growth rates over the period 1984 to 1988.
e. Relative performance measures based on average annual growth rates over the period 1985 to 1988.
f. Industry data is an aggregate of MCI Communications, United Telecommunications, and Telecom USA Inc.
Source: U.S. Department of Commerce, S&P Compustat, and the Cellular Telecommunications Industry Association.

As Exhibit 13 shows, the industries in the innovation group have experienced higher growth rates in shipments and capital expenditures relative to the respective benchmarks in every single case. Among the three innovation industries, the computing equipment industry registered the strongest relative performance in shipments, expanding 12 percentage points faster than both the nonelectrical machinery industry and the manufacturing sector and almost 8 percentage points faster than the private nonfarm economy. In capital expenditure growth this industry also ranked number one. Rather impressive relative growth rates are apparent in the pharmaceutical preparations and semiconductor industries as well.[13]

Relative performance calculations for quality-of-life–related industries paint a similar picture in that the intensive high-yield issuers in our sample have recorded growth rates in sales and capital expenditures that exceed all the benchmarks (see lower portion of Exhibit 13). Among the group, the cellular phone industry stands out as the best relative performer. Growth in sales and capital expenditures since 1984 has been explosive, outpacing the benchmarks — both its own industry and the private nonfarm economy — by roughly 50 percentage points for sales and by over 60 percentage points for capital expenditures. Noteworthy as well are the long-distance telephone, cable television, motion picture, and educational and social service industries.

Taken together, the relative performance of industries in the innovation/quality-of-life sector suggest that high-yield bonds have played an integral role in fostering economic growth and investment during the 1980s. To be sure, other forms of external capital have also been employed to facilitate corporate growth in these industries. However, growth of many of these firms would have been retarded without the development of the high-yield bond market, especially given the general malaise of the U.S. commercial banking system during the 1980s, resulting from problematic LDC, petroleum, and real estate–related loans and the relatively high cost of equity capital caused by biases in the U.S. tax structure.

---

13. It should be pointed out that shipments and capital expenditure growth in the computing equipment and semiconductor industries has slowed dramatically in the past few years, reflecting chiefly ongoing structural adjustments. Thus, the data shown in Exhibit 13 undoubtedly overstates the current relative performance of these industries. For a general discussion of these and other issues, see Stephen S. Roach, "The Technology Trap," *Economic Perspectives,* Morgan Stanley, December 15, 1989.

EXHIBIT 14 *U.S. Trade Balance in Selected End-Use Categories*

End-Use Category	Nominal Trade Balance, Surplus/Deficit (−) (in Billions)						
	1978	1980	1982	1984	1986	1988	1989
Computers	$0.84	$1.37	$1.04	$2.08	$1.66	$2.19	$3.56
Computer Accessories, Peripherals	2.30	4.63	5.20	3.04	1.73	1.19	1.73
Semiconductors (Integrated Circuits)	−0.27	−0.56	−1.51	−3.09	−1.89	−3.88	−3.18
Pharmaceutical Preparations, Medical and Dental	0.78	1.23	1.44	1.18	0.98	0.63	0.66
Motion Pictures, T.V., and Other Media	N.A.	0.92	1.00	1.19	1.56	2.53	N.A.
Memo Item: All Nonpetroleum Products	9.58	51.25	23.23	−58.88	−119.27	−84.61	−65.61

Note: Data for 1989 is January through August, expressed at an annual rate. N.A. stands for "not available."
Source: U.S. Department of Commerce and the Motion Picture Association of America.

Moreover, when assessed from a global competitiveness perspective, the high-yield market has helped the United States meet the challenge from abroad. As Exhibit 14 shows, with the exception of semiconductors, the United States has run trade surpluses over the past decade on goods and services produced by high-yield intensive innovation/quality-of-life industries.[14] These surpluses — especially the growing balances in computers and in motion pictures, T.V., and other media products — stand in sharp contrast to the massive nonpetroleum merchandise trade deficits the United States has experienced during the 1980s.

The High-Yield Market in the 1990s

The decade just ended witnessed the development of a market for corporate control that facilitated the restructuring of companies in mature industries seeking to regain their competitive edge, as well as an explosion of new products and services generated by dynamic, infant industries. In the 1980s, the high-yield bond market played a pivotal role in both of these constructive developments; about one-third of new issue proceeds were used to finance LBOs and financial restructuring in the market for corporate control, while nearly another third provided crucial support for the fast-growing innovative/quality-of-life industries.

In the 1990s, we expect the market for corporate control to remain a stern disciplinarian of companies with free cash flow in mostly mature industries. But in earlier research, we have concluded that a successful market for corporate control sows the seeds of its own periodic destruction.[15] We constructed a "squander index," which attempts to gauge the volume of free cash flow that is invested internally in unprofitable projects, and found that after reaching extraordinarily high

---

14. Interestingly, the trade deficit in semiconductors to a large extent stems from an insufficient supply of capital, even though this industry has been an intensive issuer in the high-yield market. This inadequate supply has hindered the ability of U.S. producers to meet growing foreign competition. For more on this issue see Dr. Robert N. Noyce, remarks before the U.S. House of Representatives Joint Subcommittees of the Science, Space and Technology Committee, Washington, D.C., November 8, 1989.

15. See John D. Paulus and Stephen R. Waite, "Mergers and Acquisitions Activity in the 1990s," *Special Economic Study,* Morgan Stanley, November 17, 1989.

levels in the first half of the 1980s, this index fell sharply in the second half during the LBO boom years and currently has settled at a low level. This suggests that the $151 billion of LBOs completed from 1986 to 1989 eliminated considerable squandering of free cash flow, both directly through the transactions and indirectly by encouraging management in companies with free cash flow but not involved in LBOs to pay out such cash to suppliers of capital in order to avoid asset undervaluation and possible takeover.

With the principal motivator of the market for corporate control, namely, the misuse of free cash flow, no longer as prevalent in America's mature industries, the LBO wave appears to have crested. But, though a continuation of leveraged buyout activity at the levels of 1986 to 1989 seems highly unlikely in the 1990s, the success of such a large percentage of the completed deals and the existence of a mature mechanism for facilitating transactions seem to imply that the market for corporate control should remain active, with the amount of leveraged buyouts below that of the frenzied boom years.

In contrast, the fast-growing, innovative/quality-of-life industries should increase their usage of high-yield financing. As we pointed out, these industries generally have been growing much more quickly than the economy overall and therefore account for an increasing share of national output. Their expanding size and the gradual further maturing of the high-yield market — including such recent innovations as the CBO (collateralized bond obligation), which should enhance liquidity in the market — point to more, not less, high-yield financing for these dynamic industries.

Thus, in the 1990s new issue volume in the high-yield market should remain near though probably below the levels experienced in recent years, that is, between $20 billion and $30 billion per year in 1989 dollars, assuming regulations are not imposed to restrict the use of this market. But the share of new issues financing the market for corporate control should shrink, while that of the fast-growing innovative/quality-of-life industries should rise. Since the latter type of funding, rightly or wrongly, generally is viewed more favorably than the former by the public, the high-yield market in its second decade should finally gain a measure of respect as it comes to be viewed as a vital source of finance for a dynamic, competitive America.

2

Evolution of the High-Yield Market

J. Thomas Madden, CFA
Senior Vice President
Federated Investors

Joseph Balestrino, CFA
Investment Analyst
Federated Investors

A retrospective view of the high-yield market allows us to categorize development into three evolutionary periods: (1) early capital markets from 1900 to the 1930s; (2) postdepression and postwar from the 1930s through the mid-1970s; and (3) the new issue era, commencing in the late 1970s.

Early Capital Markets

In general, issuance of high-yielding securities has historically been associated with intense corporate activity, rapid change, and new business formation in the United States. At various critical points in economic history, high-yield securities have played a major developmental role. Some of today's blue chip, investment-grade companies that started out by issuing below-investment-grade securities that paid higher yields include U.S. Steel, General Motors, IBM, and Goodyear.[1]

The high-yield bond is not as novel an investment concept as some market observers suggest. In the late nineteenth century, entrepreneurs

---

1. *1989 High Yield Market Report: Reviewing the Issues,* Drexel Burnham Lambert, Beverly Hills, CA.

like Henry Frick and Andrew Carnegie issued preferreds with substantial dividends to acquire and finance coal properties and other industrial investments in Pittsburgh. This innovation in the 1890s was the historical equivalent to today's high-yield bond. Since financial markets in that period favored equity investments, high-yielding preferred stocks found ready buyers and provided access to long-term growth capital. With comparable U.S. government securities and high-grade railroad bonds yielding 3 percent and 4 percent, respectively, high-yield preferred stocks were offered at 7 percent. Surprisingly resilient performance during and after the mid-1890s depression entrenched preferred stocks as an acceptable alternative for sophisticated investors until the Great Depression. Then, as now, the investment promised high returns to the investor to be paid from cash flow generated by the assets, either through operations or asset sales.

The medium to lower rated bond market itself has a similar long history in U.S. capital markets. In the period from 1900 to 1927, 40 percent or more of new bonds issued had fixed charge coverage on an after-tax basis of 1.4 times or less; in the period 1900 to 1915, *average* fixed charge coverage, after tax, was 2.0 times or less.[2] Moody's Investors Service began offering ratings of railroad bonds in 1909, with public utilities and industrials coming later in 1914. The peak of the rating movement was the period 1924–1935, with ratings assigned to over 98 percent of corporate bonds outstanding. Railroads and public utilities were heavy borrowers in the early twentieth century, issuing over 85 percent of all corporate bonds outstanding prior to 1920. The majority of these rated bonds were investment grade; 85.4 percent carried an investment-grade rating in 1928. By 1940, the percentage of corporate bonds with investment-grade ratings had fallen to 56.4 percent.[3]

The performance of the bond market in the period 1900–1943 is exhaustively analyzed in Braddock Hickman's seminal study, *Corporate Bond Quality and Investor Experience*.[4] The study documents the record of what would today be called high-yield or "junk" bonds

---

2. W. Braddock Hickman, *Corporate Bond Quality and Investor Experience* (Princeton: Princeton University Press and the National Bureau of Economic Research, 1958).
3. Ibid.
4. Ibid.

through the period. Hickman's classic summary includes the observation that the higher life span returns on lower rated debt, net of defaults, emerged only when broad "aggregates of corporate bonds are considered over long investment periods.... [T]he results reflect the experience of all investors over long periods... rather than that of any particular investor over any given short period."[5] The study clearly illustrates the volatility of returns to high-yield bond holdings and the influence of both business cycle and capital market conditions over such returns. One lesson Hickman teaches is that the successful high-yield investor must examine both the fundamentals of the issuer and the conditions and participants in the market itself. These twin pillars of useful analysis and portfolio management are detailed in Chapter 10.

Postdepression/Postwar Periods

The postdepression/postwar periods continued to be dominated by railroad bonds, particularly for below-investment-grade issues. In the aftermath of the Depression, the "flight to quality" opened a yield spread of over 660 basis points between U.S. Treasuries and Baa industrials by May 1932. During this period, many bonds became what bond buyers and sellers call "fallen angels" (investment-grade bonds that fall to lower quality as issuer fundamentals erode) and, in fact, such fallen angels constituted the bulk of high-yield securities up until the late 1970s. In 1932, for example, Shell Union fell from A to Ba; its 5 percent bond of 1947 traded at $.47 on the dollar.[6]

Hence, in American capital markets between the late 1930s and mid-1970s, the high-yield universe was predominantly composed of fallen angels initially issued as investment-grade bonds. In the early 1930s, such high-yield securities provided a powerful investment opportunity in that heightened fears of default spurred by rating agency downgrades, sharp declines in the equity markets, and the onset of the Great Depression subsequently proved excessive. By 1934, Shell Union bonds

5. Ibid., p. 14.
6. Charles Montanaro, *An Historical Perspective of the High Yield Bond Market 1929–1989,* Drexel Burnham Lambert.

traded above par. As one observer notes: "In practice, not a single rail-road issue over $40 million in size and not one industrial issue over $20 million actually defaulted at that time."[7] By 1946, the U.S. Treasury to Baa yield spread had narrowed to 80 basis points.

From the end of World War II up to the late 1970s, the high-yield market continued to be dominated by rail issues and fallen angel industrials. The term "junk bonds" apparently originated in the early 1970s and initially referred to such bonds originally issued as investment grades but subsequently downgraded. Penn Central Corporation and Chrysler Corporation are examples of junk bonds created by rating downgrades in the 1970s. The progress of hundreds of issuers of lower rated debt, for example MCI, Harley Davidson, Turner Broadcasting, and Tele-Communications suggest the term is both inaccurate and a wrong-headed metaphor for this market as a whole.

New Era—Late 1970s to the Present

The modern high-yield market is really a phenomenon of the late 1970s, when the predominance of fallen angels began to subside with the emergence of a new issue market. Prior to 1977, high-yield companies (those not qualifying for investment-grade ratings) were basically limited to short-term bank debt or private placements, being unable to issue debt in the public market. Financial intermediaries largely controlled the availability and terms of debt capital to such companies. From the borrower's vantage point, banks and insurance companies were in the driver's seat.

Changing economic conditions in the late 1970s spurred the creation of original issue high-yield debt for growth companies and those firms that previously relied on bank debt and other financial intermediaries for funding. The late 1970s saw accelerating inflation, mirrored in high and rising interest rates, which substantially increased the cost of capital, jeopardizing the survival of many companies. At the same time (and for the same reasons), the total return performance of high-grade corporate and government security portfolios suffered as their prices fell in response to rising rates. Investors began to view yields

---

7. Ibid.

available in the junk market in a more attractive light. A simple example of investor interest is the explosive growth in the number of high-yield mutual funds from only a handful in the late 1970s to approximately 90 such funds in 1989, with assets of over $30 billion.[8]

Accelerating inflation was a major impetus to high-yield market growth in other ways, as it set the stage for accelerating high-yield debt creation. Such inflation reduced real borrowing costs and rewarded debtors relative to creditors.[9] At corporations, high inflation rates translated into easier pass-through of costs and higher nominal income relative to debt service. (The example of the family that borrowed in the early 1970s to purchase a home and whose income rose with inflation into the 1980s illustrates the principle: The value of the house rose, the income available to service mortgage debt rose, but the debt service on the mortgage remained the same.) Hence, growing companies found debt financing more attractive; oil and gas related, steel, and manufacturing companies were issuers of high-yield bonds. Examples include Sharon Steel (1979) and energy companies such as Smith International (1979) and Texas International (1977).[10]

In response to interest rate volatility and the inverted yield curves that were the bane of the credit markets in the late 1970s and early 1980s, banks and insurance companies generally backed away from providing long-term, fixed-rate loans. Borrowing short to lend long was a recipe for disaster when short-term rates rose above loan yields, creating negative interest rate margins. Thus, demand for growth capital began to shift toward the original issue high-yield market and much growth in new high-yield issuance can be viewed as simply substitution for bank debt. In the process, hundreds of companies found access to long-term, fixed-rate growth capital, via a "new" approach that used a new version of forgotten financing tools initially seen in the late nineteenth century. The market of "emerging credits" had developed again, and in similar circumstances of strong growth and rapid economic change.

---

8. Lipper Analytical Services, Inc.
9. Real interest rates are usually measured by subtracting an inflation measure from nominal bond yields. For example, if a bond has a coupon of 10 percent, but inflation is 11 percent, the real rate is (10 percent − 11 percent) or −1 percent. When real rates are negative, borrowers are rewarded relative to creditors.
10. *High Yield Handbook,* First Boston, New York, 1989.

EXHIBIT 1   *High-Yield Market Growth, Dollars (in Billions) at Year End*

Year	High-Yield Debt	Year	High-Yield Debt
1977	$24	1983	$43
1978	26	1984	59
1979	28	1985	82
1980	30	1986	125
1981	32	1987	159
1982	35	1988	183

Source: Drexel Burnham Lambert.

Between 1977 and the mid 1980s the bond market came to realize that risks of default did not justify excluding high-yield bonds from portfolios, because net returns after the effects of defaults were positive and competitive with investment-grade returns.[11] Initial buyers were individuals and mutual funds, followed later by pension plans, insurance companies, and financial institutions including savings and loans. Exhibit 1 depicts the dramatic growth in high-yield debt from approximately $24 billion outstanding in 1977 to an estimated $183 billion outstanding at year end 1988. New issuance totaled over $174 billion over this same time frame, nearly $120 billion of which was issued from 1986 to 1988.[12]

Much recent high-yield market literature has documented both new high-yield issue growth and its underlying rationale.[13, 14] Particularly significant in fostering such growth were three major contributing factors: (1) U.S. corporate tax policy and the 1981 Economic Recovery Tax Act (ERTA); (2) the decline of common stock prices in the 1980–82 period and declines in inflation, which favored acquisitions; and

11. Edward I. Altman, *Default Risk, Mortality Rates, and the Performance of Corporate Bonds* (Research Foundation of the I.C.F.A., 1989).
12. *1989 High Yield Market Report, Financing America's Future,* Drexel Burnham Lambert.
13. Ibid.
14. Jane Tripp Howe, *Junk Bonds, Analysis & Portfolio Strategies* (Chicago: Probus Publishing, 1988).

(3) deregulation of financial intermediaries. Each of these factors is worth examining.

ERTA and the Tax Preference for Debt versus Equity. Accelerated depreciation provisions of ERTA, which was passed in 1981, had the effect of significantly increasing corporate cash flow. Readers should consider more generally that the U.S. tax code effectively *subsidizes debt* by allowing interest as a deductible expense. On the other hand, the tax code penalizes equity, because dividends must be paid from after-tax income. Progressive realization of this simple truth led to higher levels of debt on the average corporate balance sheet through the 1970s and 1980s. This process culminated in the mid- to late-1980s with the introduction of the leverage buyout/management buyout (LBO/MBO) financed in part by deferred interest bonds, whose interest was deductible even though the issuer made no cash outlay for interest expense. (Congress moved to limit such deductions in 1989.)

Low Inflation and Falling Stock Prices. With stock prices and accompanying asset values relatively low following the early 1980s recession, many firms found returns from the acquisition of operating companies superior to internal investment opportunities. New issue high-yield debt was increasingly used to finance such acquisitions.

Deregulation of Financial Intermediaries. Rising nominal interest rates and an inverted yield curve, resulting from accelerating inflation, had several effects. Investors became increasingly dissatisfied with low regulated yields on time deposits and pressed regulators for relief. Banks and S&Ls found that paying depositors higher deregulated returns to invest those deposits at what was hoped would be a positive margin was a dicey proposition, as short-term rates turned higher and more volatile. One solution for investors was to disintermediate banks and thrifts—cut out the middleman. The decade saw growing direct investment in assets such as money market mutual funds, mortgage-backed securities, and high-yield debt.

Deregulation of interest rate caps paid on deposits also meant that banks and insurance companies grew more reluctant to provide 5- to 10-year term loans to smaller, "middle market" companies, given the growing risks of funding such assets in the new environment. Thus, yield-hungry investors, along with issuers ready to finance growth with term debt, met in the new high-yield marketplace.

Recent Conditions.   To recap, the principal change in markets for less than investment-grade debt in the late 1970s was the discovery by corporate issuers and the corporate finance departments of a handful of broker dealers of a potential market for new bond issues of less than investment grade. As noted earlier, an important reason for the opening of this market was the yield curve inversion in the late 1970s and early 1980s and the powerful reluctance the inverted curve created on the part of traditional corporate lenders like banks and insurance companies to grant credit for terms in excess of three to four years. While both Bear Stearns and L. F. Rothschild, among others, were early underwriters of lower rated debt for their clients, there can be no doubt that Drexel Burnham Lambert, under the leadership of Michael Milken, was intelligent and aggressive in exploiting and developing this new market. Nor is there any question in the minds of most veterans of the high-yield market that Mr. Milken's commitment to secondary market liquidity for the growing number of issues was a prime force in the growth of this market.

It is not within the scope of our exposition to detail the recent evolution of the high-yield market or the role played by Drexel Burnham Lambert, First Boston, L. F. Rothschild, Prudential-Bache, Morgan Stanley, Donaldson Lufkin Jenrette and others in the market's evolution. The reader is again cautioned that the road traveled by these firms, the clients, and customers was not lacking in detours and potholes. It is well worth reemphasizing a major point, however; the successful investor through this period scrutinized the investment banker as carefully as he/she did the issuer.

Before embarking on an examination of the recent period, some statistics are useful in dispensing with the perception that *most* high-yield deals are the result of hostile takeovers — leveraged buyouts (LBOs) or other "deals" rather than ordinary financing objectives. In fact, high-yield proceeds over the 1980–1988 period break down as follows:[15]

---

15. Drexel Burnham Lambert, *1989 High Yield Market Report, Reviewing the Issues*. Op. cit.

- internal growth and development, 59%
- acquisition financing, 36%
- unsolicited takeovers, 5%

Additionally, industry diversification of the market is illustrated in Exhibit 2. As shown, no single category of high-yield issuer constitutes more than 8 percent of the total, and the top four categories combined total less than 30 percent.

Lastly, to accentuate a point made at the outset, intense business activity is historically associated with increased debt financing, which serves as an essential component of such business growth. The period from the late 1970s to the present, accompanied by the powerful forces of a long business cycle, deregulation, easy fiscal policy, and accelerating change in economics and technology, has a clear parallel in the first three decades of this century, which saw a parallel growth in low-grade debt.

Use of proceeds in early high-yield offerings, in the main, focused on the terming out of bank debt and augmenting of working capital. Thus, the use of proceeds of new high-yield issues in the late 1970s paralleled that of investment-grade corporate bond offerings. Issuing companies included early advocates of high leverage like American Financial, led by Carl Lindner, and Rapid American, under the guidance of the irrepressible and shrewd Mishalum Riklis. The oil and gas boom of the late 1970s and early 1980s provided the high-yield market with a host of energy issuers. (Some of these were Texas International, Petro-Lewis, Western Company of North America, Global Marine, and Crystal Oil. Many of these issuers experienced problems as inflation slowed.) The recapitalization of LTV contributed heavily to high-yield bonds outstanding. Another major source in the early 1980s was the downgrading of nuclear generation–exposed utilities ("glow bonds" in Street slang) like Long Island Lighting, Public Service of New Hampshire, and Commonwealth Edison. The excesses in energy/energy services and the problems of basic industry in the 1981–1982 recession led to high default rates for these sectors, but overall the expanding high-yield market weathered the early 1980s successfully.

Another powerful force began to shape the market in the middle of the decade—the leveraged buyout. William Simon's remarkably

EXHIBIT 2   *Outstanding High-Yield Issues
by Industry at Year End, 1988*

Industry	Percentage of Total High-Yield Debt Issues
Air Transport	3
Auto/Vehicle	2
Banks/S&L's	3
Building Materials	4
Cable/Broadcasting	8
Chemicals	2
Consumer Products	2
Containers	3
Data Processing/Electronics	3
Diverse Manufacturing	1
Diversified	4
Filmed Entertainment	1
Food/Beverage	3
Gaming	3
Healthcare Facilities Supplies	2
Homebuilders	2
Insurance/Finance	3
Leisure/Amusement	4
Lodging	2
Machinery	1
Oil & Gas	7
Paper	1
Publishing	2
Railroads/Equipment	2
Real Estate/Development	1
Restaurants	1
Retail—Food & Drug	7
Retail—General	7
Services	1
Shipping/Transport	1
Steel	2
Telecommunications	2
Textiles	2
Utilities	4
Unclassified	2
Miscellaneous	2
Total	100

*Source: 1989 High Yield Market Report: Financing America's
Future,* Drexel Burnham Lambert, 1989.

successful LBO of Gibson Greetings, purchased in 1982 for $80 million and taken public eighteen months later for $290 million, was an early example of leveraged transactions that took aggressive advantage of the tax code's preference for debt over equity, discussed earlier. The attractiveness of leveraged acquisitions done on either a friendly or hostile basis, combined with the growing power of the high-yield market to raise large amounts of capital in short periods of time, created a volatile financial brew. The high-yield market began a steady transformation from "ordinary corporate purpose" financings to LBO/MBO transactions, an activity in which leading Wall Street firms including Drexel Burnham Lambert took a prominent role.

Notwithstanding much ill-informed commentary in the financial press, many leveraged transactions in the 1980s were great successes for their investors. Even a cursory examination of deals like Metro Media, Cain Chemical, Triangle Pacific, American Standard, Container Corp., and others provides powerful evidence of the usefulness of the high-yield market as a tool for smart, aggressive entrepreneurs in the acquisition of cheap assets. The record of Kohlberg, Kravis & Roberts, even with the recent problems of its Jim Walter deal, provides further evidence of this point.[16] We believe that with the passage of time, the positive effects of privatizing corporations and allowing U.S. capital investments to move from lower returns to higher returns through use of leverage will eventually be demonstrated empirically.

But the long economic expansion of the 1980s undeniably has led to excesses. Recent conditions in the high-yield market reflect correction of these excesses. We address this correction at the close of Chapter 10. It is precisely this more difficult environment that emphasizes the need for a careful and thoughtful approach in managing high-yield portfolios. In Chapter 10, some aspects of this approach are examined.

---

16. KKR had no court-supervised reorganizations in over 30 deals before Jim Walter. High-yield debt used to finance many of these transactions has generally paid as agreed. Equity investors in these transactions were handsomely rewarded.

3

The International Market for High-Yield Securities

Les B. Levi, Ph.D.
Vice President
High Yield Research
Merrill Lynch

Joseph C. Bencivenga
Director and Manager
High Yield Research
Salomon Brothers Inc

The extraordinary growth of the high-yield market through the 1980s was driven by several factors: the growing acceptance of leverage by corporate issuers, deregulation in the capital markets, the trend toward disintermediation, the demand for high-yielding instruments conditioned by the high interest rates of the late 1970s and early 1980s, the swelling supply of institutional funds in the United States, and the increased participation of foreign investors in the U.S. capital markets. International participants in the high-yield market have been an important source of investment capital and have also contributed to the market's growth. In the future, with new regulatory constraints imposed on the U.S. savings and loan industry and restrictions on high-yield investments by insurance companies and banks, the international arena appears to offer one avenue of potential growth for the high-yield market. Today, a relatively small portion of corporations and institutions in fewer than two dozen countries invests or issues in the high-yield market. In the 1990s we are likely to see an expanded interest in the technology of U.S. subordinated debt markets as well as an increased focus on investment opportunities.

In many respects, the international high-yield market today resembles the domestic U.S. market in the early 1980s. Many foreign buyers are engaged in a learning process, gradually familiarizing themselves with individual credits, industries, and types of securities before moving into the broader marketplace. For many, only the most familiar, high-quality, actively traded issues will do. To illustrate, RJR Nabisco's debt has been the single most popular credit among overseas investors, as it is with U.S. investors, followed by names like McCaw Cellular, Viacom, Duracell, and Revlon. Some foreign buyers will purchase only high-quality increasing-rate notes (IRNs), reflecting a preference for short maturities, stepped-up coupons, and commitment fees.[1]

The international segment's importance to the high-yield market is evident in the way new issues are structured—that is, with an eye toward satisfying foreign investors' risk profiles. For that reason, we are seeing more floating-rate coupons (over 90 percent indexed off the London Interbank Offered Rate, or LIBOR) and more IRNs. The RJR Nabisco transaction, which we will examine more closely later in this chapter, has specific tranches expressly designed for the international marketplace, whether the overseas commercial banks that purchased the $13 billion in RJR's senior debt or the institutional investors that bought the $5 billion in IRNs in the first round of subordinated debt financing and the $250 million of "floaters," or floating-rate notes, in the permanent financing.

International Participation in the High-Yield Market

Generally speaking, international participation in the high-yield market consists of two types of activity: foreign investment in U.S.-issued, dollar-denominated high-yield securities and foreign issuance. Foreign investment, which began over only the last few years, has gained considerable momentum as overseas institutions, led by Japan, have geared up to manage high-yield portfolios and to engage in high-yield credit research. Today, international investors make up 10 percent of the high-yield market, holding more than $20 billion in dollar-denominated high-yield securities. We are likely to see the expansion of this

---

1. Commitment fees are fees paid to induce buyers to commit to purchase securities in complex transactions. These fees are usually one-half to one percent of the purchase price.

market throughout the 1990s, especially as the number of management buyout transactions and leveraged acquisitions by foreigners increases.

The issuance of high-yield securities by overseas corporations has proceeded slowly for a number of reasons, mainly because of the nature of the relationships between banks and corporations within many countries. For example, though the Japanese are the most active foreign buyers of high-yield bonds, the country's banks provide very low cost short-term capital to domestic corporations under generous terms; these loans, which are almost automatically rolled over, are frequently exchanged for equity in the corporations. The net result is that most Japanese corporations have continual access to lower costing capital and need no high-yield debt. Moreover, Japanese corporations are required by the Ministry of Finance to issue the equivalent of single A–rated paper; if necessary, credit quality must be enhanced by a bank letter of credit. What we are likely to see in Japan are more yen-denominated high-yield issues by U.S. corporations, such as the ¥14 billion offering by Coastal Corp. that was distributed directly to Japanese investors in 1988. In the United Kingdom, however, the nascent market in mezzanine debt, which is mostly in loan form, is the first step in the development of an indigenous public high-yield market. The next step, of course, is the securitization of these mezzanine loans, which should lead to a more liquid market. Much like the growth of the U.S. market from 1986 through 1989, the growth of this market should parallel growth in management buyouts (MBOs) and merger and acquisition activity within the United Kingdom in the next decade. Interestingly, Australian corporations have been among the largest issuers of high-yield debt after U.S. corporations, including issues from John Fairfax Group, the country's largest newspaper publishing company, and Linter Textiles, the country's largest textile/apparel concern.

Many innovations have been implemented in high-yield securities over the last decade, and this technology in turn has been exported overseas. Increasing-rate notes, split coupon securities, pay-in-kind instruments, and extendable reset notes have found acceptance in international portfolios. Subordinated or mezzanine debt is itself an innovative product that the United States has exported; in the United Kingdom, continental Europe, Japan, and the Pacific Rim countries, the only type of financing available to invest in previously had been senior secured debt or equity.

EXHIBIT 1   Selected Increasing-Rate Note Issues over $100 Million

Description	Coupon	Priority	Maturity	Amount Issued ($MM)	Rate Reset
Anacomp	13.0000	senior subordinated	09/02/91	250.0	Reset monthly at the greater of: 13% or 3-month LIBOR + 430 BP, increases by 50 BP/quarter during the first year and 25 BP/quarter thereafter.
Food 4 Less Supermarkets	13.3125	senior subordinated	07/15/96	125.0	Reset monthly at the greater of: 13.3125% + Spread or 3-month LIBOR + 400 BP + Spread. Spread is 0 BP for the first quarter, increasing by 50 BP/quarter thereafter.
G Industries	14.0000	senior subordinated	03/15/94	283.0	Reset monthly at LIBOR + 375 BP, increasing by 50 BP/quarter to 12/15/90.
Rexene Products	13.1875	senior	07/15/92	350.0	Reset monthly at the greater of: 3-month LIBOR + 387.5 BP or 13.1875%, increasing by 50 BP/quarter for the first 8 quarters and 40 BP/quarter thereafter.
Rexene Products	14.3125	senior subordinated	07/15/92	150.0	Reset monthly at the greater of: 3-month LIBOR + 500 BP or 14.3125%, increasing by 50 BP/quarter for the first 8 quarters and 25 BP/quarter thereafter.
RJR Holdings Capital	13.5625	first subordinated	02/15/97	1,250.0	Reset monthly at the greater of: 13.4375% or 3-month LIBOR + 400 BP, increasing by 50 BP/quarter from 5/15/89 to 5/15/91 and 25 BP/quarter thereafter.
Uniroyal Chemical Acquisition	12.6250	senior secured	10/30/94	300.0	Reset monthly at the greater of: 3-month LIBOR + 375 BP or 12.625%, increasing by 50 BP/quarter for the first 2 years and by 25 BP/quarter thereafter.

International Investors in High-Yield Securities

In the last few years, buyers in Japan, the Mideast, the United Kingdom, and Europe have become more comfortable with U.S. high-yield securities for their portfolios. Several investment trends may be noted. First, high-yield issues that sell well overseas usually are well-known, high-quality issues with strong cash flow coverage of interest.[2] Many are in noncyclical businesses like consumer nondurables and have readily identified brand names. Foreign investors have also shown a preference for floating-rate paper that is indexed to an interbank rate such as LIBOR (see Exhibit 2), investing in it outright or swapping into it. Floating-rate debt matches their liabilities, which are frequently floating-rate bank loans. Additionally, many international investors prefer short maturities, once again to match their liabilities, and, like U.S. investors, are attracted to debt securities that include equity kickers.[3] Finally, overseas investors have had some difficulty accepting subordinated debt because such debt is a relatively new concept in foreign countries. In Japan, for example, the word for subordinated debt translates as "inferior" or "bonds no one wants." Corporations traditionally raise capital either through senior secured debt with the banks or through equity offerings.

For these reasons, quality increasing-rate notes (IRNs) have been popular among European and Japanese institutions. IRNs, which usually are redeemed in less than 12 months despite stated maturities of five to eight years, are frequently senior and structured with floating-rate coupons usually indexed off LIBOR; the coupons are increased quarterly, usually by 25 to 50 basis points, and the notes are callable any time at par (see Exhibit 1). Many are accompanied by commitment fees. In a typical IRN private placement structured today, 10 percent to 25 percent of the buyers are non-U.S. institutions. Similarly, floating-rate notes are frequently purchased by overseas investors (see Exhibit 2).

The swap market has also played an important role in opening up the U.S. high-yield market to European and Japanese investors. Using

---

2. Cash flow is earnings before depreciation, interest, and taxes, or EBDIT. Historically, EBDIT coverage of interest expense has ranged from 1.0x to 1.5x in typical subordinated debt offerings.
3. Warrants or common stock issued at a minimal cost with the debt securities.

EXHIBIT 2   *Selected Floating-Rate Note Issues over $100 Million*

Description	Priority	Coupon (%)	Maturity	Rating		Amount Outstanding ($MM)
				Moody's	S&P	
Beatrice	senior subordinated floating-rate note	12.987	11/01/97	B3	B+	100
Clark Oil & Refining	first mortgage floating-rate note	11.562	07/15/94	B1	BB	100
Continental Cablevision	senior subordinated floating-rate note	11.562	11/01/04	NR	NR	100
Hasbro	subordinated variable-rate note	10.563	12/01/95	Ba1	BBB-	50
Owens-Illinois	variable-rate note	11.125	04/01/96	B1	NR	394.4
RJR Holdings Capital	subordinated floating-rate note	12.412	05/15/99	B1	B+	250
Union Texas Petroleum Holdings	senior subordinated floating-rate note	10.500	11/01/92	Ba3	BB+	100

swap transactions, investors can transform fixed-rate, dollar-denominated high-yield bonds into floating-rate and nondollar obligations. Interest rate swaps enable investors to manage interest rate risk more effectively by matching assets with liabilities, which are often floating-rate bank loans. Currency swaps can insulate investors against foreign exchange exposure by hedging. Thus, a swap transaction can effectively turn a portfolio of fixed-rate, dollar-denominated high-yield bonds into floating-rate yen bonds. (For more on this see the section on swap transactions later in this chapter.)

Regulatory Issues in the International High-Yield Market

Although several regulatory restrictions on investments in high-yield securities have emerged over the last few years in the United States, most notably the prohibition on investments by savings and loan institutions and the expected insurance company restrictions, there has been little regulatory activity in the international high-yield market. The Right Honorable Robin Leigh-Pemberton, Governor of the Bank of England, has taken the position that high-yield debt is an acceptable investment by U.K. institutions as long as buyers understand the risks and are adequately rewarded for taking those risks.[4] Governor Leigh-Pemberton also indicated that the current levels of MBO activity in the United Kingdom are acceptable. Japan's Ministry of Finance, which oversees most investing institutions, has made no express pronouncements on high-yield securities, but is watching developments in the high-yield market.

Structuring Transactions for the International Marketplace: The RJR Nabisco Case Study

The financing of RJR Nabisco's leveraged buyout in February 1989 illustrates how new issues are structured to create interest on the part of international buyers. The enormous size of the transaction — at some

---

4. "Corporate Gearing and Takeovers," speech delivered at the Biennial Dinner of the Institute of Bankers in Scotland, 23 January 1989.

$31 billion, the largest ever — required that Kohlberg Kravis Roberts (KKR) line up non-U.S. banks and institutional buyers in order to complete the transaction. Many believed that $25 billion of debt could not be raised in the United States alone. But as a high-quality credit with strong brand names and in noncyclical industries, RJR had strong appeal to overseas investors and the bond offering was oversubscribed.[5]

The $25 billion financing was done in several tiers. At the senior level, some $13 billion in bank debt was placed, much of it with foreign institutions. The bank loans consisted of three tranches: a $5.25 billion term loan and revolver, a $6 billion asset sale bridge facility, and a $1.5 billion bridge refinancing facility. Of the $13 billion of bank debt, more than $6 billion was purchased by foreign banks, which included approximately 20 Japanese banks, 10 European banks, and a number of Canadian banks.

Two strategies were used in structuring the debt to overcome difficulties presented by the transaction's size. First, the LBO was structured conservatively, with a debt to total capitalization ratio of only 74 percent rather than the usual 90 percent to 100 percent for leveraged buyouts; a large capital cushion of some $8 billion was beneath the bondholders, consisting mainly of "cramdown" debt and preferred and common stock. Secondly, generous commitment fees were offered to the bank debt holders and bondholders along with equity kickers, which boosted their expected total rate of return. The banks received $380 million of fees, or just under 3 percent of the bank facilities (instead of the usual 1 percent). Bondholders received commitment fees and warrants that amounted to as much as 12 percent of the principal amount of bonds. The sponsor and underwriter recognized that equity and commitment fees are important to international buyers.

In the first round of $5 billion subordinate financing, Drexel Burnham intended to place privately $3 billion of IRNs and to provide a $2 billion bridge loan. But the enormous popularity of the offering eliminated the need for the bridge. One reason the bonds sold so quickly in Europe and Japan was that many banks were already familiar with the company's credit quality, because they had reviewed RJR in connection with the $13 billion of senior bank debt already

---

5. Demand for the bonds exceeded the amount being offered.

placed. For the interim financing, $5 billion of first and second sub-ordinated increasing-rate notes was issued in February 1989 and was oversubscribed. The terms of the IRNs were as follows: The senior tranche (first subordinated IRNs) carried a coupon of 400 basis points over three-month LIBOR; the second tranche (second subordinated IRNs) was set 500 basis points over LIBOR. The spread on both would be increased 50 basis points each quarter from May 1989 through May 1991 and 25 basis points afterwards. In May 1989 the company took all but $1 billion of the IRNs out at par and replaced them with per-manent financing. Of the $5 billion of IRNs, European and Japanese investors subscribed to more than $1 billion and in the end purchased about $750 million.

Within the $4 billion of RJR's permanent financing, one tranche was designed expressly for Japanese and other foreign buyers. The $250 million of subordinated floating-rate notes, set at 385 basis points over three-month LIBOR, was designed for and purchased by for-eign investors. Additionally, the $1 billion of IRNs that remained out-standing is held in part by foreign investors. Because there is only a limited quantity of RJR floating-rate debt ($250 million), many Japa-nese investors bought RJR's 13.5 percent subordinated debentures of 4/15/01 and used interest rate swaps to turn the bonds into floating-rate obligations.

Japanese Investors in
High-Yield Securities

By the mid-1980s, the Japanese began to emerge as the most aggressive foreign buyers of U.S. high-yield issues. Several factors have spurred the increase of Japanese investments in the high-yield market over the last several years. First, there was a growing amount of U.S. dollar-denominated currency accumulated by the Japanese during the 1980s. This excess liquidity resulted from Japan's low GNP growth rate, a large trade surplus, a relatively high individual savings rate (averaging 18 percent versus 5 percent in the United States), and the widespread overfunding of corporate pension funds. Second, there has been a move toward deregulation in Japan, giving institutions more flexibil-ity in making investment decisions and acquiring foreign investments.

For example, institutions under the jurisdiction of the Ministry of Finance previously were restricted to investing up to only 10 percent of their assets in foreign investments in 1980; today they are allowed to invest up to 25 percent in foreign assets. Third, the development of new financial technology in Japan, particularly swaps, allows institutions to offset interest rate and currency risk, which in turn makes high-yield debt, as well as other nonyen, fixed-rate investments, more attractive.

Financial technology has been an important element in Japanese finance in the 1980s. "Zaitech," or high-tech financial transactions, is Japanese arbitrage, which institutions there began practicing only in the 1980s. Using technologies such as interest rate and currency swaps, many institutions have managed to earn money consistently. In fact, for some large Japanese industrial corporations, Zaitech is their most profitable business segment. Importantly, Zaitech has enabled many Japanese institutions to invest in the high-yield market, making high-yield instruments more attractive because interest rate risk and currency risk can be substantially mitigated. Indeed, most of the Japanese money invested in the high-yield market is Zaitech-related. Through Zaitech, Japanese investors with high-yield bonds lock in spreads. Swaps have enabled Japanese investors to gain more flexibility.

Primarily because of Japan's trade surplus, the country's excess liquidity has been building up throughout the 1980s, with its capital account growing steadily. In 1980, for example, Japan had a $2.3 billion cash inflow, but by 1987 that had turned into a $137 billion outflow. This capital, a large portion of it in U.S. currency, was chasing profitable investment opportunities abroad. Beginning in the early 1980s, so much Japanese capital was directed to U.S. government bonds that current estimates put Japanese holdings at approximately 20 percent of the U.S. government market.

Japan entered the high-yield market cautiously because subordinated debt was unfamiliar to buyers. The earliest transactions, which took place in 1984, involved only senior paper, including collateralized issues and unrated mortgage issues; leasing companies purchased select high-yield utility issues, such as Philadelphia Electric, Detroit Edison, and Cleveland Electric. Because these investors had previous experience with the regulated utility industry, the move to the high-yield utility sector was easy. Other names that appealed to early buyers because of their recognizable brands included Texaco, Playtex, Beatrice, and Turner Broadcasting. The Japanese institutions that today invest in high-yield products include insurance companies, trust banks, mutual funds, trading companies, and leasing companies.[6]

Another important segment of the high-yield market was opened up to the Japanese when increasing-rate notes were introduced in 1985. The Triangle Industry IRNs were sold in 1985 with an up-front commitment fee and a rate pegged to LIBOR. IRNs frequently match maturity constraints and are floating rate, which Japanese institutions prefer. For many Japanese banks, IRNs offer a more attractive alternative to bridge financings, which are inherently difficult to trade and therefore more risky.

Japanese banks have played an important role in domestic LBOs, providing funding that has been estimated at 20 percent to 30 percent of the bank financing for the largest U.S. transactions. Importantly, the participation of Japanese banks in LBO lending syndicates has resulted in more extensive credit analysis of U.S. high-yield companies. Japanese institutions became more familiar with high-yield companies when U.S. commercial banks started syndicating LBO bank debt with Japanese banks. Once Japanese banks began doing more credit analysis on those companies they were making loans to, it was natural for the banks to invest in the bonds. As we saw, Japanese banks were responsible for approximately $6 billion of the more than $13 billion of RJR Nabisco's bank loans, followed by the commitment of over $1 billion by Japanese institutions in the first round of RJR's subordinated debt financing. Once a bank evaluates and then buys the senior loan of a company, it may also feel comfortable with the more subordinated issues of the same company.

Japanese investments in high-yield bonds are growing dramatically. In 1988, for example, some $2.5 billion was invested in the high-yield market. For the first nine months of 1989, approximately $4 billion was moved into the high-yield market. Additionally, Japanese institutions are investing in American LBO funds — that is, equity funds for

---

6. See Edward I. Altman and Yoshiki Minowa, "Analyzing Risks, Returns and Potential Interest in the U.S. High Yield Debt Market for Japanese Investors," Salomon Brothers Center for the Study of Financial Institutions, Graduate School of Business Administration, New York University, Working Paper No. 461 (May 1988).

leveraged buyouts. After observing the high returns in these funds, Japanese investors encouraged U.S. sponsors to develop Japan-based funds. In the last few years, U.S. sponsors like Coniston Partners, Kohlberg Kravis Roberts & Co., Wasserstein Perella & Co., Inc., and Clayton & Dubilier, Inc., opened up LBO funds, which have attracted an estimated $2 billion.

Japanese investors are at an early stage in the learning curve. They tend to invest in familiar industries such as consumer goods and petroleum; within those industries they invest in familiar names. Until recently, these investors relied almost exclusively on the U.S. credit rating agencies to determine credit quality. Today, a growing number of Japanese institutions have developed in-house research capabilities and thus have become more open to investments in high-yield debt securities.

However, there is also an attitude of cautiousness among Japanese investors today. Investments in troubled U.S. LBOs such as Campeau, Ohio Mattress, and Southland, and privatizations such as DFC, a New Zealand company that did not successfully complete its transaction, resulted in significant losses. In response, Japanese institutions are scrutinizing deals more carefully and the Ministry of Finance is reassessing Japanese investments in LBOs.

The U.K. Market

In the United Kingdom, as well as in much of Europe, there has traditionally been a small market for corporate debt, particularly long-term, fixed-rate issues, but that may be changing. The U.K. "bulldog" market of long-term, fixed-rate, sterling-denominated corporate bonds is composed of only the highest quality blue chips, often the most senior paper in the capital structure. U.K. corporate issuers frequently go to the Eurobond market to raise funds because there are far more buyers there, and many institutions buy no debt instruments except for government bonds, or gilts. Because of the conservative nature of U.K. institutional investors, U.K. corporate debt is usually secured, and only companies with the highest credit ratings issue unsecured debt. An alternative to the domestic sterling market is the Eurosterling market.

In the 1980s, there was a surge of new issuance of corporate debt in the United Kingdom as a result of both a declining supply of U.K. government debt and recent legislation that made it easier for corporate issuers to issue directly in their own name without withholding tax. Also, institutional buyers have become more comfortable with corporate debt, and a large and liquid sterling swap market for currency and interest rate swaps has developed over the last few years. In 1986, for example, some £3 billion in fixed-rate, sterling-denominated corporate bonds was issued by some 51 issuers; in 1987, approximately £5.3 billion was issued by 72 issuers; and in 1988, £6.3 billion was issued by 74 issuers.[7]

A new and growing segment in the U.K. market is the sterling-denominated mezzanine debt issued by U.K. companies. Most mezzanine debt is issued in connection with management-led buyouts and, more recently, leveraged acquisitions. Most is in loan format, usually floating rate, at usually 200–400 basis points over LIBOR. Accompanying most mezzanine debt are common stock warrants or some other form of equity kicker. Recent total internal rates of return for U.K. mezzanine debt have been in the 20 percent to 30 percent range. In the next stage in the development of the U.K. high-yield market, which likely will follow the path of the early U.S. high-yield markets, these loans will probably be securitized as high-yield bonds. As the United Kingdom and Europe prepare for deregulation in 1992, there is likely to be an increase in corporate restructurings, including MBOs and acquisitions. This will probably increase the issuance of mezzanine debt in Europe and the United Kingdom (we will say more on this later).

In 1988, the United Kingdom's 3i, the leading underwriter of mezzanine debt (see Exhibit 3), underwrote and syndicated £30 million of mezzanine loan facilities in the £359 million MBO of Bricom Group. Some other recent mezzanine offerings included BPCC and Crockfords Casino. BPCC, the largest printing company in the United Kingdom, was sold by Robert Maxwell to management. In the transaction, £177 million of senior debt and a £40 million subordinated loan were issued. Crockfords issued £10.5 million of mezzanine debt. Large

---

7. David Carter and Chris Beresford, *Management Buyout Statistics: 1 October 1989* (London: KPMG Peat Marwick McLintock, 1989).

EXHIBIT 3 *Leading Mezzanine Arrangers*[a]

	Number of Deals Led	Total Value (£m)	Average Size (£m)
3i	13	187	14
Bankers Trust	9	300	33
Barclays/BZW	7	74	11
County NatWest/Nat West	7	70	10
SecPac/SPHG Equity	5	38	8
Phildrew	4	14	4
GE Capital	3	580	193
PIC Capital	3	109	36
Standard Chartered	3	88	29
Bank of Boston	2	13	7
Charterhouse	2	24	12
Chase	2	11	6
Citicorp	2	15	8
Kleinwort	2	17	9
Others	14	202	14
(Eliminate duplications)	(6)	(250)	
	72	1,492	21

a. As of 1 October, 1989.
Source: KPMG Peat Marwick McLintock.

transactions like Gateway and B.A.T. will be generating more mezzanine debt issues (see Exhibit 4).

The MBO market has been growing rapidly in the United Kingdom (see Exhibit 5). As Exhibits 6 and 7 indicate, mezzanine debt constitutes a sizable portion of a typical MBO financing. In 1980, there were an estimated 100 MBOs valued at £40 million, with an average transaction size of under £400,000. By 1988, some 400 MBOs were transacted with an aggregate value of £5 billion, averaging £12.5 million in transaction size. Of these, approximately 10 were financed in part by mezzanine debt.[8] A greater portion of MBOs in 1989 are being financed by mezzanine debt.

This market for mezzanine debt is likely to grow as MBOs and other leveraged transactions increase in the United Kingdom and Europe

8. Ibid.

EXHIBIT 4 *The Ten Most Highly Leveraged MBOs over £50MM*

	Date	Total (£m)	Equity (£m)	Mez-zanine (£m)	Debt (£m)
British Syphon	2/89	53	2	15	36
Pontins Holidays	3/87	60	3	6	51
Cope Allman	2/88	265	20	–	245
EIP	12/88	62	5	17	40
Gateway	7/89	2,375	200	375	1,800
Bricom Inds	7/88	405	39	30	336
BPCC	1/89	265	28	40	197
NFC	1/82	59	8	–	51
London Clubs	5/89	120	19	40	61
Response	10/88	97	17	24	56

Source: KPMG Peat Marwick McLintock.

EXHIBIT 5 *Estimate of Total of U.K. Management Buyouts*

Year	Number	Value (£m)	Average Size (£m)
1980	100	40	0.4
1981	180	130	0.7
1982	200	550	2.8
1983	220	240	1.1
1984	200	270	1.4
1985	250	1,070	4.3
1986	300	1,320	4.4
1987	350	3,270	9.3
1988	400	5,000	12.5
1989[a]	300	5,570	18.6
	2,500	17,460	7.0

a. As of 1 October, 1989.
Source: KPMG Peat Marwick McLintock.

EXHIBIT 6   *Debt/Equity Distribution in U.K. MBOs* [a]

Year	Total Value (£m)	Equity (£m)	Mez- zanine (£m)	Debt (£m)	Debt Ratio (1)[b]	Debt Ratio (2)[c]
1981	45	30	—	15	0.5	0.5
1982	470	195	—	275	1.4	1.4
1983	160	45	—	115	2.5	2.5
1984	170	85	—	85	1.0	1.0
1985	860	230	120	510	2.7	2.0
1986	950	300	100	550	2.2	1.7
1987	2,780	810	210	1,760	2.4	2.0
1988	4,440	1,210	280	2,950	2.7	2.3
1989[d]	4,950	790	780	3,380	5.3	3.2

a. This table includes substantially all (approximately 95%) of the value of U.K. MBOs, though it does not include some U.K. MBOs for which data was not available.
b. Mezzanine treated as debt.
c. Mezzanine treated as both equity and debt in equal parts.
d. As of 1 October, 1989.
Source: KPMG Peat Marwick McLintock.

and as the average transaction size gets larger (see Exhibit 7). In 1986, some £180 million of mezzanine debt was issued; in 1987, £210 million; in 1988, £280 million; and for the first nine months of 1989, £780 million.[9] More mezzanine debt would have been issued if there had been a stronger buyer base. Today, commercial banks in the United Kingdom are steady buyers of only small pieces of mezzanine debt — some £2–£3 million parcels, perhaps two to three times a year. In contrast, very few of the United Kingdom's 150 insurance companies or pension funds invest in mezzanine debt. For this mezzanine market to grow, a larger universe of buyers with a greater number of credit analysts is needed.

One of the first investment vehicles that have enabled European institutions to become familiar with subordinated debt is the mezzanine fund, a pool of institutional money raised to invest on a dedicated basis in MBOs and other leveraged transactions. First Britannia Mezzanine, N.V., the first mezzanine fund targeted at Europe, was formed

9. Ibid.

EXHIBIT 7 *Use of Mezzanine Debt in U.K. MBOs*

Year	MBOs Using Mezzanine Debt			Total MBOs		% of Deal Covered by Mezzanine	% of MBOs Using Mezzanine	Average Size of Mezzanine Layer (£m)
	Number	Amount of Mezzanine (£m)	Total Value of Deals (£m)	Number	Total Value of Deals (£m)			
1985	5	123	430	22	850	29	23	25
1986	7	96	370	28	960	26	25	14
1987	14	213	1,570	35	2,770	14	40	15
1988	24	282	1,800	54	4,470	16	44	12
1989a	23	778	4,200	47	4,990	19	49	34
	73	1,492	8,370	186	14,040	18	39	20

a. As of September 15.
Source: Peat Marwick McLintock.

EXHIBIT 8 *First Britannia Capital Structure*

(a) £125 million Senior Loans/Notes; 5 year maturity; LIBOR + 1⅝ %;
    Investment-Grade Rating (BBB equivalent with strong covenants) —
    interest coverage 1.75x, asset coverage 1.50x.

(b) £45 million Subordinated Loans/Notes; 10 year maturity; LIBOR +
    3%; BB equivalent rating; own covenants — interest coverage 1.25x,
    asset coverage 1.10x.

(c) £23 million Preferred Stock; 12 year maturity; LIBOR + 5% (PIK for
    at least first 2 years).

(d) £7 million Common Stock
    (i) £1.6 million Class A Common — DBL
    (ii) £5.4 million Class B Common — Strip Investors

• Categories (b), (c), and (d.ii) were sold as a "strip," the minimum strip
  investment being £817,777 (£500,000 + £255,555 + £62,222).

• Return from strip is 23–30%, depending upon portfolio returns — very
  high for a debt instrument. Modeling is conservative. Existing assets
  imply a return in excess of 30%.

---

in December 1988 and has £200 million in capitalization; £125 million
senior debt (rated BBB), £45 million junior capital (rated BB), £23
million preferred stock, and £7 million common stock (see Exhibit 8).
The approximately 40 institutional subscribers purchased the senior
debt or strips of the junior capital. Although the fund can invest in
any country in Western Europe and in any currency, it typically seeks
debt of stable, predictable manufacturing businesses. The investments
are generally in loan format and are not securitized. Mezzanine funds
like First Britannia, along with others such as Charterhouse Buyout
Fund ($250 million) and funds run by Schroder Ventures and Generale
Occidentale, are credited with allowing U.K. and European investors
to become familiar with subordinated debt.

High-Yield Issues for the
International Market

Over the last several years, an increasing number of high-yield issues
have been tailored for the international marketplace. What follows
are some examples. As discussed earlier, many U.S. high-yield issuers

are pursuing foreign capital more aggressively by structuring their new issues as foreign currency–denominated (e.g., Coastal and Kronos) or floating rate (Continental Cablevision). Also, the recent increase of MBO and acquisition activity in the United Kingdom and Europe is playing an important role in the issuance of new high-yield subordinated debt by non-U.S. companies (for example, Isosceles/Gateway, Magnet, La Cote Desfosses). For foreign companies such as Australia's John Fairfax, the high-yield market offers access to U.S. capital.

MBO- and Acquisition-Related High-Yield Debt: Non-U.S.

Isosceles/Gateway.   In April 1989, Gateway, a U.K. supermarket chain, was the target of an unsolicited takeover bid by Isosceles, a U.K. bidding group. Using S. G. Warburg as its banker, Isosceles raised £3.18 billion for the acquisition, which consisted of various layers of senior and subordinated debt and equity. These included:

five senior debt tranches:
   £1.04 billion bridge facility — 18 months
   £600 million bridge facility — 1 year
   £620 million bridge facility — 3 years
   £170 million term loan — 7 years
   £375 million revolving credit — 7 years

one subordinated bridge facility: £175 million — 8 years

two mezzanine debt tranches:
   £100 million at LIBOR + 300 basis points (and warrants)
   £150 million at LIBOR + 350 basis points (and warrants)

The £250 million of mezzanine debt was accompanied with an equity kicker in the form of warrants.

La Cote Desfosses.   The leveraged acquisition of La Cote Desfosses, a financial newspaper in France, was implemented with split coupon mezzanine debt. In January 1989, after a year of negotiations, Georges Ghosn purchased Cote for FFr261 million. The debt was sold in strips: purchasers of the FFr43 million of equity in DesFosses International, the acquisition holding company, were required to buy also the FFr46 million of subordinated debt. The financing was structured as follows:

senior debt: FFr89 million — floating rate

subordinated debt: FFr46 million — pays 9% for two years and then
12% for five years

equity: FFr43 million

deferred payment of FFr83 million over five years to former owner.

Magnet.   A building materials retailer headquartered in Yorkshire,
England, Magnet could not have completed its £630 million March
1989 MBO without financing it with £190 million of mezzanine debt.
Magnet, the largest U.K. public company to go private, was bid on
by DMWSL, the buyout group. The following outlines the financing:

two senior debt tranches:
£65 million bridge loan at LIBOR +175 basis points — 120 days
£300 million term loan — 6 years

mezzanine debt:
£160 million senior subordinated notes at LIBOR +175 basis
points — 8 years
£30 million junior subordinated notes at LIBOR +350 basis
points — 8 years

equity: £110 million

John Fairfax.   Australia's premier newspaper publisher, John Fairfax, was acquired in an A$2.6 billion leveraged buyout in November
1987. Part of the bank debt was refinanced in January 1989 with A$450
million of privately placed senior subordinated and subordinated debentures, high-yield securities uniquely designed for an international
market.

In the refinancing, the company's objective was to raise money outside of Australia, which has no subordinated debt market, and to issue Australian currency–denominated bonds in order to match its assets. At the time of the offering, the non-Australian buyers of the issue
asked for some protection against foreign exchange risk. Normally,
the swap market would enable investors to hedge, but because Fairfax
needed to issue debt with a 10–12 year maturity (swaps do not extend
so long) there was a need for a built-in currency hedge. This hedge was
provided through Foreign Exchange Appreciation Rights, or FEARs,
which were issued along with the bonds. The FEARs are a currency

"makewell" feature entitling bondholders to receive a guaranteed rate of return (subject to a cap) at the time of principal payment, despite the effects of currency fluctuations. The cap enables the company to limit its foreign exchange exposure. The securities consisted of two Australian dollar–denominated bonds, A$300 million of 18 percent senior subordinated debentures and A$150 million of 18.5 percent subordinated debentures, which were issued with the nondetachable FEARs as well as 25 percent of the company's equity.

U.S. High-Yield Debt for International Buyers

Coastal Corporation. Coastal, a Texas-based energy company, has issued high-yield bonds in foreign currencies in order to have greater access to capital. Issues include a September 1988 offering of SFr80 million of 5.75 percent bonds due 1988–93 and ¥14 billion of 6.3 percent senior loans due 1995.

Kronos International. Headquartered in West Germany, Kronos International is the fourth-largest manufacturer of titanium dioxide pigment in the world. As part of a 1989 refinancing, Kronos took out a seven-year Deutsche Mark (DM) 1.6 billion secured term loan facility and issued DM400 million of eight-year subordinated notes.

The principal subsidiary of NL Industries, an American company, Kronos International has most of its operations in West Germany, where it has a 30 percent market share. Kronos used DM-denominated loan facilities and notes in order to match its liabilities with its assets.

Continental Cablevision Inc. In November 1989, Continental Cablevision, a Boston cable television company, offered international investors $100 million of 15-year floating-rate Eurobonds with interest that increases progressively from 300 basis points over the 3-year LIBOR in the first year to 650 basis points above LIBOR in the final year.

1992: High-Yield Opportunities in the United Kingdom and Europe

The deregulation of Europe's financial markets scheduled for 1992 is expected to result in a surge of demand for high-yield securities by investors and a sharp increase in issuance by European companies. To compete effectively with Japan and regain market share in crucial manufacturing sectors, European companies will need long-term, relatively low-cost capital that offers flexibility. Since the early 1980s, high-yield bonds have provided American industry with that sort of capital.

In anticipation of a less regulated environment by 1992, many European companies have begun to restructure their operations. Simultaneously, companies in non-EEC countries, seeking footholds in the EEC, are seeking to acquire companies in member countries. European industry, largely rebuilt with strong family ownership after World War II, is maturing, and questions of succession are arising. Growth into conglomerates is now being assessed by institutional investors and management, and a redefinition of corporate strategies is leading to a concentration on core businesses.

Subordinated debt financing opportunities are likely to emerge as divisions are sold or subsidiaries divested when these companies restructure. In addition, the recent strong economic conditions in Europe are making it possible for entrepreneurial management to pursue growth through acquisition. Indeed, many recent transactions illustrate the growth of this market (see Exhibit 9). Younger entrepreneurs, averse to dilution of equity, are often more receptive to leverage in order to finance acquisitions. The consequent wave of MBOs should make Europe ripe for mezzanine financing.

Elsewhere around the world acceptance of high-yield investments is occurring gradually. In the Middle East, banks began buying high-yield securities in 1986 as their U.S. branch offices were made profit centers. Pacific Rim countries such as Korea, Taiwan, and Singapore are only now starting to look for opportunities in the high-yield market. In the future, as our global marketplace expands, high-yield securities should find increasing acceptance.

Swap Transactions

The following example demonstrates how swaps are used in the international market.

Assume an investor purchases a single high-yield issue: $1 million of the XYZ 13.5 percent coupon bond maturing 12/01/96 currently

EXHIBIT 9 *Selected 1989 Cross-Border and Non-U.S. Acquisitions Involving Bridge Financing*

Target	Country	Acquiror	Country	Transaction Value ($MM)	Amount of Bridge ($MM)
The Gateway Corp. PLC	U.K.	Isosceles PLC	U.K.	3,296[a]	2,060
Magnet PLC	U.K.	Investor Group	U.K.	1,085[a]	270
Coalite Group	U.K.	Anglo United PLC	U.K.	760[a]	314
Anchor Glass Container	U.S.	Vitro SA	Mexico	721[a]	295
Pacific Resources	U.S.	Broken Hill Proprietary	Australia	378	400
WA Krueger Co.	U.S.	Ringier AG	Switzerland	306	190
Dunkin' Donuts	U.S.	DD Acquisition	Canada	279[a]	180
SSMC Inc.	U.S.	Semi-Tech Microelectronics	Hong Kong	279[a]	140
Scotty's Inc.	U.S.	GB-Inno BM SA	Belgium	146[a]	146

a. Pending or partially completed.
Source: Securities Data Corporation.

priced at par. The cash flows to the investor from this asset are fixed payments of 13.5 percent semiannually for the seven years until maturity.

The investor, however, may prefer to receive regular floating-rate payments either if he or she believes that interest rates are going to rise or to meet floating-rate liabilities, which is frequently the case with overseas institutions. This is accomplished with an interest rate swap.

Interest Rate Swap

An interest rate swap is the contractual agreement between two parties to exchange interest rate flows. Two main uses of swaps are hedging and altering the interest rate structure of a portfolio by creating synthetic securities. The swap is accomplished by the two parties exchanging fixed- and floating-rate interest flows; interest rate swaps do not affect principal.

The purchase of a fixed-rate asset in combination with an interest rate swap duplicates the direct purchase of a floating-rate asset. In the example, the fixed cash flow is 13.5 percent semiannually. The swap is structured such that the investor makes fixed semiannual payments at 8.65 percent (the swap rate) and receives in return (floating) six-month LIBOR-based cash flows for the same seven-year term as the original investment. (Note that the maturity of the swap can be earlier than that of the asset, in which case the original fixed-rate cash flows resume upon termination of the swap.)

After the swap the situation looks like this:

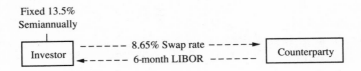

The investor receives the original fixed cash flows at 13.5 percent semiannually. A fixed semiannual payment of 8.65 percent is then made in exchange for floating-rate cash flows at six-month LIBOR. The net result is a floating cash flow of LIBOR plus 4.85 percent semiannually.

Fixed receipt	13.50%
Floating receipt	LIBOR
Fixed payment	− 8.65%
NET CASH FLOW	LIBOR + 4.85%

This transaction offers various advantages to the investor.

- Interest rate swaps can accommodate any desired investment structure, with maturities ranging from 1 to 10 years.
- The liquidity and depth of the swap market enable the investor to return at any time to the original fixed-rate position by arranging a swap reversal.
- Swaps can be tailored to match call provisions of bonds.

Currency Swap

A currency swap is the contractually agreed transfer between two parties of their interest rate flows, which are denominated in two different currencies. Unlike an interest rate swap, the currency swap involves a transfer of principal at either origination or maturity of the swap at a predetermined spot exchange rate.

A synthetic fixed-rate foreign bond is created by combining a fixed-rate, U.S. dollar–denominated asset with a currency swap. In the example, the fixed-rate, U.S. dollar–denominated asset can be converted into a fixed-rate, Deutsche Mark (DM)–denominated asset with the purchase of a currency swap. At initiation of the swap, the spot DM/USD exchange rate is 1.7965, and the 7-year DM swap rate is 8.14 percent semiannually. The DM investor must first purchase dollars to invest in the bond:

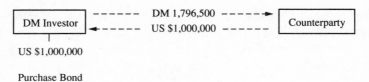

Purchase Bond

The DM rate that the counterparty is willing to pay in return for the investor's coupons is 12.90 percent. Thus the semiannual cash flows from the bond are as follows:

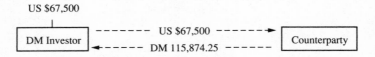

EXHIBIT 10

YEN spot exchange   143.80
        7-year swap rate   10.83% p.a.
 	
        initial flow:
                Yen   ¥143,800,000
                USD   1,000,000
 	
        semiannual flows:
                USD   67,500
                Yen   ¥7,786,770
 	
        principal flow:
                USD   1,000,000
                Yen   ¥143,800,000
	SWF spot exchange 1.6055
	        7-year swap rate 11.78% p.a.
	
	        initial flow:
	                Swiss Franc SFr 1,605,500
	                USD 1,000,000
	
	        semiannual flows:
	                USD 67,500
	                Swiss Franc SFr 94,563.95
	
	        principal flow:
	                USD 1,000,000
	                Swiss Franc SFr 1,605,500

STG   spot exchange   1.5604
        7-year swap rate   17.83% p.a.
 	
        initial flow:
                Pounds   £640,861.32
                USD   1,000,000
 	
        semiannual flows:
                USD   67,500
                Pounds   £57,132.78
 	
        principal flow:
                USD   1,000,000
                Pounds   £640,861.32
	FF spot exchange 6.1300
	        7-year swap rate 15.02% p.a.
	
	        initial flow:
	                French Franc FFr 6,130,000
	                USD 1,000,000
	
	        semiannual flows:
	                USD 67,500
	                French Franc FFr 460,363
	
	        principal flow:
	                USD 1,000,000
	                French Franc FFr 6,130,000

In addition to the final coupon above, principal is exchanged at maturity of the swap (at 12/01/96):

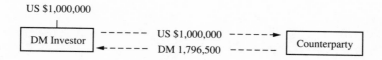

The semiannual foreign currency flows are based on the principal amount and the swap rate. Thus, 12.90 percent on the DM1,796,500 principal yields 115,874.25 semiannually.

The advantages to the investor of a currency swap are similar to those described for an interest rate swap.

The cash flows for other foreign currency–denominated swaps are shown in Exhibit 10.

4

High-Yield Default Losses and the Return Performance of Bankrupt Debt: 1977–89

Gregory T. Hradsky
Associate
The First Boston Corporation

Robert D. Long, CFA
Managing Director
The First Boston Corporation

Default risk has always been a controversial topic associated with the high-yield bond market. Several large defaults in 1989 fueled the debate and led one financial publication to declare that in 1990 junk bonds are "out" and Treasury bonds are "in." The well-publicized Asquith[1] default study raised the level of apprehension by proclaiming that the default rate was much higher than previously thought. However, when citing these comparisons, the press neglected to mention that the default rates in the Asquith study were cumulative rates, not the annualized rates of previous studies. In fact, the Asquith study's annualized rates support the conclusions of prior studies, including Edward Altman's[2] and First Boston's.[3]

---

1. Paul Asquith, David W. Mullins, Jr., and Eric D. Wolff, "Original Issue High Yield Bonds: Aging Analyses of Defaults, Exchanges, and Calls," *Journal of Finance* (September 1989), pp. 923–951.
2. Edward I. Altman, "Measuring Corporate Bond Mortality and Performance," *Journal of Finance* (September 1989), pp. 909–922; and Edward I. Altman, "The Anatomy of the High-Yield Bond Market," *Financial Analysts Journal* (July–August 1987), pp. 12–25.
3. See our earlier work on defaults in Gregory T. Hradsky and Robert D. Long,

We have updated our default study, which examines the effect of defaults on the high-yield bond market for the years 1977–1989. Actual prices have been used to measure the loss to investors. Our study also includes the negative impact of distressed exchange offers, which has been a popular alternative to an outright default or Chapter 11 filing both for issuers and investors. The results show that default losses have been much smaller than the risk premium paid to investors for assuming the additional default risk associated with investing in high-yield bonds. We also examined the price behavior of defaulted securities by tracking their excess returns two years prior to and after default to determine whether any patterns existed in the returns on bankrupt debt. The data indicates that investors uncover the signs of distress long before default and suggests a potential trading strategy for investing in bankrupt debt.

Default Rates and Losses

We have defined default as an uncured failure (i.e., beyond the 30-day grace period) to make a required interest or principal payment, the filing of a bankruptcy petition, or the initiation of a distressed exchange offer. Distress is defined as an exchange for securities with a lower principal amount or interest rate.

The loss in principal value is computed by subtracting the price at issuance from the price at the end of the month of default or exchange and then dividing by the original issue price.[4] This percentage is then multiplied by the principal amount outstanding at the time of default. One half of the annual coupon payment, which represents the value of lost interest income, is added to this amount. The losses

"High Yield Default Losses and the Return Performance of Bankrupt Debt," *Financial Analysts Journal* (July–August 1989), pp. 38–49; Robert D. Long and Gregory T. Hradsky, "The First Boston Default Study," *The High Yield Handbook* (New York: The First Boston Corporation, 1989); and Robert D. Long and Gregory T. Hradsky, "A Closer Look at Defaults and Exchange Offers," *The High Yield Handbook* (New York: The First Boston Corporation, 1988).
4. If warrants or stock were attached, their market value was subtracted from the issuance price. The issuance price of defaulted debt that was previously involved in a distressed exchange offer was adjusted to prevent the double counting of losses (i.e., the month-end price during the exchange was substituted for the issue price).

are then summed and divided by the corresponding universe figure for the year to arrive at the default rates.

The study's universe of securities comprises all straight debt defaulting or involved in a distressed exchange offer; convertible securities were excluded. Original issue high-yield debt is defined as all public debt rated split BBB or lower. The universe of defaulted securities spans the time period from January 1, 1977, to December 31, 1989. The study used 1977 as the starting point because it represents the inception of the modern-day high-yield bond market. Price data is monthly, starting at the beginning of 1975 and running through the end of 1989. Price data was obtained from First Boston and supplemented by Tradeline, Moody's Bond Record, and S&P Bond Guide.

Default Results

Our study shows the market-weighted average default loss rate from 1977 through 1989 to be 1.87 percent, including all distressed exchange offers and fallen angels (see Exhibit 1). When fallen angels are excluded, the rate drops to 1.51 percent. Fallen angels account for nearly a third of the par value of defaulting issues, but only 20 percent of the total loss to investors. The lower loss number can be attributed to Texaco's strategic default in 1987. Its bonds suffered an average total loss of only 18.5 percent — 12.8 percent excluding coupon loss — and the default accounts for 19 percent of the universe of defaulted securities. The weighted average principal loss over the 13-year period is 49.5 percent. From 1977 to 1989, 170 companies defaulted or announced exchange offers on a total of 384 bonds.

Nearly $7.3 billion of public debt defaulted or was involved in a distressed exchange offer during 1989, resulting in a default loss rate of 2.53 percent. This figure is based on an average amount of high-yield debt outstanding (as of June 30, 1989) of $215.2 billion. The 2.53 percent rate is higher than the historical experience of 1.87 percent over the 13 years from 1977 to 1989. This is due primarily to a principal loss of 68.1 percent for 1989 that was more severe than the historical weighted average loss of 54.2 percent (not including Texaco). The onslaught of negative news confronting the high-yield market during the last four months of the year fomented widespread fear that a recession would result in a massive wave of defaults and restructurings. This accentuated the difference between strong and suspect credits and hit

EXHIBIT 1 *Default Loss Rates, 1977-1989*

Year	High-Yield Straight Debt Universe[a] (millions)	Defaulted Principal Amount[b] (millions)	Dollar Principal Loss (millions)	Principal Loss (%)	Total Loss Including Coupon (millions)	Default Loss Rates (%)	Without FA Debt
1977	$8,479.0	$585.4	$288.9	49.35	$308.5	3.64	2.74
1978	9,401.0	265.2	83.5	31.48	92.6	0.99	0.64
1979	10,675.0	126.5	17.1	13.51	22.8	0.21	0.08
1980	15,125.0	257.1	149.3	58.08	162.1	1.07	0.60
1981	17,362.0	349.7	115.7	33.09	131.1	0.76	0.09
1982	18,536.0	1,038.3	622.7	59.97	670.7	3.62	0.70
1983	28,233.0	379.4	133.1	35.09	155.0	0.55	0.44
1984	41,700.0	408.9	184.2	45.05	207.3	0.50	0.34
1985	59,178.0	2,055.8	796.8	38.76	920.0	1.55	1.55
1986	92,985.0	4,319.0	2,210.7	51.19	2,454.4	2.64	2.22
1987	121,827.0	7,485.0	1,833.0	24.49	2,286.0	1.88	1.13
1988	163,618.0	3,661.2	1,955.6	53.41	2,173.7	1.33	0.96
1989	215,202.0	7,298.4	4,967.6	68.06	5,444.8	2.53	2.49
Totals		$28,230.0	$13,358.2		$15,028.9		

Weighted Averages	1977-89	Without FA Debt
Default Loss Rate	1.87%	1.51%
Principal Loss	49.50%	54.98%

a. Midyear figures; Source: First Boston, S&P, and Moody's for 1977-86.
b. Includes distressed exchange offers.
Source: The First Boston Corporation.

EXHIBIT 2 *Default Loss Rates, 1977–1989*

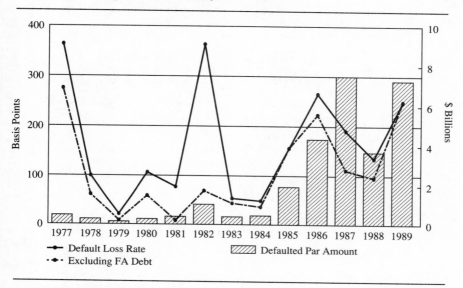

Source: The First Boston Corporation.

distressed securities particularly hard, resulting in the higher principal loss number. In fact, the 1989 principal loss is not that far from the recession-plagued 1982 experience of 60.0 percent.

Pattern of Defaults

Exhibit 2 shows the pattern of annual defaults in fallen angels and original issue high-yield debt. The relatively high dollar amounts of defaults during 1985–1989 may be partially explained by the increased use of bankruptcy filing as a strategic rather than financial device, with the intent of avoiding legal, labor, regulatory, and other problems. Many of the largest "defaults," including Texaco, Hillsborough Holdings, and Public Service of New Hampshire, have significant strategic elements. As such, the decline from issue price is less than average for many of these securities, because strategic defaults generally have been much less harmful to bondholders than financial insolvency. Another explanation for the higher numbers is the dramatic growth in the high-yield market, thereby increasing the number of securities that could potentially default.

EXHIBIT 3 *Defaults by Industry*

Industry	1989			1977–1989		
	Number of Companies	Principal Amount (millions)	Percent	Number of Companies	Principal Amount (millions)	Percent
Air Transportation	0	$0.0	0.0	3	$188.7	0.7
Chemicals	0	0.0	0.0	5	261.0	0.9
Consumer (Distribution/Retail)	2	304.0	4.2	8	1,730.6	6.1
Consumer (Manufacturing)	2	194.6	2.7	9	660.9	2.3
Containers	0	0.0	0.0	1	11.0	0.0
Energy (Oil & Gas)	0	0.0	0.0	28	8,052.1	28.5
Entertainment (Film)	1	23.4	0.3	5	601.0	2.1
Financial (S&L/Insurance/Banks)	15	3,037.4	41.6	32	4,316.6	15.3
Food (Distrib./Restaurants/Storage)	1	510.0	7.0	4	631.2	2.2
Gaming (Hotels/Leisure)	2	1,050.1	14.4	8	1,263.2	4.5
General Industries	0	0.0	0.0	15	842.3	3.0
Healthcare	0	0.0	0.0	7	819.0	2.9
Housing (Bldg. Materials/Real Estate)	2	1,286.1	17.6	11	2,027.2	7.2
Information & Technology	0	0.0	0.0	7	767.4	2.7
Media (Broadcasting/Cable/Publishing)	2	537.1	7.4	6	837.1	3.0
Metal & Minerals	0	0.0	0.0	7	2,841.9	10.1
Transportation (Surface)	4	355.7	4.9	12	1,073.2	3.8
Utility	0	0.0	0.0	2	1,305.6	4.6
Totals	31	$7,298.4	100.0	170	$28,230.0	100.0

Source: The First Boston Corporation.

EXHIBIT 4 *Defaults by Industry, 1977–1989*

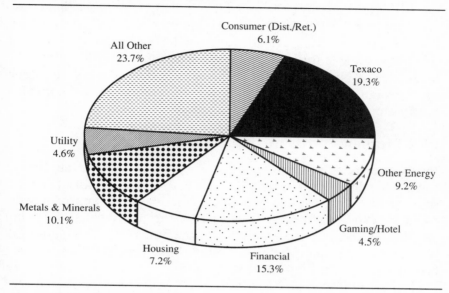

Source: The First Boston Corporation.

Industry Concentration

In the past, defaults were concentrated primarily in the energy and steel industries (see Exhibits 3 and 4). The year 1989 witnessed a shift in this trend, with the bulk of defaulting debt occurring in the financial sector. A total of 31 companies defaulted during 1989. Fifteen financial companies defaulted on $3.0 billion of debt (42 percent of the total), including three of the five largest defaults: Integrated Resources, Lomas Financial, and Southmark. There were also nine savings and loans that defaulted on $675 million of bonds. The largest default was Hillsborough Holdings, which had $1.2 billion of public debt outstanding and made housing the second highest industry concentration, with 18 percent of the total. The securities of Eastern Airlines were not included in our numbers despite the company's March Chapter 11 filing, because the bonds, mostly equipment trust certificates backed by airplanes, never stopped making interest payments. The Kelsey-Hayes (Fruehauf) exchange offer was also omitted, because the exchange was not distressed and was contingent on the sale of the company to Varity Corp., which guaranteed the new debt.

The data indicates that cyclical sectors appear to be more susceptible to default. Energy (29%), financial (15%), steel (10%), and housing (7%) lead the list with the largest amounts of defaulted debt over the past 13 years. Media (3%), food products (2%), and containers (0%) have some of the lowest numbers. The bankruptcy filing by Public Service of New Hampshire demonstrates that defaults can occur even in a noncyclical industry such as public utilities, proving that industry alone is not adequate protection against default.

Risk Premiums versus Actual Default Losses

Investors demand a premium over a comparable risk-free rate for assuming the default risk associated with investing in corporate bonds. In an efficient market, this premium in theory should approximately equal the expected future loss experience for all investors. We compared our default rate calculations for the past 13 years to high-yield spreads to determine whether investors have been sufficiently compensated for the risk undertaken.

The First Boston High Yield Index (FBC Index) was used as a proxy for the high-yield market, and the yield on similar-maturity Treasury bonds was used for the risk-free rate. The risk premium is the spread at the beginning of the year between the FBC Index and Treasuries. We then subtracted the yearly default rates from the risk premiums to determine whether any excess premiums had been paid.

For the 13-year period, high-yield investors received a weighted average risk premium of 436 basis points. This compares favorably with the historical default loss experience of 187 basis points, suggesting that investors were overcompensated by 249 basis points (Exhibits 5 and 6). The FBC Index began the 1989 year with a spread of 448 basis points and lost 253 basis points from defaults, resulting in an excess premium of 195 basis points. Given all of the negative press surrounding the high-yield bond market, the Index widened to 790 basis points at the beginning of 1990, implying that bond investors expect the worst for the year.

Return Behavior

We also examined the performance of defaulted issues over a four-year period, that is, two years prior to and after default for debt de-

EXHIBIT 5 *Risk Premiums vs. Actual Losses (in Basis Points)*

Year	Yield Spread[a]	Default Losses		Excess Premiums	
		Default Rates	Without FA Debt	Excess Premiums	Without FA Debt
1978	414	99	64	315	350
1979	299	21	8	278	291
1980	271	107	60	164	211
1981	351	76	9	275	342
1982	388	362	70	26	318
1983	430	55	44	375	386
1984	267	50	34	217	233
1985	373	155	155	218	218
1986	425	264	222	161	203
1987	538	188	113	350	425
1988	459	133	96	326	363
1989	448	253	249	195	199
1990	790				

Weighted Averages	1978–89	Without FA Debt
Yield Spread	436	436
Default Loss Rate	187	151
Excess Premium	249	285

a. Spreads based on subtracting the YTM on comparable maturity Treasuries from the yield-to-worst figure for the FBC High Yield Index at the beginning of the year; pre-1987 uses the 10 Year; pre-1982 are Index estimates.
Source: The First Boston Corporation.

faulting between 1977 and 1988. In calculating the impact of default, excess returns were used to isolate the effect of default from general market movements. The Blume–Keim (BK) Index for Lower Grade Bonds[5] was used as a proxy for the market returns. The BK Index was chosen because defaulted securities are removed from it two months

5. Marshall E. Blume and Donald B. Keim, "Return Indexes for Lower Grade Bonds 1977–1987," Rodney L. White Center for Financial Research, 1988.

EXHIBIT 6   *Risk Premiums vs. Default Losses, 1978-1990*

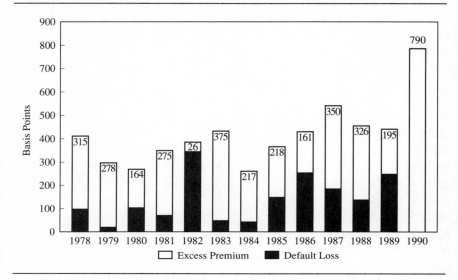

Source: The First Boston Corporation.

after the default event. Because the objective was to isolate the impact of default, we did not want an index that included the performance of these bonds. Excess returns were calculated on a monthly basis by subtracting the index total return from each security's total return for the month. Accrued interest was computed by dividing the semiannually compounded coupon rate by 12 and adding the result to the bond price. Interest was not added during the month of default or thereafter, because most defaulted issues trade flat.

Cumulative excess returns (CERs) were computed by summing the weighted averages over time. Mean prices, returns, and standard deviations were calculated, as well as weighted averages, to give the reader a sense of the dispersion in the data. The number of bonds for each computation is included also. The number of bonds used in the monthly calculations drops off gradually after the default date. There are two reasons for this. First, our price data for this analysis ends in 1988; therefore, it was not possible to collect data until two years after default on debt defaulting in 1987 and 1988. Second, prices were not available for all securities for the entire post–two-year period as a result of the pricing services dropping them or the bonds becoming worthless. There is also a lower number of bonds for the two-years-prior calculation. The BK Index starts in 1977, so we were unable to calculate returns for the full two years prior to 1977 and 1978.

Results

As can be seen in the graph of the CERs in Exhibit 7, most of the decline in value occurs before the default announcement (Exhibit 8 contains a monthly listing of the excess returns). The downward trend is evident 17 months before default and becomes markedly visible approximately during the 11th month prior to the event. The decline becomes very steep 5 months before and bottoms out at the 5th month after. The CER then rises for several months (five) before returning to a secondary low. This second trough is shallower than the first and is followed by another upward trend. These peaks sometimes are the result of asset sales, a recovery in business fortunes, or the acquisition of the company by another firm. It is also possible that the low point is created by money managers who want to avoid showing positions in

EXHIBIT 7 *Excess Returns (All Debt)*

Month	Weighted Average Return (%)	Mean Return (%)	Standard Deviation (%)	Number of Bonds	Par Amount ($)	CER (%)
−23	0.09	−0.09	4.86	222	12,958	0.31
−22	−0.38	−0.41	4.62	229	13,355	−0.07
−21	1.29	0.39	6.33	236	14,026	1.22
−20	0.17	−0.20	5.59	236	14,041	1.39
−19	−0.48	−0.52	6.24	239	14,414	0.91
−18	0.10	0.23	6.49	240	14,284	1.01
−17	−1.27	−0.26	10.84	244	15,319	−0.26
−16	−0.94	−0.77	5.38	252	16,031	−1.20
−15	−0.36	0.00	5.77	258	16,510	−1.56
−14	−0.50	−0.90	5.26	259	16,563	−2.06
−13	−0.45	−0.49	5.27	261	16,600	−2.51
−12	−0.01	−0.07	6.26	267	16,885	−2.52

EXHIBIT 7 *Continued*

Month	Weighted Average Return (%)	Mean Return (%)	Standard Deviation (%)	Number of Bonds	Par Amount ($)	CER (%)
−11	0.70	−0.80	6.91	267	17,010	−1.82
−10	−1.06	−0.31	8.98	269	17,225	−2.87
−9	−0.65	−1.40	9.41	271	17,687	−3.52
−8	−1.14	−1.30	8.76	268	17,564	−4.66
−7	−1.82	−2.25	10.63	275	18,240	−6.49
−6	−1.46	−1.06	10.95	280	18,659	−7.95
−5	0.38	−0.07	9.63	282	18,931	−7.57
−4	−2.23	−2.74	11.39	280	19,111	−9.80
−3	−4.64	−3.96	12.84	282	19,460	−14.44
−2	−6.07	−5.36	15.85	284	19,670	−20.51
−1	−3.45	−2.48	24.62	283	19,645	−23.97
0	−10.95	−11.04	26.45	280	19,447	−34.92
1	−3.02	−2.70	18.63	282	19,298	−37.94
2	−1.39	−2.30	18.06	276	19,100	−39.33
3	−0.56	−1.84	18.46	277	18,854	−39.89
4	−5.35	−4.60	16.03	270	18,592	−45.24
5	−0.38	−1.22	19.33	261	18,344	−45.62
6	0.82	2.62	32.14	250	18,000	−44.80
7	2.60	1.31	16.85	246	17,359	−42.20
8	3.91	1.49	14.50	237	16,889	−38.29
9	2.42	3.34	19.91	227	15,887	−35.87
10	2.72	3.57	17.93	226	15,872	−33.15
11	−1.42	−3.24	16.38	216	15,650	−34.57
12	−1.90	0.44	28.26	202	15,082	−36.47
13	−1.33	0.10	16.84	196	14,817	−37.80
14	−0.26	−0.11	12.00	199	14,962	−38.06
15	−2.31	−0.82	18.37	186	14,079	−40.37
16	−1.33	0.35	18.21	178	13,290	−41.70
17	1.45	2.99	22.17	178	13,318	−40.25
18	1.16	0.02	14.48	177	13,288	−39.09
19	2.03	2.08	15.18	170	12,573	−37.06
20	1.56	0.12	17.08	169	12,738	−35.51
21	4.54	2.99	20.52	142	7,504	−30.97
22	−1.12	−0.60	16.88	133	6,944	−32.10
23	3.90	3.73	13.77	132	6,965	−28.19
24	−1.79	−0.93	7.16	124	6,589	−29.99

Source: The First Boston Corporation.

EXHIBIT 8   *Cumulative Excess Returns, 1977–1988*

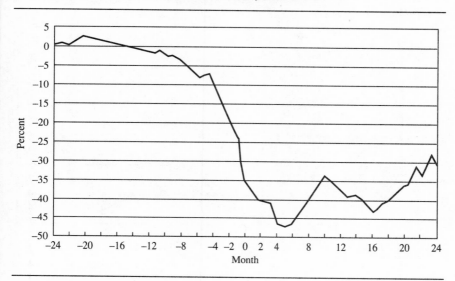

Source: The First Boston Corporation.

defaults and become sellers at almost any price. As the price declines worsen, investors specializing in bankrupt securities see an opportunity to buy what they perceive as excessively cheap bonds.

As one might expect, the volatility of returns, as measured by the standard deviation, increases as default becomes imminent (11th month prior) and remains high for the two years following default. Average volatility is the highest for original issue high-yield debt.

For original issue high-yield debt, the pattern of the CERs resembles that of the combined group (see Exhibit 9); the only difference is that the troughs and peaks are at much deeper levels. This is in line with expectations, because original issue high-yield companies are usually leveraged at the time of issuance. Fallen angels have a moderating influence on the severity of the price declines. As the largest fallen angel, Texaco's bonds are responsible for this, because of both the strategic nature of its bankruptcy and the huge amount of debt involved. As mentioned earlier, Texaco constitutes 19 percent of the universe of defaulted securities. When Texaco is excluded from the calculation,

EXHIBIT 9   *Cumulative Excess Returns: Original Issue High-Yield, 1977–1988*

Source: The First Boston Corporation.

the CERs closely follow the pattern of the group as a whole, with the exception that the declines are more severe (Exhibit 10).

Return Patterns

There is a pattern in these returns. The graphs suggest investing in bankrupt securities at approximately the fifth month after the default or distressed exchange offer and selling during the tenth month. No doubt real-life investing will not conform perfectly with this pattern. However, a strong case can be made for diversification given the wide range of returns on specific securities. A number of so-called vulture funds have been formed during the past year to take advantage of inefficiencies in the trading of bankrupt securities.[6] Some of these funds utilize a diversified portfolio approach as well as firm-specific analysis.

6. Marcia Parker and Marlene Givant Star, "$1.5 Billion Targeted for Ailing Firms," *Pensions & Investment Age* (March 6, 1989), pp. 1, 39.

EXHIBIT 10　*Cumulative Excess Returns: With and Without Texaco Debt, 1977–1988*

Source: The First Boston Corporation.

Conclusion

An understanding of the impact of default may be useful in estimating the future return of a given high-yield portfolio under various scenarios. It may also be useful in making comparisons with other markets, such as investment-grade bonds. However, it is important to note that high-grade investors have also experienced a significant "default" rate in the last few years. In addition to outright default, investors lose market value from a decline in rating to noninvestment-grade status as well. The RJR Nabisco leveraged buyout underscored this point. When the deal was announced, the entire corporate bond market declined as spreads widened and investors came to the realization that size alone does not afford protection. Given the large numbers of downgrades in recent years, the default rate for investment-grade securities might be surprisingly high.

In this chapter we have demonstrated that the risk premium paid on high-yield bonds over the past 13 years has more than compensated investors for the default losses they have suffered. In fact, investors received an excess premium of 249 basis points. This study has also shown that the cumulative excess returns of defaulted securities exhibit a marked downward trend as early as 18 months prior to default. Investors uncover the signs of financial distress long before the default announcement, as the return patterns show. The patterns also suggest that there is the potential to reap substantial gains by investing in the securities of bankrupt companies.

Although the absolute dollar amount of defaults in 1989 seems huge, the high-yield bond market is much larger than most observers realize. More importantly, a substantial part of the default rate is already reflected in security prices, so that high-yield market returns have already absorbed much of these losses. Bonds of issues such as Southland may actually rise in a default, considering their extremely depressed market levels at present. Given the current Index spread of 790 basis points, investors appear to have a comfortably large margin against future default risk.

Although the historical default experience is of great interest, the universe of debt issues has undergone dramatic change with the large increase in both fallen angels and underwritten high-yield issues. To assume that future default rates and price trends will resemble the pattern of the past may be misleading. New systematic and specific risks have been created by the wave of leveraged acquisitions and the general increase in leverage of corporations in both the high- and low-grade sectors.

SECTION II

High-Yield Bonds and Their Analysis

5

High-Yield Deferred Interest Securities: Evolution and Characteristics

Sam DeRosa-Farag
Assistant Vice President
The First Boston Corporation

Deferred interest securities (DISs) are fixed income securities that have no coupon payment for a specified interval, allowing the issuer to defer interest costs. High-yield DISs have been issued in several forms: zero-coupon bonds, issued without a coupon at a deep discount and redeemed at par when held to maturity; step-coupon bonds, whose initial coupon is below the market rate, with the discount making up for the difference; zero-fixed (or Zerfix) coupon bonds, a type of stepped-coupon security whose coupon is initially set at zero and moves after a specified period to another specified rate; and payment-in-kind (PIK) securities, whose coupons are in the form of additional securities for a specified period of time.

History of the DIS Market

The first DIS high-yield bonds were zero-coupon bonds, mostly senior notes, issued in the early 1980s. Issuers, primarily in the media industry, reasoned that their rapid growth rate would compensate investors for the risk of deferral of interest. Such a financing would also allow for the payment of bank debt amortization in the years immediately

EXHIBIT 1   *The High-Yield Universe, 1985 Weighting by Coupon Type*

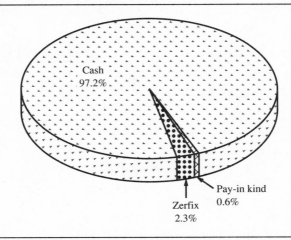

Source: The First Boston Corporation.

after issuance. Investors were attracted by the promise of cash flow growing more quickly than the accretion rate, and most all of these issues performed well.

Merger and acquisition activity in 1985–1986 spurred the issuance of zero-fixed and PIK securities offered in exchange for common stock (cramdowns). Approximately 3,000 M&A transactions were structured in 1985, 270 of which had a value in excess of $100 million and 36 of which had a value of over $1 billion. In contrast, 1984 M&A activity totaled only about $15 billion. (See Exhibit 1.) By 1987 the high-yield DIS market had grown rapidly and offered a number of large issues in a variety of industries and with a range of maturities, deferral periods, and seniority. Sophisticated analytical techniques were developed to analyze various capital structures and to identify appropriate tranches in the capital structure in which to invest.

The stock market crash of 1987 prompted more focus on the covenants of high-yield issues, and restrictions were initiated on the ability to repay junior securities in a number of large issues. The growing use of an interest coverage test in covenants ensures that no additional debt can be added to the detriment of the DIS or the credit. Also, several variations on the DIS structure have evolved, including PIK/Zerfix resets and increasing-rate notes that are partially PIK.

Originally, deferred interest securities were used as a substitute for bank debt or in conjunction with it; hence, DISs were issued at a senior level in the capital structure. During the 1986–1988 period, cramdown DISs were issued as the most junior security in the capital structure. Recently, a return to more senior DISs was fueled by a need to make the securities more acceptable to investors and by an opportunity to lower the blended cost of financing for the issuer. By year-end 1989, a wide range of DIS issues could be found at all levels of the capital structure.

Growth of the Deferred Interest Securities Sector

The fastest growing sector of the high-yield market in the 1985–1989 period was the DIS sector, which includes Zerfix debt, PIK debt, and PIK preferred stock. By year-end 1989, deferred pay issues accounted for $45 billion, 21 percent of the par value of the high-yield universe (Exhibit 2). The high level of M&A in this period generated increasing amounts of arbitrage-related cramdown paper, much of which is DIS.

EXHIBIT 2 *The High-Yield Universe, 1989 Market Value Weighting by Coupon Type*

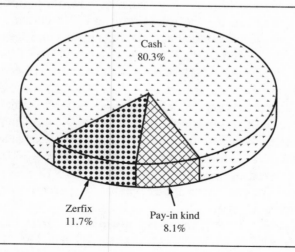

Source: The First Boston Corporation.

EXHIBIT 3   *First Boston High Yield Cash Index vs. Zerfix and PIK Preferred*

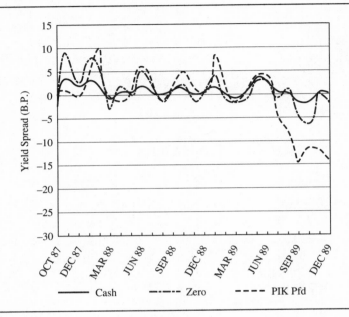

Source: The First Boston Corporation.

Returns on this sector have been volatile in recent periods, as shown in Exhibit 3. In 1988, Zerfix bonds returned 21.6 percent versus 12.8 percent for cash-paying securities; PIK debentures on average returned 14.1 percent. PIK preferred stocks averaged a return of 24.9 percent, aided by early retirement of several issues that had been trading at large discounts to the call or tender price. Because some deferred interest securities are junior to cash-paying bonds, the interest rates are typically among the highest paid by the issuer. As a result, companies often retire these issues as early as cash flow from asset sales or operations permits. On the other hand, 1989 returns were −33.0 percent for the PIK preferred index, −8.9 percent for the PIK debt index, and −10.1 percent for the Zerfix index, versus 2.3 percent positive return for cash-paying securities.

The PIK debt market is relatively new and has grown rapidly from $1.7 billion in 1987 to $8.0 billion at the end of 1989. The PIK preferred universe has also grown rapidly. The PIK preferred market more than doubled in size with the distribution of the RJR PIK debt. The PIK preferred market also experiences exchanges of PIK preferred into PIK debt securities. A number of issuers have exchanged their preferred for debt, such as Viacom, RJR, and TWA. The exchange usually occurs on the date on which an issuer expects to be a taxable entity, when interest expense can be deducted before tax instead of after tax for preferred dividends.

Because of the large supply of new issues in 1988–1989, along with unfavorable market conditions, prices of most issues were depressed, particularly those of preferreds. Investors also saw that preferred securities in bankruptcies, such as Revco, had very little value. Traditional high-yield investors were slow to expand into this sector because of the equity aspect of these junior securities. Equity investors also have been slow to look at these securities because of the complicated yield calculations required and the fixed income component of returns. Thus, PIK securities have fallen between the cracks of the two major security classes. However, the creation of $9 billion of PIK securities in the RJR Nabisco transaction generated greater investor awareness and participation in this sector. In fact, the early purchasers of the RJR PIK securities have been aggressive equity and individual investors, like traditional high-yield buyers. Although DISs are riskier than more senior cash-paying debentures, demand may grow as more investors find that above-average returns over larger periods justify the additional volatility and credit risk.

New Evaluation Methods
for a New Market

The foundation of fixed income security analysis is cash flow coverage of interest expense. The lack of a cash coupon and the relatively low level of seniority in the capital structure, however, make traditional cash flow coverage analysis of deferred interest securities inadequate for DIS instruments. In general, the volatility of these securities is higher than that of cash-paying bonds; therefore, price movements have a larger impact on returns. As a result, investors may benefit from analysis of liquidation as well as of cash flow coverage.

The performance of deferred interest securities in the past has been more related to events such as asset sales than to earnings or cash flow. Thus, total asset coverage is a key measure of creditworthiness for the sector. This is particularly relevant for preferred stocks, where small variations in valuations may have a substantial impact on asset coverage. Because of the large size of some of the preferred issues, preferred dividends may substantially reduce total cash flow coverage ratios. For example, although the pro forma cash interest coverage of RJR was 1.4 times cash flow, the total interest and preferred dividends were covered only 1.0 times at issuance.

Another useful measure of relative value from the fixed income perspective is the spread over the next-most senior cash-paying security. This measures the incremental yield over the next-most senior cash-paying security of the same issuer. As shown in Exhibit 4, spreads for the Zerfix and PIK debenture markets have ranged between 100 and 250 basis points over the cash-paying market but widened to 400 basis points at the end of 1989. While PIK preferreds initially traded 300–400 basis points over the cash-paying market, the October 1987 stock market crash opened spreads to the 800 basis point level. By year-end 1988, the huge new supply added additional pressure; spreads reached 1,000 basis points and yields of 25 percent became common. In 1989, a number of legislative issues, a large supply, and a number of highly publicized defaults resulted in a general weakness in that sector, carrying spreads to 1,200 basis points by the end of 1989 (see Exhibit 5).

Liquidation value may be an important determinate of returns. A number of companies have insufficient operating cash flow to cover total interest and preferred dividends. Thus, proceeds from asset sales are used to meet debt service obligations. Because of the uncertainty regarding asset sales, risk is considerably greater for these issues. Furthermore, even if the preferred is covered sufficiently by asset values, equity holders may not wish to liquidate at a price with little upside return, which may be adverse to the long-term health of the credit. However, all of these issues are trading at large discounts to par or call; thus, price appreciation may contribute significantly to returns, particularly if a security is retired early or if perceptions of credit conditions improve quickly. A number of other key measures should be analyzed in a DIS, such as the cash flow growth rate versus the accre-

EXHIBIT 4   *Deferred Interest Securities Yield Spread vs. the Next-Most Senior Ranking Security*

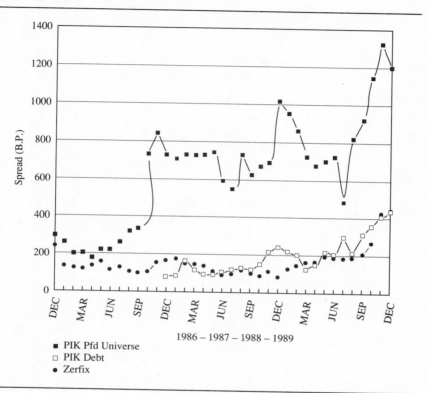

1986 – 1987 – 1988 – 1989

■ PIK Pfd Universe
□ PIK Debt
● Zerfix

Source: The First Boston Corporation.

tion rate of the DIS issues and the improvement of total interest coverage, and a fundamental analysis of the issuer should be made.

Finally, liquidity and covenants are important measures of value. The credit's amortization schedule and its ability to generate free cash flow, along with any carveouts that enable credits to conduct either capital investment to increase cash flow beyond the accretion rate or asset sales for use of proceeds, all impact the value of the security.

In case of senior Zerfix/PIK issues, a number of these securities have a warrant attached. Seniority, coupled with upside from the equity

EXHIBIT 5 *Deferred Interest Securities Average Yield to Worst of Zerfix, PIK Debt, and PIK Preferred Sectors versus First Boston High Yield Index (Cash)*

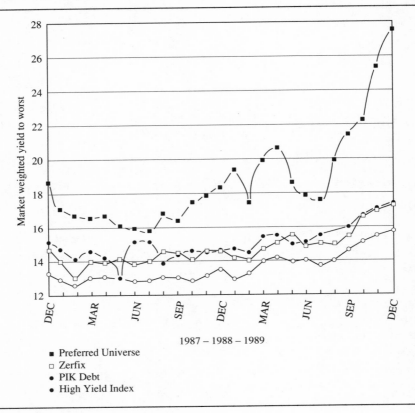

- ■ Preferred Universe
- □ Zerfix
- ● PIK Debt
- ● High Yield Index

Source: The First Boston Corporation.

participation, makes these securities more attractive than the junior cash pay.

Historical Performance of the Deferred Interest Sector

DISs tend to outperform in a bull market and lag in a bear market. During 1988, the deferred interest sector outperformed the First Boston High Yield Index, and individual deferred interest issues offered some of the highest returns. A number of issues, such as the Borg-

EXHIBIT 6

	1988 Actual Returns	1989 Actual Returns	1989 Monthly Return Volatility
FBC HY Index cash-paying issues	12.80%	2.27%	1.05%
Zerfix Index	21.56	−10.10	2.22
PIK Debt Index	14.10	−8.82	1.45
PIK Preferred Index	24.90	−33.01	3.22
Deferred Interest Market Weighted	20.35	−9.26	2.34

Warner 0/14 percent and the CJI PIK preferred issues, delivered returns of over 60 percent. On the other hand, the DIS market sector underperformed cash-paying securities in 1989 (see Exhibit 6).

Deferred interest securities historically have been both the most junior securities in a capital structure and the most expensive piece of financing for issuers. A successful credit will usually retire these securities as early as possible. Examples of early retirement have included Borg-Warner, CJI-Triangle, Burlington, and Amsted Industries. Unsuccessful issues often result in little value for deferred interest securities in a distressed liquidation scenario.

In 1988, Borg-Warner's tender for the 0/14 percent of 1999 produced a return of 68 percent and the 0/13 percent of 2007 had a return of 95 percent. CJI PIK preferred returned 107 percent when Pechiney S.A. tendered for the issue in the acquisition of Triangle in 1988. Burlington and Amsted also saw gains of 30–40 percent. In order to better measure the performance of the deferred interest sector, First Boston has created a number of indices to measure their performance: PIK Preferred Index, PIK Debt Index, and the Zerfix Index. The total returns for the PIK indices assume that a buy-and-hold strategy is utilized. Exhibit 3 shows the relative performance measured by monthly returns of each sector from October 1987 to December 1989.

Average Yield Spread versus Next Cash Pay

The lack of cash payments and the more junior nature of deferred interest securities cause them to trade at spreads above cash-paying securities. PIK debt and Zerfix debt usually trade relatively close to each other if seniority is similar at spreads between 100–200 basis points on average above the next-most senior cash-paying security. PIK preferred issues show a wider range of spreads, with an average of 1,200 basis points above the next-most senior issue by the end of 1989. Zerfix and PIK debentures yield identical future cash flows (assuming the PIK security pays in kind throughout the PIK period). However, volatility is much lower for PIK debentures and returns tend to vary less than on Zerfix issues. Furthermore, the issuer has the option to pay in cash on a PIK and may be able to call the issue earlier than zeros, which are usually callable only at par at the cash accrual date. As a result, PIK debentures of high-quality issues may trade like high-coupon cash cushion bonds with low volatility and high current yield.

PIK preferreds tend to fall into a higher and a lower quality group. The higher quality sector trades at an average 200–300 basis point spread off the next-senior security, in the same range as other deferred pay securities. (See Exhibit 7.) Issues in the lower quality sector often trade at a 1,000 basis point spread off the next-most senior security and behave more like equity securities. The high-quality sector was not as dramatically affected by the October 1987 crash or poor market conditions in September of 1989 as the low-quality sector was.

Volatility

Deferred interest securities have higher volatility, on average, than cash-paying securities. The PIK preferred universe, being more junior than the Zerfix and having a small number of issues, has the highest volatility. Most of the volatility results from the lower quality preferreds, which react strongly to events. The more volatile issues had

EXHIBIT 7 *Spread vs. Next-Most Senior Security (in basis points)*

	Dec 87	Dec 88	Dec 89
Zerfix debt	158	153	434
PIK debt	150	225	426
PIK preferred	820	1050	1204

the highest returns in 1988, when they were recovering from depressed October 1987 stock market crash levels. However, in 1989 high-volatility issues such as Eastern Airline preferreds realized 50 percent returns while Interco preferreds suffered a 90 percent loss.

Volatility has proven to be a good measure of uncertainty in the high-yield market. Enron's financial performance, for example, has been improving steadily. The price volatility of the Enron 10 percent of 1998 declined from the low level of 4.5 percent to 5.00 percent in 1988 to around 1.0 percent by mid-1989. On the other hand, Super-markets General experienced an increase in price volatility. Supermarkets General had been showing improvement in coverage since the LBO, and the volatility declined steadily, until the softness in its Rickel stores division in mid-1989 raised the volatility of the bonds.

The volatility of a new issue (LBO or RECAP) typically declines to 30–40 percent of its initial volatility levels if credit improves. The volatility level of the HBJ Zerfix 0/14.5 percent of 2001 declined from the 18–25 percent level to the 5–7 percent level before the proposed new issue in November 1988 but has increased since.

On average, the volatility of a deferred interest security is twice that of a cash-paying one and a PIK preferred three to four times in the same capital structure. The volatility of a PIK debt security is less than that of a comparable Zerfix security with the same terms.

Exhibit 6 shows that the volatility of monthly returns of different sectors is consistent with price and yield volatility trends. Within each sector, the return volatility correlates with the credit and uncertainty associated with each name.

Correlation of Deferred Interest Securities with Cash Module

PIK securities have a low correlation with the cash-paying universe. Hence, the volatility of PIK securities can be partially mitigated by using them to diversify a predominantly cash pay portfolio, simultaneously enhancing returns. Exhibit 8 shows the correlation between the cash-paying issues, the Zerfix Index, and the PIK Debt Index and the PIK Preferred Index.

EXHIBIT 8   *Correlation between the
Monthly Returns, Cash Paying Module*[a]
vs. Deferred Interest Security Sectors

Zerfix Module	0.96
PIK Debt Index	0.69
PIK PFD Index	0.64

a. Oct. '87–Dec. '89.

Our correlation study indicates that the more senior the issue is in the capital structure, the higher the correlation with Treasuries; the lower in the capital structure, the lower the correlation. Preferreds have a high correlation with the common stock of the same issuer, if such exists. Exhibit 8 shows that preferreds have a lower correlation with the cash module than do Zerfix instruments. The low correlation of the PIK debt index reflects the fact that these issues tend to trade very close to par and have been the least affected by event risk of the deferred interest securities sectors.

Effect of the PIK Option on Duration

The duration of a cash-paying issue is shorter than the duration of a pay-in-kind security. When EAL elected to change from paying cash to PIK for the E, F, and G series early in 1988, to conserve cash in anticipation of the strike, the security characteristic changed. Exhibit 9 shows that the price/yield curve of the EAL preferred had a steeper slope when paying in kind (i.e., longer duration) than when it paid in cash. Because the issue pays a higher PIK dividend than the cash rate, the change in duration in this case is dramatic; however, even when the issue has a PIK rate equal to the cash rate, duration is higher for PIKs, resulting in a greater change in price for a given change in yield.

The effect of the PIK option on the price/yield relationship is one of the main differences between Zerfix and PIK debt. The other difference is that a PIK has the option to pay in cash or kind; hence, the issuer can stop the compounding effect of interest at any time, if covenants permit. That option is estimated to be worth around 25–50 basis points. That is the mean spread between a Zerfix and a PIK issue of

EXHIBIT 9   *Yield to Worst Analysis, Price/Yield Curve*

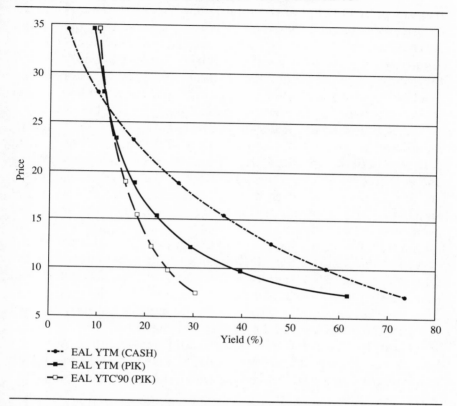

- -●- - EAL YTM (CASH)
- -■- EAL YTM (PIK)
- -□- EAL YTC'90 (PIK)

Source: The First Boston Corporation.

the same structure and *pari passu* in the same credit. Safeway is an example of an issuer that elected to pay cash, leading the issue to trade at a 100 basis point narrower spread. This tightening was due to both the issue becoming a cash pay, implying credit improvement, and the higher call price after November 24, 1988, of 102.9 percent.

Yield Calculation for DIS

Most Zerfix securities accrete at their offering yield to maturity. Zer-fix securities offered at a yield lower than their stated coupon accrete to a discount to par on the specified date, with that discount accreting over the remaining life of the security. On the other hand, if a Zerfix security is offered at a yield higher than its stated coupon, the security accretes to a premium to par on the specified date, with that premium amortized over the remaining life of the security. The book value of the security at any time is the cost basis multiplied by the purchase yield of the security. That enables a number of issuers to book a gain if they purchase the security at a price lower than its book value.

The cash flow of PIK securities is identical to that of Zerfix securities. Zerfix securities have been offered at a discount with no interim cash flow until the specified date, after which cash coupons commence and continue to maturity. In a PIK, fractional bonds ("baby bonds") are distributed in lieu of cash. While PIK issues tend to have a face value of par, the number of securities grows over time, with fractional bonds distributed *pro rata* to the investor's holdings; that is, an interest-on-interest effect takes place. Yield calculations assume both the bond and the baby bonds are held to maturity. PIK issues trade with the quoted price including accrued interest, even if the issuer has elected to pay cash interest, because the accrued interest on PIKs is a function of the market price of the securities. For identical securities, the yield is higher for a PIK security below par and vice versa. Because a large number of PIK securities trade at a discount, securities like the Southland 13.5/14.5 percent of 1995 or EAL Series D, E, F have a higher PIK rate than cash rate, to compensate holders for the discount.

Appendix

Tax Treatment of Dividends

Domestic corporations receiving taxable dividends on stock investments in other U.S. companies are generally allowed a 70 percent dividend-received deduction if they have maintained a "risk" position in the security for at least 46 days. Because the top marginal corporate tax rate is currently 34 percent, a 70 percent dividend-received deduction yields an effective tax rate of 10.2 percent [$34\% \times (100\% - 70\%)$].

A distribution by a corporation is a taxable dividend only if it is paid out of current or accumulated earnings and profits. The excess of a distribution over its taxable component first reduces the investor's basis in the stock and is then taxable as a capital gain to the extent that it exceeds the basis.

Pay-in-Kind Preferred Stocks

Dividends paid in kind on preferred stocks are treated as distributions on the underlying stock to the extent of the fair market value of the new stock distributed. The fair market value is generally measured as the average of the high and low trading prices on the date of the distribution.

"Extraordinary" Dividends

To combat tax abuses, the tax law limits the availability of the dividend-received deduction when large (extraordinary) dividends are paid. Generally, if a taxable dividend is paid on a stock that has not been held for at least two years on the announcement date, the 70 percent dividend-received deduction will be recaptured when the stock is sold. (Procedurally, the deduction is tentatively allowed at the point of the dividend if the general 46-day holding period is met, and the basis of the stock is reduced at the point of sale.) A taxable dividend is generally considered extraordinary if it exceeds 5 percent of the basis of preferred stock and it exceeds 10 percent of the basis of the underlying stock (in the case of another stock being paid).

New Tax Law

In 1989 the tax law disallowed the deductibility of interest on deferred interest securities unless the security meets certain criteria. The new law will not allow deductibility if the security has more than five years of maturity and has a significant original issue discount, or if its yield at offering is in excess of 600 basis points from the comparable Treasury. If the offering yield is between 500 and 600 basis points from the comparable Treasury, then the portion that is disqualified is determined by the yield; the higher the yield, the less interest is deductible. The tax law will permit a deduction if interest is paid in a lump sum within the first five years of issuance.

Issues outstanding before July 10, 1989, have been grandfathered. On the other hand, if a security does not qualify under the new tax law, it would for tax purposes be treated as a preferred stock. Though that would lead the issuer to pay the PIK debt interest from after-tax earnings, it entitles corporate holders to the same deductions as preferred stock, that is, a 70 percent dividend-received deduction.

6

Collateralized Bond Obligations

Robert Gerber
Vice President
Fixed Income Research
The First Boston Corporation

Securitized high-yield bond transactions, commonly known as collateralized bond obligations (CBOs), are the most recent addition to the asset-backed securities (ABS) market. Like many ABSs, CBOs typically offer multiple classes of securities collateralized by financial assets. In the case of CBOs, high-yield corporate bonds are used as collateral.

CBOs are created using the structuring techniques developed for collateralized mortgage obligations (CMOs). A special-purpose entity is formed to acquire financial assets and issue securities backed by those assets. Collateral cash flows are used to pay bondholders. Bonds are divided into several classes, or tranches, which differ according to their priority and/or timing of cash flows. As a result, individual CBO classes do not resemble their high-yield collateral in credit quality or investment performance.

CBOs, like other asset-backed securities, are generally created because of differing performance requirements among investors; by rearranging cash flow priorities, securities backed by the pooled assets have a higher market value than the collateral itself. With CBOs, there is a credit reallocation. Multiple security classes, which differ in their credit exposure to the high-yield market, are created. Investors with a variety of tolerance levels can exchange credit risk for security

EXHIBIT 1   *Historical Net Premiums, High-Yield Market*

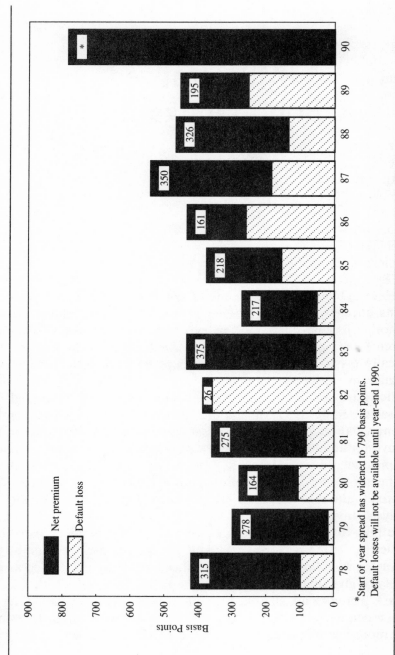

Source: The First Boston Corporation.

yield. For example, investors who believe that future default and recovery experience for noninvestment-grade credits will not be significantly worse than they have been historically will prefer the highest yielding tranches; those who are concerned that defaults or losses might sharply rise would prefer the lower yielding, investment-grade senior tranches. In this way, significant yield premiums in the high-yield market are distributed to investors according to their risk/return preferences. Exhibit 1 presents the historical beginning year spread to Treasury notes, net of default losses, of the First Boston High Yield Index.

All structured financings are fundamentally similar — collateral cash flows generate bond payments. Specific bond structures, however, reflect the credit risk and repayment characteristics of the underlying collateral. Therefore, CBOs, CMOs, and bonds backed by credit-card receivables and automobile loans differ with respect to the timing and predictability of principal repayments.

CBOs must be offered as private placements in order to avoid onerous leverage limitations and the registration and reporting requirements imposed by the Investment Company Act of 1940. Mortgage and other asset-backed securities enjoy an exemption from these requirements and can thus be efficiently issued as public securities. Historically, private placements have been less liquid than public securities because, by statute, only a small number of sophisticated investors may participate in an offering. Proposed SEC Rule 144A, if adopted, would liberalize registration/reporting requirements and might increase efficiency and liquidity in the traditional private placement markets.

Investor acceptance of CBOs requires a thorough understanding of the product. This report contains a product description, a discussion of the elements of security structure, an outline of the determinants of credit quality and agency rating criteria, and a sample investment analysis. Investors already familiar with CMOs, private label mortgage pass-throughs, or asset-backed securities will find many similarities.

Any complex security requires additional effort at first. The availability of investment-grade senior notes in the CBO structure, together with a conservative rating process and attractive performance profiles, warrants the attention of investors in the corporate, government, and mortgage sectors.

Security Structure

CBOs are typically issued by a limited partnership and/or corporation, depending on tax and legal considerations. The issuer's sole purpose is to acquire high-yield corporate bond collateral and to issue debt and equity (partnership interests or common stock). A portfolio manager selects the initial portfolio and provides ongoing management of the collateral pool. The manager, or an affiliate, typically holds a significant equity interest, and thus has a strong performance incentive. Exhibit 2 is a flowchart of a hypothetical CBO.

The rules governing collateral management and how cash flows are passed to CBO investors define the security structure. These rules can vary among CBOs. Moreover, the market is relatively young and new structures will continue to evolve. Structural features, however, must provide investor confidence as to credit quality and investment performance. As a result, certain elements are common to all CBOs, namely, collateral eligibility requirements, cash flow prioritization, overcollateralization, and ongoing portfolio management.

EXHIBIT 2 *Hypothetical CBO Flowchart*

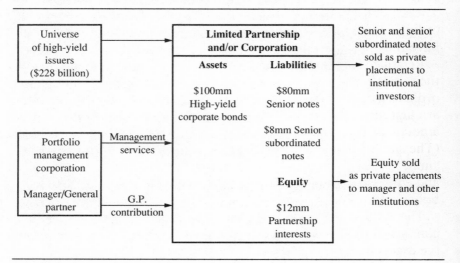

Source: The First Boston Corporation.

Rules directing cash flows are of two kinds. Some determine the average lives of the CBO debt. Pioneered in the CMO market, these rules only indirectly affect security credit quality — bonds with longer maturities, because they are outstanding longer, may have increased risk of cash flow disruption. Other rules set cash flow priority in the event of losses on the collateral and thus influence credit quality.

Two methods are currently used to alter the average lives of CBO classes — interest-only periods and accrual periods. Senior and senior subordinated bonds typically have an interest-only period during which interest, but not principal, is paid to bondholders. At the conclusion of the period, cash flows are also used to retire bond principal in order of seniority. Sometimes the most junior debt is an accrual or Z bond. Rather than making cash payments, interest is added to the principal balance of accrual bonds until the more senior bonds have been retired. The cash, which otherwise is payable, is reinvested in the CBO during the accrual period. Afterward, the Z bond receives interest in cash and principal paydowns.

Exhibit 3 is an example of directing collateral cash flows to vary CBO classes' average lives. The collateral has a $200 million principal value and an average coupon of 13 percent. For the sake of simplicity, it is assumed that none of the collateral is called, sold, exchanged, matures, or defaults. The senior and senior subordinated bonds have coupons of 10 percent and 13 percent, respectively, paid semiannually. The senior notes have a three-year interest-only period; the senior subordinated notes begin principal receipt in year 10, once the senior notes have fully paid down.

Relative credit quality among the security classes is determined by their cash flow priorities — senior debt, senior subordinated debt, subordinated debt (if any), and equity. If collateral defaults occur, losses are first absorbed by the equity interest. Losses in excess of the full amount of the equity are passed through to the subordinated debt. (The subordinated debt is frequently sold along with the equity as a "unit.") Only if the senior subordinated notes, subordinated bonds, and equity are completely eroded by collateral defaults are the senior bonds affected.

The "equity cushion" for senior and senior subordinated classes consists of the initial principal value of the most junior security and the excess interest spread available to the equity for payment or reinvestment. Excess interest is generated by the difference between the

EXHIBIT 3   *CBO Cash Flows ($ millions)*

Year	Senior Class		Senior Subordinated Class	
	Interest	Principal[a]	Interest	Principal
1	16.0	—	2.1	—
2	16.0	—	2.1	—
3	16.0	1.0	2.1	—
4	15.8	2.0	2.1	—
5	15.5	11.7	2.1	—
6	14.2	16.8	2.1	—
7	11.6	40.4	2.1	—
8	8.2	27.0	2.1	—
9	4.7	49.5	2.1	—
10	0.6	11.6	2.1	10.2
11	—	—	0.4	5.8
12	—	—	—	—
Total	118.6	160.0	21.4	16.0

a. There is one principal payment occurring in month 36, which
is accounted for in the third year.
Source: The First Boston Corporation.

interest income from the collateral and interest expense on the CBO
debt. In some recent transactions, this cushion has allowed senior notes
to weather, without loss, annual collateral default rates in the range
of 15 to 20 percent, well in excess of the 3 percent historical average
for high-yield bonds. Reflecting the relationship between cash flow
priority and credit quality, senior debt usually receives a single- or
double-A rating, whereas the remaining securities are typically not
rated.

Varying cash flow priority is a method that separates security characteristics from those of the collateral. Senior notes are substantially
removed from collateral performance; only under exceptional circumstances will collateral performance affect these bonds. The equity interest, however, can be considered a leveraged position in the collateral.

Credit quality of the CBO debt is enhanced by several structural
characteristics: ongoing portfolio management, collateral quality and
diversification restrictions, overcollateralization, and excess collateral

interest flows. Some CBOs, especially senior tranches in the Euromarket, may also have guarantees of principal from surety agents, which result in triple-A ratings. Structural elements in combination can affect bond performance and, although there is no standard formula, attaining an investment-grade rating on CBO senior debt places a number of restrictions on the mix of features.

The portfolio manager monitors the collateral, reinvests collateral cash flows, and acts to minimize credit losses on the portfolio. Portfolio management restrictions, which vary among issues, are introduced to prevent "trading down" in collateral quality.

In the typical CBO, collateral reinvestment rules differ between the amortization and interest-only (noncall) period. During the interest-only period, to the extent certain asset coverage tests are met, all collateral principal collections are reinvested in eligible high-yield bonds; if replacement high-yield collateral is unavailable, these funds are reinvested in bonds with at least an A rating. In some structures, all excess cash flows are likewise invested. If coverage tests are not satisfied, some or all cash flows in excess of interest payments on senior notes are used to restore coverage levels. With some deal structures, these excess cash flows are reinvested in high-grade reserve securities, thus effectively defeasing the senior notes during the interest-only period. In other cases, excess cash flows are used to prepay senior notes. During the amortization period, all collateral principal cash flows are applied to the most senior securities outstanding.

Two types of coverage tests are used to protect CBO bondholders in the event of collateral defaults — overcollateralization (O/C) and interest coverage (I/C) tests. These tests impose minimum required ratios of outstanding collateral principal to CBO debt and collateral interest income to that of the CBO securities. These ratios depend on whether senior CBO notes have been retired. For example, the minimum O/C and I/C might be 120 percent and 140 percent when senior debt is outstanding and 110 percent and 115 percent when only senior subordinated debt is outstanding.

Unless default rates are very high, collateral interest payments will exceed those on CBO debt, and these excess interest cash flows can be used to restore coverage ratios. As a result, the timing of defaults, as well as their absolute level, will affect the performance of CBO debt. For example, suppose CBO securities pay 10 percent interest and the collateral pays interest at 13 percent. For each year the collateral pays without defaulting, additional excess interest of 3 (13 – 10) percent is available to increase credit support for security holders.

As described above, many features determine the structure of a CBO. A heterogeneous market requires that each CBO be examined on its own merits. The actual mix of features in a particular issue, however, is responsive to rating agency requirements, which systematically take into account the entire structure.

Credit Quality and Rating

CBO senior notes are typically rated by one or more of the rating agencies. Duff & Phelps, Fitch, Moody's, and Standard & Poor's will rate CBOs. Most CBOs are rated by Moody's and/or Standard & Poor's, both of which evaluate these securities based on collateral quality, quantity of credit support, and legal soundness of the transaction. Ratings are based on the security's ability to withstand "stress tests." Stress level is equal to the product of collateral default incidence and average loss per default. The stress tests require the rated notes to withstand collateral default and loss rates well in excess of historical experience.

Rating criteria are similar between the two major agencies. Differences in approach, however, do exist. Standard & Poor's primarily derives its requirements from a "worst case" scenario, a multiple of the historical default experience of the high-yield bond market. Moody's relies more on an "expectations" approach. Probability models are used to forecast expected loss severity, which depends on the initial credit rating of the collateral. A weighted average, or expected, stress level is used to determine credit enhancement requirements. A conservative adjustment is then added to these levels.

Although rating approaches vary slightly, general principles regarding collateral performance apply to both agencies. A detailed discussion of Standard & Poor's criteria, provided later in this section, addresses these guidelines. Credit analysis begins by defining a standard of comparison, known as a "base case pool," according to a set of characteristics. Although the agencies will evaluate any potential deal structure, if the particular collateral's characteristics are not up to base case pool quality, default probability is assumed to increase, and the ability to absorb larger losses via additional credit enhancement is necessary to obtain the desired investment-grade rating.

A base case pool is a well-diversified portfolio of relatively high quality. Guidelines for maximum industry (5 percent) and issuer (2 percent) par value concentrations are set. Thus, the health of the entire pool is not vulnerable to the idiosyncratic risk of a small group of issuers or to the fortunes of a few industries. Moreover, the pool must be composed of fixed-rate, nonconvertible, cash-paying bonds, at least 60 percent of which have an implied BB or better senior debt rating and none of which has an implied senior debt rating below B.

Once the CBO is issued, the portfolio manager monitors the collateral for changes in quality. Restrictive trading rules and diversification requirements encourage portfolio managers to follow long-term investment goals rather than short-term trading strategies. In practice, these constraints have tended to make trading infrequent.

Collateral substitution may occur in several circumstances. During the interest-only period, principal collections are reinvested in substitute high-yield collateral. Throughout the life of the CBO, the manager, subject to varying reinvestment requirements such as credit support levels and portfolio diversification, can trade out of securities either to avoid default on credit risk securities or to recognize gains on appreciated securities.

Portfolio quality may change over time due to upgrades and/or downgrades. The manager is not obligated to improve the portfolio in the event that ratings decline. If certain minimum thresholds are not met, however, portfolio trades are allowed only if they improve the portfolio's rating profile.

Trading powers granted to managers differ across CBOs. In some cases managers are not permitted to trade down in collateral quality; in other instances they are allowed some flexibility in this regard. When available, this flexibility is very limited, because rating agencies require a commensurate increase in credit support. For example, suppose the original senior implied collateral quality was 60 percent BB-rated collateral and 40 percent B-rated collateral, but the manager is allowed to trade down to a 50/50 split. The rating agency would set credit support requirements based on the lower 50/50 split.

For each rating level, Standard & Poor's specifies a worst case collateral loss scenario that a base case pool must be able to withstand without loss to the rated CBO tranche. Exhibit 4 summarizes stress

EXHIBIT 4   *Collateral Default Frequency,*
Base Case Pool

Desired CBO Rating (Moody's/S&P)	Cumulative Default Frequency of Collateral to Be Withstood (%)	
	Moody's[a]	Standard & Poor's
Aaa/AAA	67	67
Aa/AA	52	50
A/A	47	38
Baa/BBB	40	32

Stress Test Default Timing

Year	Loss (%)	
	Moody's	Standard & Poor's
1	50	5
2	10	30
3	10	30
4	10	30
5	10	5
6	10	—

	Recoveries	
	Moody's	Standard & Poor's
Senior Secured	30	40
Senior	30	25
Subordinated	30	15
Accrued Interest Included	No	No
Cash Flow Delays upon Default	0	6 months

a. Moody's does not define a base case pool. Information contained in this exhibit has been compiled by applying the Moody's rating criteria to an "approximate" base case pool.
Source: The First Boston Corporation, with data supplied by Moody's and Standard & Poor's.

test components for Standard & Poor's and Moody's. For Standard & Poor's, recoveries on defaulted collateral are assumed to take six months and equal 40 percent for senior secured collateral, 25 percent for senior unsecured collateral, and 15 percent for junior unsecured collateral. Moody's, however, assumes a 30 percent recovery on all defaulted collateral.

Collateral default/loss rates are difficult to predict. Investors can find comfort with rating agency requirements that are consistent with their record of prudently rating financial assets and the historically low default rates of high-yield bonds. As with all investments, however, historical experience is no guarantee of future performance.

CBO Investment Performance

CBOs are typically offered at yields well in excess of Treasuries, mortgage-backed securities, and comparably rated corporate securities. As shown in Exhibit 5, yield spreads of the senior class to seven-year Treasury securities have recently been quoted in the neighborhood of 200 basis points. Thus, CBOs offer a considerable yield advantage over comparable securities unless annual default rates exceed five times their historical experience.

EXHIBIT 5   *Recent Yield Spreads*

Security	Coupon	Spread to Treasuries	Average Life
Three Rivers CBO Partners I			
Class A Bonds	9.26%	197 b.p.	7 yrs.
Equitable Capital Diversified Holdings II			
Class 1 Senior Notes	10.10%	185 b.p.	5 yrs.
Class 2 Senior Notes	10.45%	210 b.p.	8.5 yrs.
Direct Placements			
A-Rated Corporate	—	110 b.p.	7 yrs.
Public Security			
A-Rated Industrial	—	85 b.p.	7 yrs.
Private Label Mortgage Pass-Through			
AA-Rated	—	170 b.p.	8 yrs.

Source: The First Boston Corporation.

EXHIBIT 6   *Generic CBO Balance Sheet*

Assets

$200mm par amount high-yield bonds

Weighted average coupon:	13.2%
Weighted average yield:	14.0%
Weighted average maturity:	8.5 yrs.
Weighted average rating:	B/B2

Capitalization

	Average Life	Expected Final	Spread to Treasuries	Interest-Only Period
$160mm Senior Nts.	6.6 yrs.	10.0 yrs.	200 b.p.	3 yrs.
$16mm Senior Sub. Nts.	10.4 yrs.	11.5 yrs.	500 b.p.	9 yrs.
$24mm Equity	—	—	—	—

Source: The First Boston Corporation.

All fixed income securities are exposed to some forms of risk. Although collateral defaults can potentially erode CBO yield, similarly rated corporate bonds are exposed to event risk and similar default risk over time. In order to receive equal ratings, the probability-weighted magnitude of these risks must be approximately equal. In this context, the yield advantage of CBOs is noteworthy.

The generic CBO described in Exhibit 6 can be used to illustrate some investment implications of the CBO's yield advantage. Suppose that recoveries on defaulted collateral average 40 percent. In the exhibit, defaults must exceed 15 percent per annum for the senior class to be affected. For the senior subordinated tranche, this number is approximately 7 percent. Moreover, defaults must rise above 16 percent per year for the return on the senior class to fall to 9.5 percent, the rate on A-rated corporate bonds. This breakeven default analysis is quite conservative—if default rates on high-yield bonds were to rise to such levels, defaults on today's A-rated corporate bonds might also run high.

Investment performance depends not only on eventual return of principal but also on its timing. For example, rapid return of principal on a premium bond, with an above-market interest rate, diminishes its value. Bonds with embedded call options usually have this drawback. When interest rates decline, the bond is often retired, and the investor is unable to participate in the bull market. Moreover, bonds remain outstanding longer and witness large price declines when interest rates rise. Called "negative convexity," this characteristic adversely affects the performance of many mortgage-backed securities and callable corporate bonds. CBOs, however, should not be negatively convex.

Returns on mortgage-backed securities are negatively convex because homeowners prepay their mortgages when interest rates decline in order to attain a more favorable mortgage rate. Although high-yield collateral typically is callable, the vast majority of calls tend to be independent of Treasury yield curve movements. General behavior of the high-yield market and the individual nature of specific issues contribute to this independence.

The incentive to refinance a high-yield bond is, in most cases, tied to individual credit improvement or capital structure issues. For instances in which declining interest rates motivate a refinancing, refunding opportunities are determined by high-yield market rates. Yields in the high-yield market respond to general credit concerns, anticipated macroeconomic activity, unexpected events, and market supply and demand considerations. Therefore, Treasury yield curve movements will not have a large or direct impact on the call policy of high-yield bond issuers.

Exhibit 7 breaks down high-yield bond calls by cause. As shown, the largest cause of calls has been issuer credit improvement, often providing access to funds at lower rates. Covenant restrictions, such as those pertaining to net worth and/or additional debt, are the second most frequent reason for calls. General interest rate movements, fourth on the list, account for less than 15 percent of calls. Although calls occur, they are rarely inspired by interest rate movements and as a result are almost as likely to benefit as to hurt investors.

Although somewhat unpredictable, calls have historically ranged from 3 percent to 8 percent per year of the par value of outstanding high-yield issues. Exhibit 8 shows that the generic CBO's average life is very stable, even for radically different collateral call scenarios. Negative convexity is evidenced by an unstable average life pattern; the more average life shortens as rates fall (or lengthens as rates rise), the more negatively convex the security. This should not be a concern for

EXHIBIT 7   *Causes of High-Yield Calls, 1986–1989*

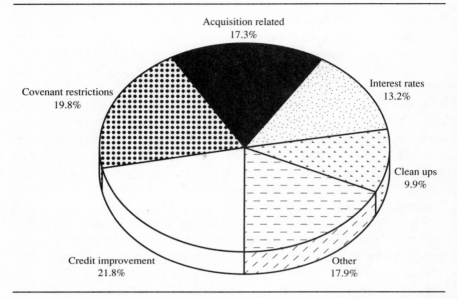

Acquisition related
17.3%

Interest rates
13.2%

Covenant restrictions
19.8%

Clean ups
9.9%

Credit improvement
21.8%

Other
17.9%

Note: "Other" includes voluntary asset sales, reverse recaps, and LBO-driven asset sales.
Source: The First Boston Corporation.

CBOs. Many mortgage-backed securities, in contrast, show significant average life variability with interest rate movements.

Lack of significant negative convexity is a great advantage of CBOs over mortgage pass-throughs. Exhibit 9 compares the performance of the generic CBO to an AA-rated 10 percent mortgage pass-through. The senior tranche of the CBO outperforms the mortgage security, especially as interest rates fall and the consequences of negative convexity become pronounced.

Investors interested in a combination of higher yield levels and increased credit exposure to the high-yield market can purchase other CBO securities. Realized collateral defaults are the main determinant of security performance. Exhibit 10 illustrates the yield/collateral default trade-off for the senior subordinated and equity classes of the CBO described in Exhibit 6.

EXHIBIT 8 *Generic CBO Average Life Sensitivity*

	Annual Default Rate (%)								
	0			2			4		
Annual Call Rate (%):	0	5	10	0	5	10	0	5	10
Senior class average life (years)	7.42	6.75	6.15	7.25	6.55	6.02	6.72	5.79	5.21
Senior sub. class average life (years)	10.21	9.78	9.43	10.78	10.39	9.96	10.56	9.82	9.34

Source: The First Boston Corporation.

EXHIBIT 9 *Comparative Price Performance*

Scenario	Private Label Mortgage Pass-Through[a]	Senior CBO Class Annual Call Rate		
		0%	5%	10%
+300 b.p.	85.2	86.5	87.4	88.1
+200 b.p.	90.1	90.7	91.3	91.8
+100 b.p.	95.1	95.1	95.5	95.8
0	100	100	100	100
−100 b.p.	103.1	105.2	104.8	104.5
−200 b.p.	103.9	110.7	109.9	109.2
−300 b.p.	105.1	116.5	115.3	114.3

a. Prices calculated using the First Boston Mortgage Prepayment Model.
Source: The First Boston Corporation.

Senior subordinated notes have recently offered yields of about 500 basis points in excess of 10-year Treasury securities. The equity cushion usually provides sufficient credit protection to withstand, without loss, default rates of about 5 to 7 percent. Depending on the security structure, the senior subordinated class can maintain an attractive investment performance even at very high default rates. For instance, the

EXHIBIT 10   *Effect of Default on Yield*

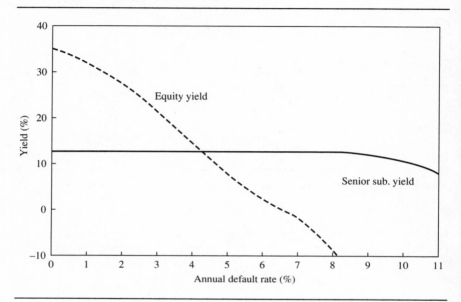

Source: The First Boston Corporation.

senior subordinated class from Exhibit 6 yields 10.86 percent at an annual default rate of 10 percent.

The equity interest is the most leveraged security class in the CBO structure. CBO equity has the highest yield and greatest high-yield market credit exposure of all CBO classes. For example, the equity interest from Exhibit 6 yields 21.45 percent if the annual collateral default rate is 3.0 percent, the market's historical average. Equity yields can vary significantly with collateral defaults — in this example ranging from 35.25 percent to 2.53 percent at annual default rates of 0 percent and 6 percent, respectively.

CBOs offer an investment-grade rating on the senior securities, a large yield spread to comparable securities, a stable average life, and the absence of negative convexity. The sample security analysis presented above can be used as a starting point for examining a CBO. Issue characteristics, however, show considerable variation, and issue-specific analysis is always necessary. Exhibit 11 lists issues completed to date.

EXHIBIT 11 *List of Outstanding Transactions*

Closing Date	Issuer	Sponsor/Manager	Total Assets	Securities Marketed	Rating (Moody's/S&P)	Agent
		U.S. Private Placements				
11/88	Long Run Bond Corp.	Imperial S&L/ Caywood Christian	$180mm	$140mm Sr.	Aaa/AAA	DBL/FBC/ML
01/89	Premier Financial	Columbia S&L	$100mm	$78mm Sr.	NR/A	DBL
05/89	Equitable Capital Diversified Holdings I	Equitable Capital Management	$200mm	$140mm Sr. $30mm Sr. Sub.	NR/A	FBC
08/89	WSGP L.P.	Wm Simon Group	$256mm	$197mm Sr. $42mm Sr. Sub.	NR/A	DBL
09/89	Duff & Phelps CBO	Duff & Phelps	$300mm	$235mm Sr. $45mm Sr. Sub.	NR/A	DBL
09/89	Chancellor Capital Holdings Ltd.	Chancellor Capital Management	$200mm	$126mm Sr. $50mm Sr. Sub.	NR/BBB	FBC
01/90	Three Rivers CBO	Westinghouse Credit	$200mm	$160mm Sr.	NR/A	DBL
02/90	Equitable Capital Diversified Holdings II	Equitable Capital Management	$200mm	$150mm Sr. $25mm Sr. Sub.	Aa/NR	FBC

EXHIBIT 11 *Continued*

Closing Date	Issuer	Sponsor/Manager	Total Assets[a]	Securities Marketed	Rating (Moody's/S&P)	Agent
		Euromarket Offerings[a]				
02/89	NJK Financial	Kidder Peabody Asset Management	$142mm	$100mm Sr. $37mm Sr. Sub.	Aaa/AAA	KP
06/89	"CBO I"	Morgan Stanley Asset Management	$300mm	$210mm Sr. $75mm Sr. Sub.	Aaa/AAA	MSI
06/89	Top Finance Ltd.	Kidder Peabody Asset Management	$100mm	$75mm Sr.	Aaa/AAA	KP
08/89	Central Secured Investments N.V.	Morgan Stanley Asset Management	$100mm	$70mm Sr.	Aaa/AAA	MSI
09/89	"CBO II"	Morgan Stanley Asset Management	$115mm	$85mm Sr. $30mm Sr. Sub.	Aaa/AAA	MSI
09/89	FGF (Bermuda)	Kidder Peabody Asset Management	$106mm	$75mm Sr.	Aaa/AAA	KP/Mitsui
12/89	Top Finance (Bermuda) II Ltd.	Kidder Peabody Asset Management	NA	$125mm Sr.	Aaa/AAA	KP
02/90	CARPS IV	Prudential Asset Management	$155mm	$155mm Sr.	Aaa/AAA	PB
Total CBO Assets			$2,654mm			

a. All senior notes issued in the Euromarket have been rated Aaa/AAA on the basis of a third party guarantee.
Source: The First Boston Corporation.

7

The Analysis of High-Yield Bonds

Jane Tripp Howe, CFA
Senior Credit Analyst
Pacific Investment Management Company

The analysis of high-yield bonds should be the same as the analysis applied to any corporate bond. The rationale behind this approach is straightforward. The purpose of credit analysis is twofold. The first purpose is to assess the risk that the company will not pay principal and interest when due. The second purpose is to determine whether the creditworthiness of the company is improving, stable, or declining. Both endeavors apply equally to the analysis of high-yield and high-grade bonds. The major difference between the analysis of the two is that the margin of safety is lower (or nonexistent) for a high-yield bond. An analyst could err in the analysis of the credit strength of a high-grade bond and still be assured of receiving the payment of principal and interest. An analyst who makes a similar mistake in the high-yield area could end up following a Chapter 11 reorganization, hoping to recoup a portion of the investment.

Overview of Basic Analysis

An analysis of any investment should proceed as an evaluation of a company rather than as an evaluation of a specific security. The attributes of specific bonds are important, but they are secondary to the basic analysis and are a function of how much risk an investor wants to take given the overall creditworthiness of a company.

The analysis of any company should begin with a general evaluation of the company's industry. Is it a cyclical, defensive, or growth industry? What are the industry prospects for the next several years in terms of growth and pricing? Are there any pending legislative actions that might affect the industry in either a positive or negative fashion? Are there any broad-based litigious issues that could significantly harm the industry?

Once this broad evaluation of the industry is complete, the analyst should proceed with an analysis of the company's return on equity (ROE) components. This evaluation gives the analyst an initial understanding of the factors that generate a company's profits. Has the company's growth been fueled by leverage, increased asset turnover, increased profit margins, or lower taxes? Can the company sustain its growth with its current operating pattern?

The next step in the analysis is the calculation of all the traditional ratios such as fixed-charge coverage, leverage, and cash flow to debt. These calculations should include the basic ratios of financial strength such as the current ratio. An analyst who calculates only a certain set of ratios, such as those relating to cash flow, may overlook a fundamental weakness in a company. Occasionally, investors are caught up in the verbiage of an LBO or other company presentation and forget to formulate their own opinions. Road shows are designed to lead an analyst's thinking to a positive assessment of the investment by presenting facts and projections in a particular sequence. This progression of facts and figures is fundamental to the marketing of an issue; it is not fundamental to analysis. The primary job of a credit analyst is to uncover all the potential factors that could negatively affect the company's creditworthiness and to balance these against all the factors that could positively affect the company. A marketing presentation only helps the analyst focus on the positives. The proper sequence for an analysis is the formulation of an independent assessment of the company and then a comparison of this assessment with opinions from the Street.

Special Considerations for
High-Yield Bonds

Although the analysis of high-yield bonds is fundamentally similar to that of any bond, there are seven areas of analysis that deserve particular care when a high-yield bond is evaluated. These are: (1) competition; (2) asset quality and marketability; (3) leverage; (4) projections of cash flows; (5) corporate structure; (6) asset coverage; and (7) management. Although each of these factors is distinct, they are interrelated. Each of these variables relates directly to the company's financial flexibility.

Financial Flexibility

Financial flexibility is the most important factor in the analysis of a high-yield bond. Unfortunately, there is no ratio to measure financial flexibility. Rather, it is a combination of several factors, including competitive position, asset quality, and cash flow. Together, these factors allow the company to survive in periods of economic stress and to prosper in periods of economic expansion.

All companies face periods of economic stress. This stress may emanate from a general downturn in the economy or, more often, a downturn in the company's particular line of business. Consider, for example, a company in the oil and gas exploration business. The downturn in this industry in the 1980s generated declining rental rates on equipment and lower utilization rates. For companies with high fixed costs, this combination decreased operating cash flow below the level sufficient to meet debt service. Many oil service companies filed bankruptcy petitions during this period. Other companies, however, survived the downturn because of financial flexibility.

Analysts often focus on financial flexibility in times of economic or industry stress. This focus is wise, because the lack of financial flexibility during such times can lead to bankruptcy. Financial flexibility is also important, however, in times of financial expansion. A successful company needs the flexibility to capitalize on expanding markets when the opportunity arises. This flexibility is particularly important to companies with large and lumpy capital requirements. Consider, for example, an automobile manufacturer that needs capital to modernize its plant as well as to take advantage of the expanding European market for American cars. Unfortunately, the automobile manufacturer in question does not have the financial flexibility to satisfy both needs. The company must therefore choose between modernizing its plant and thereby lowering its costs of production or expanding production in a quickly growing market. Whichever option management chooses, the company will not maximize its potential. A company with financial flexibility, on the other hand, could modernize its plant as well as expand in Europe. The company with financial flexibility will gain market share relative to the inflexible company.

The financial flexibility of a high-grade company is often a function of access to the capital markets. High-quality bonds are generally afforded the luxury of capital access even when their earnings are weak or negative. This access continues to be offered because the market has faith that the high-quality company will survive the downturn and return to profitability.

Capital markets do not have a similar faith in high-yield companies. This lack of faith was clearly evidenced in the temporary collapse of the high-yield market in the fall of 1989. Major offerings of high-yield bonds were deferred or cancelled during this period as investors shied away from junk bonds. This period of illiquidity in the high-yield market was short, and therefore most high-yield issuers were able to survive the temporary lack of market access. The true test of high-yield issuers will come when there is a major downturn in the economy coupled with market illiquidity. During these times, only high-yield issuers with financial flexibility will likely survive. Those companies that do survive are likely to fare well in the previously mentioned seven components of financial flexibility.

Competition

The competitive position of a company has important implications for its profitability and, ultimately, its survival. A company that is a leader in its industry often has the luxury of dictating prices. There fore, should its cost of goods sold increase, it generally has the marketing power to pass the increases through to the consumer. Under this scenario, the company will suffer only a temporary decline in profit margins. More importantly, the company probably has the financial strength to withhold the price increases and endure a decline in margins if it believes that the increased costs are only temporary and that an increase in prices would be more than offset by a decline in revenues.

A company in a weak competitive position generally will not have the luxury of dictating prices and must necessarily follow the pricing of the industry leader. This could be disastrous to a company whose margins are already low. Such a company could be driven into bankruptcy during a prolonged period where prices do not keep pace with increasing production costs.

A weak competitive position can also be damaging during periods of economic downturn. During such periods, the weak company may not have the financial resources to adequately fund research and development, capital improvements, or marketing. Although cutbacks in these areas may allow the company to remain on a healthy operating basis for the short term, such cutbacks have major negative implications for the long term. For example, if a fast-food chain were to significantly reduce its marketing budget, it would suffer a long-term loss in market share in exchange for a short-term increase in operating income.

Asset Quality and Marketability

The quality of assets and their marketability are of particular importance in determining the financial flexibility of a company. An evaluation of assets must proceed from two viewpoints. First, the analyst must determine whether the balance-sheet value of assets is a true reflection of their market value. Second, the analyst must evaluate the marketability of the assets. Often, assets on the balance sheet are drastically understated and represent pockets of value for the conscientious analyst. Once such assets are identified, the analyst must evaluate any liens on these assets that would diminish their value to an investor who is not party to the lien.

A company that has recently undergone a leveraged buyout has no such undervalued assets on its balance sheet, because its assets have been written up to market as part of the acquisition. This assignment of full value is standard procedure and instructive to the analyst, because it provides an indication of value for particular assets and, importantly, for goodwill. Generally, the values so assigned are based on appraisals. A problem can arise, however, when the appraisal value of a specific asset differs from the price it can command in a sale. Often, companies that have undergone an LBO plan to sell assets to reduce debt or meet debt service requirements. In these cases, it is paramount that the assets be marketable at prices that approximate their appraisal values. If this is not the case, the success of the LBO can be quickly unwound and the company restructured or forced into bankruptcy. This was the case in the recent bankruptcy of Resorts International. The November 1988 acquisition of Resorts International by Merv Griffin was financed by $325 million of high-yield debt. Griffin planned to fund the high debt service through a combination of cash proceeds from the debt offerings, cash flow from operations, and asset sales. Cash flow from operations was below expectations. Griffin was therefore forced to rely on asset sales to raise cash to service the debt requirements. Unfortunately for investors in Resorts, the planned asset sales were likewise below expectations. Bids for the Resorts real estate were either nonexistent or at distressed levels because of a weak real estate market and the widespread perception that Resorts must sell assets to avoid bankruptcy. This lack of marketability of assets was a major contributing factor to Resorts' bankruptcy petition in 1989.

The importance of marketability of a company's assets is epitomized in the Resorts situation. It is also important for a company that is experiencing a temporary deterioration in finances. In this case, the company could collateralize some of its assets in order to provide liquidity during a decline. A company without such flexibility could find itself without capital access.

Leverage

Issuers of high-yield debt are generally highly leveraged. A high degree of leverage should not automatically exclude a company's securities from a portfolio. The securities of many highly leveraged firms have fulfilled their interest and principal obligations.

An evaluation of the leverage of a firm should focus on three factors: (1) the total leverage of the firm in the context of the firm's rating; (2) the financial flexibility that the company possesses given its level of leverage; and (3) the likely direction of leverage.

An evaluation of the total leverage of the firm should commence with calculations of standard measures of leverage such as long-term debt/capitalization and total debt/capitalization. After these ratios are calculated, they should be compared with the median figures for these ratios to determine where they fall within the rating category. For this purpose, the analyst can use industry-specific ratios or the median figures for industrial companies published annually by Standard & Poor's, which are outlined in Exhibit 1, or industry-specific ratios.

This exercise provides the starting point for the evaluation of a company's leverage. The analyst should also consider the level of debt within the context of the market value of the equity of the firm. When leverage is viewed in the context of market values, it gives an impression of how much more debt the market thinks the company can support. To the extent that the common equity of a company is selling below book value, the leverage of the company will be understated by

EXHIBIT 1 *Median Financial Ratios for Industrial Long-Term Debt, Three-Year (1986–1988) Medians*

	BB	B	CCC
Pretax Interest Coverage (x)	2.42	1.32	0.00
Pretax Interest Coverage Including Rents (x)	1.78	1.26	0.25
Pretax Funds Flow Interest Coverage (x)	4.19	2.18	1.50
Funds from Operations/Total Debt (%)	23.4	9.5	2.9
Free Operating Cash Flow/Total Debt (%)	0.8	(4.2)	(4.0)
Pretax Return on Permanent Capital Employed (%)	12.8	9.9	0.0
Operating Income/Sales (%)	13.1	9.8	4.5
Long-term Debt/Capitalization (%)	50.5	66.1	62.4
Total Debt/Capitalization Incl. Short-Term Debt (%)	53.7	69.1	67.4
Total Debt/Capitalization Incl. Short-Term Debt (Incl. 8 Times Rents) (%)	63.8	75.1	76.5

the traditional approach. In a similar manner, the leverage of a company whose common equity is selling at a premium to book will be overstated. Market adjustments can also be made to the debt on the balance sheet.

Although the adjustment of equity and, to a lesser extent, debt is logical, this process has several drawbacks. First, it oversimplifies the leverage calculation because it does not take specific provisions of bonds into account. Consider, for example, a company whose debt is selling for 60 percent of face amount. In this case, the market-adjusted leverage calculation would indicate a debt level substantially less than that generated if debt were incorporated at par or accreted value. If this debt contained a provision for reset at par within three months, the market-adjusted calculation could be highly misleading. Another drawback of the market adjustment process is that equity and bond values can change significantly during short periods of time.

A second facet of leverage is whether leverage is likely to increase, decrease, or remain the same. This evaluation is largely a function of cash flows and earnings growth, but it is also a function of company policy. Most companies state their long-term goals in their financial reports. These goals can range from attaining investment-grade status through the reduction of debt to attaining growth through acquisition financed by additional debt.

Leverage should also be viewed in the context of the financial flexibility of the company. On the surface, a highly leveraged company may appear to have little flexibility in terms of its financial structure. This is not always the case. The analyst must examine the covenants on the outstanding debt to determine whether more debt may be issued if required. Frequently, a highly leveraged company can issue additional debt by collateralizing specific assets or by utilizing carve-outs or exceptions to specific covenants. However, although this strategy may grant the company more flexibility, it will have a negative impact on the outstanding bonds because part of the bonds' asset protection will have been removed.

Cash Flow

Perhaps the most important variable in the analysis of high-yield bonds is cash flow. The importance of cash flow is a function of the high cash requirements of high-yield issuers and their frequent lack of financing flexibility. A company might survive in spite of high leverage, illiquid assets, and a weak competitive position; it cannot survive with inadequate cash flow.

The determination of a company's cash flow on a pro forma basis should commence with an evaluation of its historical sources and uses of cash. Historical cash flows are generally perceived to be useful in the analysis of high-grade issuers because historical results are viewed as good indicators of future results. High-yield analysts correctly do not attach as much importance to the historical numbers because they have less predictive value for high-yield issuers. Historical cash flows are useful, however, in that they give the analyst some measure to judge the validity of assumptions used to generate pro forma cash flows. For example, if a company historically generated cash flow growth of 10 percent per year, the analyst should question a pro forma suggesting that this annual growth will accelerate to 25 percent.

The analyst should formulate pro forma cash flows and then determine whether this level is sufficient to meet interest and principal repayments as well as capital expenditures. In this formulation, care should be taken to ensure that the assumptions are reasonable. For example, if a large percentage of the company's debt is floating rate, conservative assumptions should be made concerning interest rates. The pro formas should also be sensitive to the time frame under which any pay-in-kind securities are required to become cash paying.

Corporate Structure

Many high-yield bonds have complicated capital structures. These structures and their implications for asset coverage and fixed-charge coverage must be incorporated into an analysis. This incorporation is required because high-yield issuers often have a holding company structure. Under this structure, the operating subsidiaries and generally the assets of a company are far removed from the holding company. This is of great significance if the debt being analyzed is at the holding company level and there are several layers of senior debt at the operating level. Just as an analyst should consider all of the factors that could negatively affect an issuer, the analyst should also focus on the lowest level of debt in a corporate structure. Although the particular issue that is being evaluated may be secure from an earnings point of view, if a default occurs at the holding company level, the whole company will be affected. Although this approach is quite straightforward, it is not always clearly presented. For example, if a company is issuing a new bond at the operating level, too many analysts focus only on the financial parameters of the issuing subsidiaries and not on the total leverage of the company.

Asset Coverage

Asset coverage should be approached in terms of quality of assets, the corporate structure, and absolute levels of coverage. Asset coverage should be calculated using market valuations when possible. These can then be discounted appropriately to recognize the fact that assets sold to satisfy claims are generally liquidated at some discount to market.

Investors should also be cognizant of any encumbrances (current or potential) that might be placed on the assets. Consider a company that owns a $200 million asset. If this asset provides security for both a $100 million first mortgage bond and a $100 million second mortgage bond, the coverage is thin but at the one-to-one level. However, the coverage afforded holders of the second mortgage bonds declines rapidly if the value of the asset decreases at all.

Management

Management is a critical element in the success of any firm. Good management can fulfill the potential of a firm, but poor management can deplete this potential. Although good management is difficult to quantify, an assessment must be made. Often this assessment is simply a mirror of management's historical performance. If the company has performed well relative to the industry, management generally will be perceived favorably. An assessment of a new management team after an acquisition is more difficult. One approach is to determine how well the members of the team performed in their prior positions. If these prior positions were unrelated to the current industry, a cautious approach is warranted. Generally, management ownership of a significant part of the equity of the company is favorable. In such a scenario, the management team has the dual incentive to perform well at their jobs and to increase the value of their equity holdings.

Brokerage Houses and the Rating Agencies

High-yield research was virtually nonexistent during the late 1970s, when the high-yield market was first expanding. Fortunately, research in the high-yield area has grown. Currently, the major rating agencies, including Standard & Poor's, Moody's, Fitch, and Duff & Phelps, all have a high-yield area. Additionally, more brokerage houses are providing research. Although this research is sound, it is no substitute for your own analysis. Outside research should be viewed as a complement to analysis.

8

Valuing Assets

Kenneth P. Bann
Associate Director
Bear Stearns & Company, Inc.

Raymond S. Cheesman
Vice President
Bear Stearns & Company, Inc.

High-yield bonds are, in most cases, subordinated to senior debt and are not secured by the issuer's assets. In most cases, the proceeds from the sale of an issuer's assets must go first to the repayment of the senior (bank) debt secured by those assets. The remainder of the assets may then be used to pay down the subordinated debt. Therefore, the valuation of a high-yield issuer's assets in relation to debt levels is essential to determine risk/value in high-yield bond investments.

As seen in the 1980s, the repayment of a part of the financing of a recapitalization or LBO depends on the need to sell assets in order to reduce debt quickly (sometimes called bridge financing). Valuing assets earmarked for sale is necessary to determine whether the plan is realistic in the current market environment.

Finally, the valuing of assets is necessary in developing a worst case scenario for evaluating risk if the company fails to generate sufficient cash flow to meet current debt servicing needs, both for interest and principal payments.

Determining the dollar value of an asset is often a tricky process. There are several methods of determining value, all of which have some substantial shortcomings. The use of a variety of methods, however, can produce a range of values for an asset and a check of the accuracy of the value derived from each method. The values depend on a number of key factors that cannot be predicted with certainty.

These factors are: the asset's earnings over the next several years, the level of interest rates, and the risk/reward ratio demanded by the marketplace. The purpose of this chapter is to explore the methods currently used to place a range of values on a high-yield bond issuer's assets.

Net Present Value of Future Cash Flows

The net present value (NPV) method (also known as the discounted cash flow model) of valuing a company is widely used and simple to understand. It is made up of two components. The user must first forecast the company's net cash flow to a future point, usually 5 to 10 years in the future. The user must also choose a discount rate to be applied to the cash flow stream. This method attempts to compress future values into a potential price for a company today. There are, however, two major potential problems with this method.

First, for numerous reasons it is very difficult to project cash flow from operations into the future. The competitive and regulatory environments in most businesses change very rapidly today, as do the fiscal and monetary policies of governments around the world. All these factors affect cash flow and the ability to project cash flow.

The second pitfall concerns the choice of the discount rate. Traditionally, interest rates in this country were stable, but in the 1970s and 1980s they became quite volatile. There are also separate costs involved for equity versus debt. Finally, tax consequences also have changed over the last several years because of the declining corporate tax rates which have made debt closer in cost to equity for capitalizing a company.

Through careful study of historical financial statements and current operating trends, cash flow forecasts can be generated. A discount rate can also be found by using a company's weighted average cost of capital (WACC). The WACC can be generated by adding the after-tax cost of debt multiplied by its percentage of the capital structure to the cost of equity multiplied by its percentage of the capital structure.

After deriving the potential value of the company based on assumptions concerning both the cash flow projections and discount rate, a financing package can be crafted to fit this situation.

Comparison of an Asset with
Recent Asset Sales

One of the more popular methods of determining an asset's value is to compare it with other, similar assets that have been recently sold. Generally, this method consists of taking the price paid for the asset sold and dividing that price by various financial measurements of the asset to determine a range of prices for it. For example, suppose a tire manufacturing company with sales of $400 million, earnings before interest, taxes, and depreciation (EBITD) of $25 million, operating income of $15 million, and net income of $4 million is sold for $200 million. The sale price is .5 times the asset's sales, 8 times its EBITD, 13.3 times its operating income, and 50 times its net income. If we were to value another tire manufacturing company, we could apply these same multiples to its sales, EBITD, operating income, and net income to come up with a range for its value.

The best financial measurements to use in deriving the multiples for an industrial company are EBITD, operating income, and free cash flow. The latter is defined as EBITD minus capital expenditures. These financial measurements represent the funds available to support the capital needed to acquire the asset. Because the asset will be acquired with some combination of debt and equity, these financial measurements represent the funds available to pay off or provide a return to these types of capital. The use of multiples of sales generally is less conclusive, because the operating margins of the assets compared could be vastly different. The use of a multiple of net income is also inconclusive, because the assets compared may have different tax rates and debt leverage.

For evaluations of companies in industries other than general manufacturing, multiples of other financial or operating measurements may be more useful. For example, in the cable television industry, cable franchises are often measured by a dollar multiple times the number of subscribers in the franchise area. If cable franchises have been sold for $2,000 per subscriber, then any franchise can be valued by multiplying $2,000 times the number of subscribers in its franchise area. In cellular communications, franchises are usually valued as a dollar multiple of the number of pops, or potential customers, in a franchise area. Defense companies are often valued as a multiple of the company's defense-related sales. The financial or operating measurements used to value an asset in any industry can vary greatly; therefore, it is important to know for any particular industry what measurements are commonly used in order to get a proper multiple.

There are databases that keep track of asset sales and the multiples of these measurements at which they were sold, when that information is available. By using these databases for comparison we can compute a range for almost any asset that needs to be valued. However, this method, although currently very popular and easy to use, presents a number of significant problems.

The assets that we use for comparison may not be all that similar to the asset being valued and could produce inaccurate multiples. In our tire company example, we might find that the tire company that was sold made tires for the original equipment market, where the margins are thin and the demand cyclical. The tire industry asset we are valuing might make mostly specialty tires; in this market, the margins are much fatter and demand more stable. A potential buyer might be willing to pay a higher multiple of EBITD, operating income, or free cash flow for the stability and stronger margins of the specialty tire manufacturer. We could also run into trouble when comparing assets in different geographical areas. In some industries, such as home building, location can have a substantial impact on an asset's growth potential, sales, and profitability.

It is rare to find assets that have been sold that are directly comparable to an asset being evaluated. Differences in product lines, markets, margins, and management can make large differences in value. In high-technology industries, this method of comparing multiples is generally invalid, because one company's product line or assets may be on the cutting edge of technology, which could make the company very valuable despite low sales or earnings; or it could have obsolete technology, which could render the business worthless despite a strong record of sales and earnings.

The number of comparable assets that have been sold is often very small, limiting the number of transactions from which to determine the proper multiples. In the cable television industry there have been numerous transactions, yielding a constant update of the dollar-per-subscriber amount that a cable franchise is worth. However, in the furniture industry there have been only a few transactions over many years, providing only an infrequent glimpse of what these assets are worth.

The multiples paid for an asset often are affected by the financial condition of the buyer. Well-financed strategic buyers of an asset may be willing to pay substantially more than a financial buyer who will consider only the financial return of owning an asset. The strategic buyer may see advantages other than just financial in buying an asset, such as an increase in market share or entry into a market. These advantages may outweigh the near-term impact of a poor financial return from the asset being acquired. A financial buyer, on the other hand, must have a high enough return on the capital used to buy the asset to support the capital structure. This overriding need to earn a return capable of supporting the capital structure limits the amount the financial buyer can pay, despite the extra value that an asset's more qualitative aspects can add.

Values obtained from this method are most commonly derived using historical financial or operating measurements. However, the current performance of an asset can be substantially different from the recent historical performance, rendering the value obtained from a multiple invalid. If the asset's financial performance is improving or deteriorating rapidly, then the value derived from a multiple of historical performance can produce inaccurate results, especially for the financial buyer who must rely on earning a sufficient return on capital. If the asset performance is improving rapidly, the value derived from a multiple of historical results can greatly underestimate its true value; if the performance is deteriorating, then the asset's value will deteriorate and may render the financial buyer insolvent shortly after the purchase.

Comparison of an Asset with Market Values of Existing Public Companies

We can also derive an asset's value by comparing it with the values of public companies in the debt and equity markets. The public markets for bonds and stocks provide a large database of value for assets in a variety of industries. One of the major advantages of using this method is the large amount of data available for assets in almost any industry.

This method involves comparing the multiple that the marketplace is willing to pay for an asset's earnings, sales, book value, or other financial or operating measure with the asset being valued. For example, the equity of any public company trades at a certain price/earnings ratio, which can be used as a proxy for the P/E ratio of the equity of another company in the same industry. The market value of a company can also be expressed as a multiple of a variety of other financial or operating measures, such as book value, sales, subscribers, output, and so forth.

One of the major problems with this method is that public market values of a company do not have a built-in acquisition premium. The market value of any company is established relative to the market values of other companies in the same industry. The market value may not fully take into account the improvements in performance that can be achieved by a financial or strategic buyer. Therefore, a comparison with the market values of existing companies can greatly underestimate the value of an asset to a buyer that could change the asset's performance or otherwise bestow substantial benefits.

Many companies in the public markets are conglomerates, which makes it difficult to determine how much each individual asset or division contributes to their value in the public market. Eliminating these from consideration can greatly reduce the number of directly comparable companies, making the comparison less meaningful.

Liquidation Value

Liquidation valuation should be used to provide a minimum value, because this method as generally applied does not include a premium for the going concern value of a business. Liquidation value may be applied to multiple operations where each may be sold as a separate business to realize more value than the value of the whole conglomerate (as measured by its stock price). This type of analysis can also be used to find the real downside protection an investor may have from the company's assets.

In order to do a thorough liquidation analysis, a balance sheet with the most detail possible is necessary. The process of valuation then proceeds at each level, with the most liquid assets having the least discount from face value. For example, cash would be valued at its face amount. Accounts receivable normally would have some discount from face, because they take time to turn into cash and also may not be paid in full. Certain assets, such as real estate, may be worth more than their book value, even though they take time to be turned into cash.

It is very difficult to arrive at the appropriate discount to be applied to each asset class. The discount should balance the value of a truly valuable asset and the proper reductions based upon the time frame needed to realize the true value and the uniqueness of each asset. There are many reasons why assets may not sell for their book value. These can include competitive, economic, labor-related, geographic, product specific, technological, foreign, or regulatory factors, which may move positively or negatively for each specific asset. Liquidation values are fluid and can change rapidly. Liabilities generally are valued at face amount, even though in many market circumstances they can be reduced.

By following a careful analysis of the assets and then comparing this value against a company's liabilities, you can establish whether an entity is over- or under-valued based on the assumptions included in the applicable discount factors.

Ability of Assets to Support Leverage

Valuing assets by determining their ability to support leverage has become popular in the last five to six years, a period during which many assets and companies were acquired in highly leveraged transactions. It was useful as long as funds were available for leveraged transactions, because it was possible to predict the capital structure that was needed to finance an asset purchase. However, since the funds available in the junk bond market have dwindled dramatically, it has become very difficult to predict what capital structure and what level of interest rates will be needed to finance a transaction.

Until recently, asset purchases were financed at debt levels that required almost all of the asset's available cash flow be dedicated to servicing the debt. The stability of the cash flow in both strong economies and recessions was not examined with a view to its impact on the asset's debt-servicing capability. Funds sufficient to finance acquisitions were available even though the buyers had to rely on a steadily improving economy to make the acquisition work.

The use of deferred payment debt securities, such as zero-coupon bonds and pay-in-kind securities, lengthened the time during which an asset's cash flow needed to support its debt levels. The cost of these securities, however, can become very high, and the effect of compounding their coupon results in rapidly rising debt levels and ultimately very high cash interest expenses when they begin to pay cash.

This method of asset valuation involves first constructing projections for the asset, taking into account the impact of conscious decisions by management to reduce costs because of the dramatic need to conserve cash flow. It is important to construct a variety of projections under several different economic scenarios, from rapid growth to recession, because they can have a dramatic impact on the asset's value.

Exhibit 1 provides an illustration of a leveraged buyout. Here we assume an asset acquired for $800 million plus the assumption of the outstanding $50 million of 10 percent senior notes. In this illustration we have shown a steady improvement in sales, gross margins, and operating cash flow. Improvements in gross margins and reductions in selling, general, and administrative (SG&A) expenses are due to management's emphasis on reducing costs to improve cash flow. We have picked a capital structure that is typical of many leveraged buyouts. The capital structure consists of 60 percent bank debt, 2.5 percent equity, and the rest subordinated debt or preferred equity. The bank debt amortizes equally over an eight-year period. The most junior debt level, the subordinated discount debentures and the preferred stock, are both deferred payment securities that defer payment for five years. The free cash flow of this asset after cash interest payments and capital expenditures is not enough to amortize the bank debt on its own. Therefore, we have assumed the company is able to raise other senior debt through either mortgages on existing facilities or leases of equipment. Over time, the debt levels at the company decline, its equity value increases dramatically, and its coverage ratios indicate it has no difficulty servicing its debt. Therefore, we can conclude that the asset's value under this scenario is at least $850 million, because its earnings power and cash flow can support the $800 million in new financing needed to make the purchase.

EXHIBIT 1 *Example I: Growth Case*
Leveraged Buyout for $800 Million or 8 Times Operating Cash Flow

						Year					
	0	1	2	3	4	5	6	7	8	9	10
Sales	1,000	1,000	1,050	1,103	1,158	1,216	1,276	1,340	1,407	1,477	1,551
COGS	750	750	787	825	865	907	951	998	1,046	1,097	1,150
Gross Margin	250	250	263	278	293	308	325	343	361	380	401
SG&A	150	140	140	144	147	151	155	158	162	166	171
D&A	25	25	26	26	27	27	28	28	29	29	30
EBIT	75	85	98	108	119	131	143	156	170	185	201
Interest	5	94	96	98	99	99	99	93	88	85	80
Pretax	70	−9	2	11	20	31	44	63	82	100	121
Taxes	24	−4	1	4	8	12	18	25	33	40	48
Net Income	46	−5	1	6	12	19	26	38	49	60	73
Gross Margin %	25.00	25.00	25.09	25.19	25.28	25.37	25.47	25.56	25.65	25.75	25.84
SG&A/Sales %	15.00	14.00	13.33	13.02	12.71	12.40	12.11	11.82	11.54	11.26	11.00
EBITDA	100	110	123	134	146	158	171	184	199	214	230
Capital Expenditures	35	25	25	27	28	30	31	33	34	36	37
Working Capital	15	12	13	13	14	15	15	16	17	18	19
Cash Interest	5.00	81.80	81.80	81.66	80.47	78.04	74.12	93.22	88.49	85.22	79.70
Preferred Dividend		0.00	0.00	0.00	0.00	0.00	0.00	0.00	29.52	29.52	29.52
Free Cash Flow		−9	4	13	23	36	50	42	30	46	65
Principal Due		0	70	70	70	70	70	70	60	65	
EBITDA/Cash Interest		1.34	1.51	1.64	1.81	2.02	2.30	1.98	2.24	2.51	2.89

EXHIBIT 1 *Continued*

	Year										
	0	1	2	3	4	5	6	7	8	9	10
Capitalization											
Bank Debt @11.5%		480.00	480.00	410.00	340.00	270.00	200.00	130.00	60.00	0.00	0.00
Senior Notes @10%	50.00	50.00	50.00	50.00	50.00	50.00	50.00	50.00	50.00	50.00	50.00
New Senior @12%				65.92	123.11	169.91	204.37	224.31	251.97	282.24	236.23
Senior Sub. @13.5%		160.00	160.00	160.00	160.00	160.00	160.00	160.00	160.00	160.00	160.00
Sub. Disc. @15%		80.00	92.45	106.84	123.46	142.68	164.88	165.00	165.00	165.00	165.00
Preferred @18%		60.00	70.93	83.84	99.11	117.16	138.50	163.73	164.00	164.00	164.00
Common	300.00	20.00	14.72	16.11	22.41	34.46	53.19	79.68	117.43	166.41	226.27
Full Interest		93.80	95.67	97.69	98.99	99.44	98.86	93.22	88.49	85.22	79.70
Cash Interest		81.80	81.80	81.66	80.47	78.04	74.12	93.22	88.49	85.22	79.70

In a second example, shown in Exhibit 2, we show a recession case for the same asset. In order to survive the recession, the buyer can pay only $500 million for the equity of the company. The company is just barely able to service its debt in year four, and the debt levels increase over the 10-year period. Although the company quickly recovers from the recession, it would not have been able to survive had the price paid been higher and the debt structure similar to that in the first example.

Finally in a third example, presented in Exhibit 3, we show the impact of higher borrowing rates on the projections from Exhibit 1. In this case the leveraged buyout still works, although not quite as well as in the first example. The impact of higher borrowing rates is not as dramatic as the impact of a recession or a downturn in the company's business. The buyer is still able to pay $800 million for the equity of the company and assume the $50 million of existing debt.

Conclusion

There are many ways to value assets, each with its strengths and weaknesses. The advantage of using several methods is that it can produce a range of values for the asset in question and allow an examination of these values under a variety of economic scenarios. However, any asset's value ultimately depends on its future performance, which often is hard to predict over the long term, if not the short term. Whether or not the financing method of the purchase is heavily leveraged, the wrong projections about future performance will lead to substantial errors in asset valuation.

EXHIBIT 2   Example II: Recession Case
Leveraged Buyout at $500 Million

						Year					
	0	1	2	3	4	5	6	7	8	9	10
Sales	1,000	1,000	1,050	998	978	1,075	1,129	1,186	1,245	1,307	1,372
COGS	750	750	787	788	775	812	852	893	937	983	1,030
Gross Margin	250	250	263	209	203	263	277	292	308	324	342
SG&A	150	140	146	151	149	155	161	167	174	180	188
D&A	25	25	26	26	27	27	27	29	30	30	31
EBIT	75	85	92	32	28	81	90	96	105	114	124
Interest	5	61	62	60	66	71	72	71	69	69	68
Pretax	70	25	31	−29	−38	10	17	26	35	45	56
Taxes	24	8	10	−10	−13	3	6	9	12	15	19
Net Income	46	16	20	−19	−25	7	11	17	23	30	37
Gross Margin %	25.00	25.00	25.09	20.95	20.75	24.45	24.54	24.64	24.73	24.83	24.92
SG&A/Sales %	15.00	14.00	13.86	15.17	15.20	14.37	14.22	14.08	13.94	13.80	13.66
EBITDA	100	110	118	58	54	108	117	125	134	144	154
Capital Expenditures	35	25	25	27	28	30	31	33	34	36	37
Working Capital	15	15	16	12	2	10	11	11	12	12	13
Cash Interest	5.00	53.00	53.00	50.32	54.28	58.10	57.03	70.55	69.45	69.34	68.14
Preferred Dividend		0.00	0.00	0.00	0.00	0.00	0.00	0.00	17.10	17.10	17.10
Free Cash Flow		17	24	−31	−30	11	18	11	2	10	19
Principal Due		0	45	45	45	45	45	45	30		19
EBITDA/Cash Interest	2.08	2.08	2.23	1.15	1.00	1.87	2.04	1.77	1.93	2.08	2.27

Capitalization

Bank Debt @11.5%	50.00	300.00	300.00	255.00	210.00	165.00	120.00	75.00	30.00	0.00	0.00
Senior Notes @10%	50.00	50.00	50.00	50.00	50.00	50.00	50.00	50.00	50.00	50.00	50.00
New Senior @12%				20.80	96.88	171.92	206.12	233.14	267.08	294.88	284.88
Senior Sub. @13.5%	100.00	100.00	100.00	100.00	100.00	100.00	100.00	100.00	100.00	100.00	100.00
Sub. Disc. @15%		50.00	57.78	66.77	77.17	89.17	103.05	103.00	103.00	103.00	103.00
Preferred @18%		35.00	41.37	48.91	57.82	68.35	80.79	95.51	95.00	95.00	95.00
Common	300.00	20.00	40.32	21.45	-3.71	2.84	14.07	30.96	54.31	83.84	120.70
Full Interest		60.50	61.67	60.34	65.85	71.48	72.49	70.55	69.45	69.34	68.14
Cash Interest		53.00	53.00	50.32	54.28	58.10	57.03	70.55	69.45	69.34	68.14

Assumptions:
1. 5% revenue growth per year except in years 3 and 4, where there is a recession and sales decline by 5% and 2%, respectively.
2. Gross margins improve slightly in growth years but decline in recession.

EXHIBIT 3   Example III: Growth Case
Leveraged Buyout for $800 Million or 8 Times Operating Cash Flow, with Higher Borrowing Rates

						Year					
	0	1	2	3	4	5	6	7	8	9	10
Sales	1,000	1,000	1,050	1,103	1,158	1,216	1,276	1,340	1,407	1,477	1,551
COGS	750	750	787	825	865	907	951	998	1,046	1,097	1,150
Gross Margin	250	250	263	278	293	308	325	343	361	380	401
SG&A	150	140	140	144	147	151	155	158	162	166	171
D&A	25	25	26	26	27	27	28	28	29	29	30
EBIT	75	85	98	108	119	131	143	156	170	185	201
Interest	5	99	101	103	105	106	106	101	96	94	89
Pretax	70	−14	−3	5	14	25	37	56	74	91	112
Taxes	24	−6	−1	2	6	10	15	22	30	37	45
Net Income	46	−8	−2	3	8	15	22	33	44	55	67
Gross Margin %	25.00	25.00	25.09	25.19	25.28	25.37	25.47	25.56	25.65	25.75	25.84
SG&A/Sales %	15.00	14.00	13.33	13.02	12.71	12.40	12.11	11.82	11.54	11.26	11.00
EBITDA	100	110	123	134	146	158	171	184	199	214	230
Capital Expenditures	35	25	25	27	28	30	31	33	34	36	37
Working Capital	15	12	13	13	14	15	15	16	17	18	19
Cash Interest	5.00	85.80	85.80	85.79	84.75	82.48	78.75	100.52	96.31	93.68	89.18
Preferred Dividend		0.00	0.00	0.00	0.00	0.00	0.00	0.00	29.52	29.52	29.52
Free Cash Flow		−13	0	9	19	31	45	35	22	38	56
Principal Due		0	70	70	70	70	70	70	60		
EBITDA/Cash Interest		1.28	1.44	1.56	1.72	1.91	2.17	1.83	2.06	2.28	2.58

Capitalization

Bank Debt @12%	50.00	480.00	480.00	410.00	340.00	270.00	200.00	130.00	60.00	0.00	0.00
Senior Notes @10%		50.00	50.00	50.00	50.00	50.00	50.00	50.00	50.00	50.00	50.00
New Senior @12%				69.92	131.24	182.31	221.22	245.77	280.73	318.83	281.29
Senior Sub. @14.5%		160.00	160.00	160.00	160.00	160.00	160.00	160.00	160.00	160.00	160.00
Sub. Disc. @16.5%		80.00	92.45	106.84	123.46	142.68	164.88	165.00	165.00	165.00	165.00
Preferred @18%		60.00	70.93	83.84	99.11	117.16	138.50	163.73	164.00	164.00	164.00
Common	300.00	20.00	11.60	9.76	12.62	20.99	35.78	58.01	91.38	135.66	190.44
Full Interest		99.00	101.05	103.42	105.12	106.02	105.95	100.52	96.31	93.68	89.18
Cash Interest		85.80	85.80	85.79	84.75	82.48	78.75	100.52	96.31	93.68	89.18

9

Embedded Option Value and the Analysis of High-Yield Bonds

Stephen Anbinder
Vice President
High Yield Bond Group
Merchant Banking
Merrill Lynch Capital Markets

Like most fixed income securities, high-yield bonds are issued with a variety of call and other optional provisions. The call option gives the issuer the right to redeem the bond prior to its stated maturity at a predetermined price (often at a premium to its face value). The investor is therefore short an *embedded call option*. This increases the yield but introduces a reinvestment risk in the event of a call when interest rates are low. The pickup in yield is obtained at the expense of a lower (possibly negative) convexity. Conversely, an embedded put option costs the investor in yield, but improves the bond's convexity. By making early redemptions possible, embedded options act to lessen the duration and interest rate sensitivity of the bond.

Interest rate option models are used to quantify the impact of embedded options in a bond's performance. Currently, the dominant paradigm is the *option-adjusted spread* analysis. This approach involves evaluating the embedded options relative to Treasury bonds. Option-adjusted spread[1] indicates the spread to the Treasury yield curve at

---

1. For an explanation of the option-adjusted spread methodology, see Lakhbir S. Hayre and Kenneth Lauterbach, "Stochastic Valuation of Debt Securities," in *Man-*

149

which a noncallable security would be issued. It is therefore a measure of the credit quality of the issuer. The difference between the actual spread and the option-adjusted spread is the *yield value* of the option. An option-adjusted spread analysis also provides the price of the embedded option and the (option-adjusted) duration and convexity of the bond. High-yield bonds command high option-adjusted spreads.

The key to all interest rate option models is the concept of *yield volatility*. A highly volatile interest rate environment increases the likelihood that the option holder will exercise his or her right, hence it increases the option's value. An option model should be arbitrage free in the sense that it should preclude the possibility of arbitrage between different interest-sensitive securities. By using an arbitrage-free model one can identify mispriced securities and (one hopes) make a profit. Another theoretical requirement is *yield curve consistency;* that is, the model should evaluate noncallable securities in a manner consistent with the observed yield curve.

An effective way to merge these concepts is through a *binomial interest rate model*. Existing binomial models differ in degree of theoretical sophistication and computational efficiency, but they all share one important technique: *backward induction*. In this method one "diffuses" the bond price one step backward over a series of discrete time intervals by taking the average price of two adjacent nodes and discounting by the short-term interest rate. Coupon cash flows are added and option provisions are incorporated as one moves backward, until the root of the binomial tree is reached, where the current value of the security is read off.

A Cautious Approach

The development of sophisticated models to measure the value of embedded put and call options in the investment-grade corporate and mortgage sectors has resulted in important refinements in the evaluation of spreads, duration, convexity, and so on. Dealers have adopted inventory control procedures and risk management techniques to re-

---

aging Institutional Assets, edited by Frank J. Fabozzi (New York: Harper & Row, 1990).

flect these improvements, and investors have developed new optimization and indexing techniques based on this work.

The high-yield market has lagged in the application of these techniques for a number of reasons. First of all, the relative value of the option is much lower. For example, a typical high-grade security trading 75 basis points over Treasuries might have an embedded call option worth 25 basis points, or one-third of the gross spread. A high-yield bond with a similar option feature might be trading at 500 basis points over Treasuries, in which case the identical option value would account for only 5 percent of the gross spread. The importance of a correct credit judgment obviously dwarfs any concern over correct valuation of the option. Furthermore, as liquidity in the high-yield market is relatively poor, and most high-yield participants are buy-and-hold, current income–oriented investors, the short-term price volatility of a bond (which, as we will see, can be significantly affected by the embedded option) has been of less concern. However, it seems likely that as mark-to-market requirements affect a broader spectrum of high-yield investors, total return and thus interim market valuation will grow in importance.

There are a number of reasons for adopting a cautious approach in applying a quantitative technique such as option analysis to the high-yield market. As essentially a hybrid security, containing, in varying degrees, features of the debt instrument and equity instrument alike, the high-yield bond does not quite fit the parameters envisioned in the typical fixed income–oriented option valuation model. For example, although the high-yield bond has a senior position in the issuer's capital structure, similar to its high-grade counterpart, in actuality the amount of underlying equity is often meager, affording very little protection against economic or financial reversal. As a result, factors unrelated to general interest rate trends will impact market performance. Market studies confirm that the price action of a particular high-yield bond is apt to correlate much more closely to specific company and industry developments than to general changes in interest rate levels or the shape of the yield curve. Furthermore, even though the high-yield bond contains a fixed coupon, sinking fund, and maturity schedule, again looking much like its investment-grade counterpart, the frequency of deviation from this "fixed" schedule, whether due to default or recapitalization, is much higher. For example, of the 131 major high-yield issues that came to market during 1985, fully 18 percent were no longer outstanding by the end of 1988.

The high-yield market, which is currently defined to include all non-convertible bonds rated below investment grade by the major rating agencies, actually consists of securities exhibiting a wide divergence of bond versus equity market patterns. The high end of the spectrum, essentially the bonds rated B+ and above by Standard & Poor's and B1 and above by Moody's, tends most often to behave like the investment-grade market. Performance within this group is usually highly correlated. On the other hand, the lower end of the spectrum — those bonds rated B/B2 and below — might look more like a portfolio of equities, with a wider dispersion in performance and more volatile return patterns.

Another reason for caution in applying such a quantitative technique to the high-yield market relates to the inadequacy of market data. Many high-yield issues are essentially illiquid, and reliable price quotes are often unavailable. Furthermore, the market has grown to significant size only since 1984, so that the number of data points is small and application of the standard call and sinking fund features very limited. For example, refinancing decisions will often be dictated by particular indenture features rather than by the strict economic optimization that forms the basis of the typical option model.

Thus, the application to the high-yield market of the sophisticated quantitative techniques developed to measure option value carries certain risks, and results should be interpreted carefully. Still, as I will attempt to show, there is a place for such analysis, especially when used to evaluate broad market trends, to compare bonds with comparable bond/equity characteristics, and especially to better assess the potential behavior of a particular bond in a changing rate environment.

Volatility

The controlling factor in any fixed income option model is the volatility rate, which defines the potential move in yields (and thus prices) over the relevant time period and thereby indicates the probability of the embedded option having real value or being in the money in the future.

EXHIBIT 1 *Merrill Lynch Master High Yield Index and 7–10 Year U.S. Treasury Index*

Year	Range of Yields	Annual Volatility	High-Low as % Median
High Yield			
85	13.35–14.97	4.5%	11.4%
86	12.10–13.37	5.1	10.0
87	11.59–13.75	9.6	17.0
88	12.73–13.40	5.3	5.1
89[a]	13.19–13.86	3.7	5.0
7–10 Year Treasury Index			
85	8.98–11.92	15.2	28.1
86	7.03–9.08	21.8	25.5
87	7.14–9.65	15.8	29.9
88	8.14–9.24	14.4	12.7
89[a]	7.81–9.40	14.5	18.5

a. Through September.

Price history for the period 1985 through September 1989 indicates that the high-yield market is significantly less volatile than the investment-grade market. This is evident from Exhibit 1, which compares yield range and annual yield volatility of the Merrill Lynch Master High Yield Index and the Merrill Lynch 7–10 Year U.S. Treasury Index.

However, this apparent lack of volatility is deceptive. As mentioned above, the high-yield market resembles the equity market in that it is basically heterogeneous, but investment-grade bonds tend to be fungible. Generally, all Aa-rated bonds with the same coupon, maturity, and call characteristics will move in tandem, while B-rated bonds (and equities) might vary considerably in market action. Just as the volatility of a particular equity must be viewed apart from the volatility of the S&P 500, for example, so the volatility of a particular high-yield bond must be considered apart from the volatility of any comprehensive high-yield index.

Let us say that the volatility of a high-yield bond consists of two components, one reflecting general interest rate volatility and the other reflecting factors such as credit quality specific to the particular issue.

The first component would probably not deviate much across the entire sector, but the second, credit-related, factor would likely vary with a particular issue's position on the above-mentioned bond–equity spectrum. The more a particular bond is apt to react to company-specific developments — in other words, the more like an equity it behaves — the higher this second volatility component would be. Using the bond's credit rating as a reasonable indication of its position on the bond–equity spectrum, we have taken S&P's rating as a guide in assigning volatility. Of course, the market's valuation of a particular credit is often at odds with that of the rating agencies. Nevertheless, for a large sample of securities the rating is a useful proxy for credit perception and is used in this chapter to determine volatility.

In order to provide a framework for an analysis of the high-yield bond's embedded option we selected a diverse sample of some 40 issues for which reliable 1988 and 1989 market quotes are available. These bonds are listed in Exhibit 2.

In order to show the effect of the implied volatility on option value, option value has been computed using two different volatility rates: 8½ percent in Exhibit 2A (which roughly equates to the yield volatility of the investment-grade bond market) and 10½ percent in Exhibit 2B. Historical volatility confirms the fact that volatility varies with credit quality. If our 40-bond portfolio is divided in half on the basis of rating, the higher rated portion (B+ and higher) averages a 10.9 percent historical volatility; the lower rated portion (B and lower) averages a 13.0 percent historical volatility. Because these rates reflect the sharp market decline during the fall of 1989, lower volatility rates of 8½ percent for those securities rated B+ and higher and 10½ percent for those rated B and lower are used in this analysis.

Option Value

The option value represents the present value of the embedded call feature of an issue over its life, based on the probability and financial impact of exercise and assuming interest rate volatility at the implied rate. If the option value, which represents a negative feature from the investor's standpoint — the investor has in effect granted this option to the issuer for a corresponding reduction in price — is added back to the current market price, the result theoretically represents the value of a noncallable bond of the same exact terms. From Exhibit 2, it is apparent that option value varies directly with volatility. The average value of the embedded option of our 40-bond portfolio on 9/30/89 was 2.12 points using an 8½ percent implied volatility and 2.77 points using 10½ percent. From Exhibit 3, which summarizes the change in the portfolio from September 1987 to September 1989, it is also apparent that option value increases as prices rise and with the passage of time. Note the rise in option value both during the first quarter of 1988, as prices rose, and from June 1988 to June 1989, as prices remained flat. This should not be surprising, for rising prices (falling rates) make exercise of the embedded option more likely, and the passage of time makes exercise more imminent as the noncall period diminishes.

Option-Adjusted Spread

The option-adjusted spread (OAS) measures the difference between the yield of a hypothetical noncallable bullet bond of the same issuer and the Treasury yield of the same maturity. The OAS strips out the portion of the spread that compensates for the embedded option and isolates the credit/liquidity premium attached to the particular issue by the marketplace.[2]

This is a much more useful basis on which to assess relative value than the gross or unadjusted spread, which can be distorted by widely divergent embedded option components. From our portfolio in Exhibit 2, compare, for example, the Hertz-Penske 11½ percent of 1997 to the Owens-Corning 11¾ percent of 2001. Although gross Treasury spreads are roughly comparable (337 b.p. vs. 329 b.p.), the option components are significantly different. On an option-adjusted basis, the Hertz bonds are actually trading at a much wider spread to Treasuries (311 b.p. vs. 220 b.p.). Or contrast the two Burlington issues: A 3-point difference in option value (at 10½ percent implied volatility)

---

2. For a step-by-step illustration of how the OAS is calculated, see Richard W. Wilson and Frank J. Fabozzi, *The New Corporate Bond Market* (Chicago: Probus Publishing, 1990), Chapter 11.

EXHIBIT 2A   *Sample Portfolio, 8½% Volatility*

Issue (Maturity/Par Call)	S&P	Coupon (%)	09/29/89 Price ($)	1st Call (Year & Price)
Amstar 11⅜% (02/15/97/96)	B−	11.375	81.00	90 @ 107.70
Bally's Grand 11½% (04/15/96/95)	BB−	11.500	86.25	91 @ 105.11
Barry's Jewelers 12⅝% (05/01/01/00)	NR	12.625	82.43	90 @ 109.02
Best Products 12⅝% (12/01/96/93)	CCC+	12.625	102.00	89 @ 107.21
Burlington 13⅞% (10/01/96/94)	B−	13.875	103.00	92 @ 105.00
Burlington 14¼% (10/01/99/94)	B−	14.250	104.00	92 @ 105.00
Burlington 16% (10/01/03/93)	B−	16.000	55.00	93 @ 100.00
Cablevision Inds. 11¼% (02/15/02/94)	B−	11.250	88.00	90 @ 108.00
Caesars World 13½% (10/01/97/93)	BB−	13.500	102.75	92 @ 102.25
Coastal Corp. 8.48% (11/15/91/89)	BB+	8.480	97.00	88 @ 104.00
Colt Industries 12½% (10/15/01/96)	B−	12.500	103.50	91 @ 106.25
Eckerd Jack Corp. 11⅛% (05/01/01/91)	B−	11.125	85.50	91 @ 100.00
First Brands Corp. 12½% (09/01/98/95)	CCC+	12.500	100.25	91 @ 105.56
FMC Corp. 12¼% (06/01/98/94)	B+	12.250	105.50	91 @ 106.00
FMC Corp. 12½% (06/01/01/96)	B+	12.500	105.75	91 @ 106.25
GNLV Fin. Corp. 11¼% (07/15/96/95)	BB−	11.250	96.25	91 @ 105.00
Golden Nugget 13¼% (06/01/95/94)	BB−	13.250	99.75	90 @ 105.89
Heritage Commun. 11½% (07/15/97/93)	BB−	11.500	98.50	91 @ 105.00
Hertz-Penske 11½% (07/15/97/95)	BB+	11.500	99.00	92 @ 104.31
Holiday Inns 10½% (04/01/94/94)	BB−	10.500	100.50	92 @ 101.50
Holiday Inns 11% (04/01/99/98)	B+	11.000	100.00	90 @ 108.00
Home Shpping. Ntwrk. 11¾% (10/15/96/95)	B+	11.750	82.00	91 @ 105.33
Masco Indust. Inc. 10¼% (02/01/97/95)	B+	10.250	93.25	90 @ 106.25
Mueller Co. 12⅛% (07/15/96/95)	BB−	12.125	103.50	91 @ 105.39
Ocean Shwboat. Fin. 11⅜% (03/15/02/99)	B+	11.375	92.68	93 @ 105.69
Owens-Corning Fib. 11¾% (11/15/01/91)	BB+	11.750	101.00	91 @ 100.00
Owens-Illinois 12¼% (06/01/96/94)	B−	12.250	94.38	92 @ 103.50
Owens-Illinois 12¾% (06/01/99/97)	B−	12.750	95.00	87 @ 112.75
Owens-Illinois 15% (06/01/03/93)	B−	15.000	55.50	87 @ 48.856
PST Holdings 12¾% (06/01/92/92)	B	12.750	99.25	90 @ 105.10
Safeway St. Hldg. 11¾% (11/15/96/94)	B−	11.750	100.38	89 @ 107.34
Safeway St. Hldg. 12% (11/15/98/96)	B−	12.000	101.25	91 @ 106.00
Service Merchndse. 11¾% (12/15/96/93)	B	11.750	91.25	89 @ 106.71
Sowest. Forest 12⅛% (09/15/01/95)	BB−	12.125	100.50	91 @ 105.39
Stone Container 13⅝% (06/01/95/92)	BB−	13.625	100.25	89 @ 105.84
Storer Comm. Inc. 10% (05/15/03/88)	B−	10.000	81.00	88 @ 100.00
Supermkts. Gen'l. HC 14½% (09/15/97/95)	B−	14.500	105.00	90 @ 109.06
Trump Plaza Fndg. 12⅞% (06/15/98/97)	NR	12.875	101.00	91 @ 107.00
Tyler Corp. 12% (07/15/97/96)	B+	12.000	100.00	90 @ 107.33
Zale Corp. 13⅛% (06/01/07/02)	B+	13.125	98.00	92 @ 108.75
Averages	B	12.231	94.78	

Recent Historical Yield Volatility	Option Value		Spread vs. U.S. Treasuries		Modified Duration		Convexity	
	Price ($)	Yield (b.p.)	Adj.	Unadj.	Adj.	Unadj.	Adj.	Unadj.
26.4	0.08	2	748	750	4.40	4.48	0.23	0.28
8.1	0.11	3	649	652	3.96	4.06	0.16	0.23
7.4	0.38	8	762	771	4.87	5.12	0.27	0.43
22.3	2.71	56	330	386	3.14	4.48	(0.45)	0.28
12.4	1.81	39	448	487	3.38	4.16	(0.11)	0.25
9.3	4.41	77	446	523	3.49	5.00	(0.21)	0.39
12.6	5.87	116	631	748	5.33	8.65	(0.28)	0.89
7.2	1.25	23	472	494	5.31	6.11	0.06	0.57
5.2	3.56	65	393	457	3.16	4.56	(0.22)	0.31
9.8	0.03	1	174	176	1.80	1.85	(0.06)	0.05
7.6	4.90	73	291	365	3.82	5.92	(0.58)	0.55
14.2	0.93	18	517	535	5.03	5.68	0.03	0.50
10.3	2.34	43	372	415	4.03	5.25	(0.34)	0.38
5.5	5.12	88	206	293	3.02	5.17	(0.61)	0.38
4.5	6.74	98	231	329	3.13	5.99	(0.84)	0.54
8.6	0.58	13	361	374	4.06	4.50	(0.08)	0.27
12.2	0.95	24	473	497	3.15	3.74	(0.21)	0.19
N/A	1.97	39	308	347	3.82	4.92	(0.25)	0.33
11.8	1.33	26	311	337	4.13	4.93	(0.18)	0.33
20.5	0.29	6	207	213	3.14	3.38	(0.09)	0.15
20.1	1.73	30	242	271	4.40	5.51	(0.40)	0.44
23.9	0.08	2	776	778	4.06	4.12	0.20	0.25
5.8	0.53	11	320	331	4.44	4.88	(0.01)	0.32
7.0	1.95	40	263	303	3.27	4.49	(0.51)	0.27
8.7	1.32	22	403	425	5.49	6.31	0.07	0.60
N/A	7.34	109	220	329	2.87	6.15	(0.74)	0.58
15.0	0.60	14	507	522	3.82	4.21	0.00	0.25
9.9	1.16	23	518	540	4.51	5.13	(0.02)	0.39
5.0	4.30	89	660	749	4.35	8.40	(1.96)	0.85
26.2	0.01	0	464	464	2.11	2.12	0.04	0.06
9.0	1.57	33	301	334	3.61	4.55	(0.35)	0.28
8.1	2.28	40	307	347	4.00	5.26	(0.38)	0.40
17.5	0.55	13	523	536	4.10	4.47	0.02	0.28
5.2	3.93	61	314	375	4.29	6.22	(0.49)	0.57
10.9	2.57	65	457	522	2.35	3.71	(0.42)	0.19
9.1	0.72	13	457	470	5.83	6.35	0.22	0.64
15.7	2.75	55	460	514	3.36	4.70	(0.51)	0.31
8.7	1.83	35	403	437	3.95	4.99	(0.33)	0.36
8.4	1.32	26	341	368	4.01	4.86	(0.30)	0.33
13.6	3.00	44	463	508	5.08	6.45	(0.11)	0.72
11.7	2.12	39	418	457	3.90	5.02	(0.24)	0.38

EXHIBIT 2B   *Sample Portfolio, 10½% Volatility*

Issue (Maturity/Par Call)	S&P	Coupon (%)	09/29/89 Price ($)	1st Call (Year & Price)
Amstar 11⅜% (02/15/97/96)	B−	11.375	81.00	90 @ 107.70
Bally's Grand 11½% (04/15/96/95)	BB−	11.500	86.25	91 @ 105.11
Barry's Jewelers 12⅝% (05/01/01/00)	NR	12.625	82.43	90 @ 109.02
Best Products 12⅝% (12/01/96/93)	CCC+	12.625	102.00	89 @ 107.21
Burlington 13⅞% (10/01/96/94)	B−	13.875	103.00	92 @ 105.00
Burlington 14¼% (10/01/99/94)	B−	14.250	104.00	92 @ 105.00
Burlington 16% (10/01/03/93)	B−	16.000	55.00	93 @ 100.00
Cablevision Inds. 11¼% (02/15/02/94)	B−	11.250	88.00	90 @ 108.00
Caesars World 13½% (10/01/97/93)	BB−	13.500	102.75	92 @ 102.25
Coastal Corp. 8.48% (11/15/91/89)	BB+	8.480	97.00	88 @ 104.00
Colt Industries 12½% (10/15/01/96)	B−	12.500	103.50	91 @ 106.25
Eckerd Jack Corp. 11⅛% (05/01/01/91)	B−	11.125	85.50	91 @ 100.00
First Brands Corp. 12½% (09/01/98/95)	CCC+	12.500	100.25	91 @ 105.56
FMC Corp. 12¼% (06/01/98/94)	B+	12.250	105.50	91 @ 106.00
FMC Corp. 12½% (06/01/01/96)	B+	12.500	105.75	91 @ 106.25
GNLV Fin. Corp. 11¼% (07/15/96/95)	BB−	11.250	96.25	91 @ 105.00
Golden Nugget 13¼% (06/01/95/94)	BB−	13.250	99.75	90 @ 105.89
Heritage Commun. 11½% (07/15/97/93)	BB−	11.500	98.50	91 @ 105.00
Hertz-Penske 11½% (07/15/97/95)	BB+	11.500	99.00	92 @ 104.31
Holiday Inns 10½% (04/01/94/94)	BB−	10.500	100.50	92 @ 101.50
Holiday Inns 11% (04/01/99/98)	B+	11.000	100.00	90 @ 108.00
Home Shpping. Ntwrk. 11¾% (10/15/96/95)	B+	11.750	82.00	91 @ 105.33
Masco Indust. Inc. 10¼% (02/01/97/95)	B+	10.250	93.25	90 @ 106.25
Mueller Co. 12⅛% (07/15/96/95)	BB−	12.125	103.50	91 @ 105.39
Ocean Shwboat. Fin. 11⅜% (03/15/02/99)	B+	11.375	92.68	93 @ 105.69
Owens-Corning Fib. 11¾% (11/15/01/91)	BB+	11.750	101.00	91 @ 100.00
Owens-Illinois 12¼% (06/01/96/94)	B−	12.250	94.38	92 @ 103.50
Owens-Illinois 12¾% (06/01/99/97)	B−	12.750	95.00	87 @ 112.75
Owens-Illinois 15% (06/01/03/93)	B−	15.000	55.50	87 @ 48.856
PST Holdings 12¾% (06/01/92/92)	B	12.750	99.25	90 @ 105.10
Safeway St. Hldg. 11¾% (11/15/96/94)	B−	11.750	100.38	89 @ 107.34
Safeway St. Hldg. 12% (11/15/98/96)	B−	12.000	101.25	91 @ 106.00
Service Merchndse. 11¾% (12/15/96/93)	B	11.750	91.25	89 @ 106.71
Sowest. Forest 12⅛% (09/15/01/95)	BB−	12.125	100.50	91 @ 105.39
Stone Container 13⅝% (06/01/95/92)	BB−	13.625	100.25	89 @ 105.84
Storer Comm. Inc. 10% (05/15/03/88)	B−	10.000	81.00	88 @ 100.00
Supermkts. Gen'l. HC 14½% (09/15/97/95)	B−	14.500	105.00	90 @ 109.06
Trump Plaza Fndg. 12⅞% (06/15/98/97)	NR	12.875	101.00	91 @ 107.00
Tyler Corp. 12% (07/15/97/96)	B+	12.000	100.00	90 @ 107.33
Zale Corp. 13⅛% (06/01/07/02)	B+	13.125	98.00	92 @ 108.75
Averages	B	12.231	94.78	

Recent Historical Yield Volatility	Option Value		Spread vs. U.S. Treasuries		Modified Duration		Convexity	
	Price ($)	Yield (b.p.)	Adj.	Unadj.	Adj.	Unadj.	Adj.	Unadj.
26.4	0.19	5	745	750	4.34	4.48	0.20	0.28
8.1	0.25	7	646	652	3.89	4.06	0.12	0.23
7.4	0.75	17	754	771	4.74	5.12	0.22	0.43
22.3	3.37	69	317	386	3.05	4.48	(0.43)	0.28
12.4	2.27	49	439	488	3.34	4.16	(0.08)	0.25
9.3	5.27	91	432	523	3.47	5.00	(0.16)	0.39
12.6	7.07	138	609	748	5.38	8.65	(0.17)	0.89
7.2	1.97	36	459	494	5.13	6.11	0.05	0.57
5.2	4.20	77	380	457	3.17	4.56	(0.16)	0.31
9.8	0.06	3	172	176	1.75	1.85	(0.10)	0.05
7.6	6.16	91	273	365	3.72	5.92	(0.48)	0.55
14.2	1.58	31	505	535	4.82	5.68	(0.01)	0.50
10.3	3.13	58	357	415	3.89	5.25	(0.30)	0.38
5.5	5.97	102	192	293	2.98	5.17	(0.53)	0.38
4.5	8.12	117	212	329	3.08	5.99	(0.69)	0.54
8.6	0.93	21	353	374	3.93	4.50	(0.11)	0.27
12.2	1.35	34	463	497	3.04	3.74	(0.23)	0.19
N/A	2.55	50	297	347	3.75	4.92	(0.22)	0.33
11.8	1.85	37	301	337	4.02	4.93	(0.15)	0.33
20.5	0.37	11	203	213	3.07	3.38	(0.09)	0.15
20.1	2.49	42	229	271	4.20	5.51	(0.40)	0.44
23.9	0.19	5	773	778	4.00	4.12	0.17	0.25
5.8	0.86	18	313	331	4.31	4.88	(0.05)	0.32
7.0	2.56	53	251	303	3.17	4.49	(0.43)	0.27
8.7	2.05	34	391	425	5.31	6.31	0.06	0.60
N/A	8.75	127	202	329	2.94	6.15	(0.60)	0.58
15.0	0.93	22	500	522	3.73	4.21	(0.01)	0.25
9.9	1.76	34	506	540	4.35	5.13	(0.05)	0.39
5.0	5.92	120	628	748	3.99	8.40	(1.61)	0.85
26.2	0.02	1	463	464	2.09	2.12	0.02	0.06
9.0	2.13	44	290	334	3.48	4.55	(0.35)	0.28
8.1	3.07	54	293	347	3.86	5.27	(0.33)	0.40
17.5	0.89	21	515	536	3.99	4.47	0.00	0.28
5.2	5.10	78	296	375	4.15	6.22	(0.42)	0.57
10.9	3.17	80	442	522	2.34	3.71	(0.34)	0.19
9.1	1.31	24	446	470	5.61	6.35	0.15	0.64
15.7	3.57	70	444	514	3.20	4.70	(0.48)	0.31
8.7	2.59	49	388	437	3.79	4.99	(0.30)	0.36
8.4	1.92	38	330	368	3.84	4.86	(0.32)	0.33
13.6	4.28	63	445	507	4.88	6.45	(0.09)	0.72
11.7	2.77	51	406	457	3.79	5.02	(0.22)	0.38

EXHIBIT 3   *40-Bond High-Yield Portfolio*

Date	Average Price	Option Value Points	Option Value Basis Points	Spread vs. U.S. Treasuries Adjusted	Spread vs. U.S. Treasuries Unadjusted	Modified Duration Adjusted	Modified Duration Unadjusted	Convexity Adjusted	Convexity Unadjusted
09/30/87	91.37	1.26	25	344	369	4.97	5.66	0.07	0.50
12/31/87	92.51	1.30	23	439	461	4.83	5.45	0.10	0.46
03/31/88	96.89	1.70	29	374	402	4.64	5.48	(0.02)	0.44
06/30/88	97.31	2.05	34	337	371	4.54	5.49	0.08	0.46
09/30/88	96.93	2.07	37	334	370	4.35	5.31	(0.11)	0.43
12/31/88	97.04	2.66	46	283	329	4.18	5.34	(0.16)	0.44
03/31/89	94.82	2.62	48	307	355	3.99	5.26	(0.22)	0.37
06/30/89	97.52	2.67	47	387	434	3.94	5.15	(0.17)	0.40
09/29/89	94.78	2.46	45	412	457	3.84	5.02	(0.23)	0.39
Average	95.46	2.08	37	357	394	4.36	5.35	(0.07)	0.43

EXHIBIT 4 *High-Yield vs. Treasury Spread*

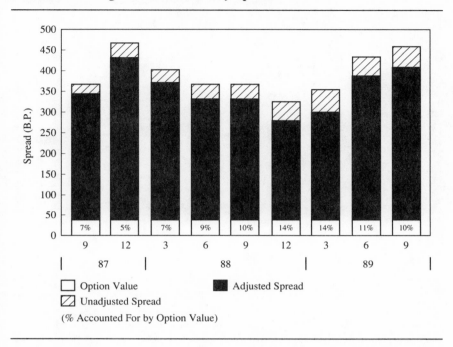

turns a 35–basis point advantage in unadjusted spread in favor of the 14¼ percent to a 7–basis point advantage in adjusted spread in favor of the 13⅞ percent.

Broadly applied, the option-adjusted spread is a more accurate reflection of the stresses operating in the marketplace at any given time than the unadjusted spread, which incorporates the option-related discount, an often volatile component of the overall spread. (The quarterly change in the option value component of the spread averaged over 11 percent during the eight quarterly periods since 9/87, while the change in the overall spread averaged less than 2 percent over the same eight periods.) Exhibit 4 contrasts the unadjusted and option-adjusted spread over Treasuries of our 40-bond portfolio since 9/87 and indicates for each quarter the percentage of the overall spread accounted for by the negative option value. Note that for our sample

EXHIBIT 5   *Quarterly Change in Portfolio Price*

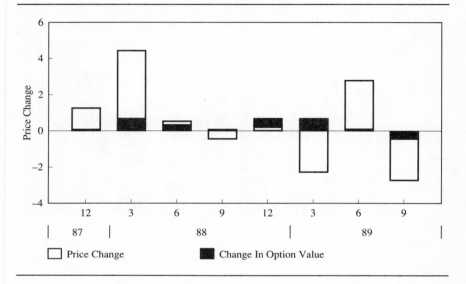

the 460–basis point gross spread at 9/89 was identical to that at 12/87. However, a doubling of the option value actually resulted in a decline in the adjusted spread from 439 basis points to 412 basis points.

Exhibit 5 isolates the quarterly price changes in our 40-bond portfolio due to the change in the value of the embedded option from the price change resulting from other factors. Note that the change in the option value can be a significant factor in any overall price change.

Using Option Value to Analyze Individual Securities

Fluctuation in the value of the embedded option as interest rates change can have a dramatic effect on the performance of a callable security. Whether the change reflects a general move in interest rates, a change in the overall spread between high-yield and Treasury bonds, or a change in the market perception of a particular credit, the resulting change in the likelihood of the issuer exercising its early call option and the consequent change in option value will directly affect the bond's price volatility.

In order to demonstrate this impact, the effect of the call feature on the behavior of one bond from our sample portfolio is measured as interest rates vary. Exhibits 6–8 examine these effects using First Brand 12½s of 1998 as a reference. Exhibit 6 projects the price action of the bond over a 500–basis point yield range and compares this to the action of an identical hypothetical noncallable bond.

The difference in price at any point along the interest rate curve is the implied value of the company's call option (read on the right-hand scale). The 0 point on the interest rate axis represents the market as of 9/30/89, with the bond trading at 100¼. For the purpose of this comparison we used an 8½ percent volatility rate to compute option value. (While the B2/CCC+ credit rating would seem to imply a higher volatility rate, in terms of market perception, First Brands trades well within the top half of the overall high-yield credit spectrum.) The noncallable bond price is simply the callable, or actual, price plus the option value. As mentioned, by adding back the negative option value, we have theoretically derived the price at which an identical, noncallable bond would trade. Note that as interest rates rise and the likelihood of call becomes more and more remote, the value of the option declines toward zero and the callable and noncallable bonds approach equality. As interest rates decline, however, and call becomes more likely, the value of the option to the issuer becomes more and more substantial, and the callable and noncallable bonds spread further and further apart.

At the current market price of 100¼, the 2.3-point negative option value translates to a 43–basis point yield differential between the callable and noncallable issue. In other words, the option-adjusted spread over Treasuries is 43 basis points lower than the 415–basis point gross spread. In a 250–basis point lower market (higher yields), the nominal ½-point option value translates to a mere 12–basis point yield or spread adjustment. However, in a 250–basis point higher market (lower yield), the option value jumps to 8 points, equivalent to a 127–basis point difference between the unadjusted and option-adjusted spread. Clearly, as markets change, adjustment for the option value in evaluating spread differentials can be crucial in deriving a meaningful measure of value.

EXHIBIT 6   Projected Price—First Brands 12.50% 1998*

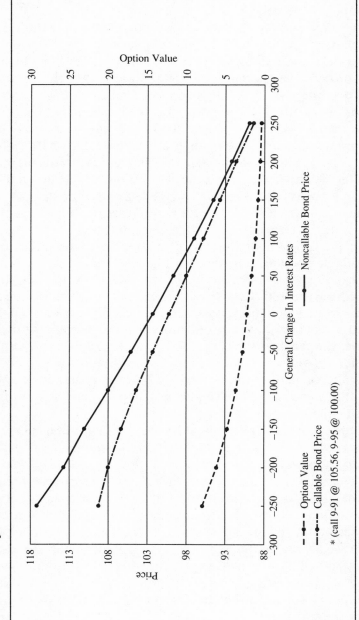

* (call 9-91 @ 105.56, 9-95 @ 100.00)

Adjusting Duration for the Embedded Option

A bond's duration, which is basically the average life of all its scheduled payments, is a widely used, reliable measure of its price volatility over small changes in interest rates. Essentially, a bond with a (modified) duration of 5 should move up and down approximately 5 percent in price given a 100–basis point change in market yields. A bond with a duration of 2 should only move up or down 2 percent for a 100–basis point shift in market yields. The correct determination of duration can thus be key in determining portfolio investment or trading strategy.

The concept of duration is based on the expectation that a bond's cash flows will follow one of a limited number of defined schedules, either to maturity or to an interim call or put date, and so on. Potential issuer default or reorganization introduces an element of uncertainty into the calculation, both as to the amount and timing of these cash flows. To the extent that substantial credit risks increase these elements of uncertainty for the high-yield market, concepts such as duration become less reliable, especially for the lower tier credits. Nevertheless, within the context of our cautious approach to such quantitative techniques, an analysis of duration can be useful, particularly in comparing issues with similar risk profiles.

Because a high coupon rate reduces duration by shortening the average life of a bond's cash flows, the high-yield market tends to be a low-duration market. For example, as of 9/30/89 our 40-bond sample had an average maturity of approximately 8½ years, but a duration of only 5.02. By contrast, an equivalent maturity Treasury would have a duration of close to 6½.

When deriving the correct duration of a bond with an embedded call option you must take into account the possibility that the bond will be called away before its scheduled maturity. The duration to maturity of our First Brands 12½ of 1998 is approximately 5¼ years. However, if the bonds were called on the 9/91 first call date, then the duration would be approximately 1½ years. As yields decline and early call becomes more likely, the bonds will trade to the 2-year call, exhibiting price volatility consistent with a duration of 1½ years. As yields rise and early call becomes less likely, the bond will trade to the

1998 maturity, exhibiting price volatility consistent with a 5¼ year duration. In the middle, however, with market yields up to 200 basis points either side of the coupon, early call is uncertain and the bonds will trade to an assumed life somewhere between the 1991 call and 1998 maturity. Exhibit 7 shows how the effect of the issuer's call option on duration varies in this area of uncertainty.

At high interest rates, with bonds trading at a substantial discount, the option reduces duration only modestly; as rates decline and early call becomes more likely, the effect on duration and thus price volatility becomes more pronounced. Referring back to Exhibit 3, note that the option-adjusted duration of our 40-bond sample was only 3.24 years as of 9/30/89. An investor or trader basing price volatility projections on unadjusted duration or (for a bond trading over par) on duration to call will obviously be oversimplifying reality.

Adjusting Convexity for the Embedded Option

Note on Exhibit 7 that the duration of the hypothetical noncallable First Brands 12½ increases steadily as yields decline. This tendency, true for all noncallable bonds, means that price volatility increases as yields decline and that for equal changes in yield up or down, the bond's price will always rise more than it falls. The extent of this differential is termed the bond's convexity.

The higher the bond's convexity the greater this difference between its price increases versus its price decline. A bond with zero convexity — short maturities generally exhibit low convexity — moves up and down at the same rate, while, for a given change in yields, a bond with negative convexity tends to move down faster than up. Note, again from Exhibit 7, that the duration of First Brands callable 12½ percent bond declines as yields drop. This, of course, is due to the growing likelihood of early retirement. The bond is therefore negatively convex. Exhibit 8 illustrates the effect. In the investment-grade market, convexity has become an especially important element in portfolio selection. For example, many indexing strategies are designed around a portfolio that matches the given index "bogey" in quality, duration, and so on, but maximizes convexity.

EXHIBIT 7   *Duration — First Brands 12.50% of 1998**

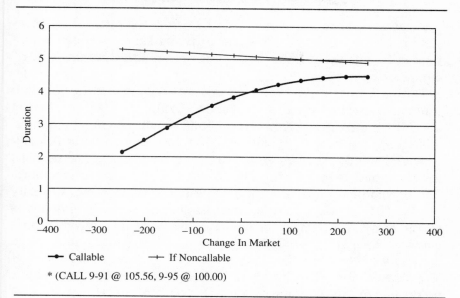

━●━ Callable   ━+━ If Noncallable

   * (CALL 9-91 @ 105.56, 9-95 @ 100.00)

EXHIBIT 8   *Convexity — First Brands 12.50% of 1998**

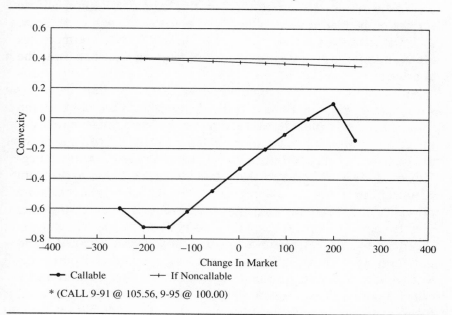

━●━ Callable   ━+━ If Noncallable

   * (CALL 9-91 @ 105.56, 9-95 @ 100.00)

Because of the preponderance of early issuer call options, the high-yield market tends to be a low-convexity market. Referring back to Exhibit 3, note that as of 9/30/89, the option-adjusted convexity of our 40-bond portfolio was −.23.

The impact of the duration and convexity factors on price volatility can be summarized by referring back to Exhibit 6. The hypothetical noncallable First Brand 12½ percent bond should move up by approximately 5¾ points (5.6 percent) for a 100–basis point market yield decline and should move down approximately 5¼ points (5.1 percent) for a 100–basis point rise in yields. This pattern reflects the combination of unadjusted duration of 5.25 years and unadjusted convexity of .38. The callable bond, however, should move up by 4⅛ points (4.1 percent) and down by 4⅜ points (4.3 percent) for equivalent market yield changes. This reflects adjusted duration of 4.03 and adjusted convexity of −.34. In effect, for a 100–basis point change in market level, the callable First Brands 12½ should trade up by only 75 basis points (4.1/5.6) and down by 85 basis points (4.3/5.1).

To put the value of the option adjustment in a real investment perspective, our 40-bond portfolio was split in half, first on the basis of unadjusted duration and then on the basis of duration adjusted for the embedded option. The price volatility of each of these subsets was measured during the first quarter of 1988, the most volatile up quarter, and the third quarter of 1989, the most sharply down quarter.

An investor correctly anticipating the early 1988 bull market and wishing therefore to purchase a volatile, long-duration, 20-issue portfolio, but basing his selection from our 40-bond universe on unadjusted duration would have shown price appreciation of *3.7* points for the quarter, for a total return of 7.5 percent over the three months. However, if his 20-bond portfolio had been selected based on option-adjusted duration, price appreciation would have been *4.2* points, providing a three-month return of 8.2 percent. By the same token, an investor correctly anticipating the mid-1989 bear market and wishing therefore to concentrate in a low-volatility, low-duration, 20-bond portfolio would have suffered price deterioration of 1.5 points if selection had been based on unadjusted duration but deterioration of only 1.3 points if based on option-adjusted duration. Total return for the quarter would have been 1.7 percent and 1.8 percent on the two portfolios, respectively. This comparison of course oversimplifies the investment decision but does indicate that use of option valuation techniques can add real value to the security selection process.

Conclusion

Most high-yield bonds are callable prior to maturity. The value of the embedded option on a particular bond will vary not only with the particular terms of the option but also with the bond's price, general interest rate level, and the perceived volatility of the issuer's creditworthiness. As the value of the option changes, due to changes in any of the above factors or simply to the passage of time, the performance characteristics of the bond will also change. Duration, convexity, and the real quality spread differential are all affected by the embedded option and the change in its value as markets fluctuate. For high-yield paper, the utility of the option valuation process is tempered by two important qualifications. First of all, it is unclear how well the quantitative techniques used to determine the impact of the embedded option are suited to a market with a significant and widely varying equity component. Second, in the context of the overwhelming fundamental credit considerations involved, the option value must be viewed as a secondary factor. Nevertheless, if applied cautiously, the techniques developed to evaluate the impact of a bond's embedded option can be beneficially applied to the high-yield sector, not only to derive a better sense of prospective market performance, but to help in the actual security selection process itself.

SECTION III

Portfolio Management

10

A Practitioner's Guide to High-Yield Bond Management

J. Thomas Madden, CFA
Senior Vice President
Federated Investors

Joseph Balestrino, CFA
Investment Analyst
Federated Investors

The objective of this chapter is to discuss some of the practical aspects of high-yield bond management in a diversified portfolio. The perspective is shaped by our experience as institutional investors engaged in high-yield bond management since the late 1970s.

High-yield bond management is, first and last, the balancing of risk and return. Any investment in subordinated debt of issuers rated less than Baa/BBB[1] with debt to capitalization ratios in the 7:10 to 10:10 range bears significant risk. (Adjusted for intangible assets, some high-yield deals have negative equity.) Issuers may default, postpone payments, force exchanges, or tender for or call debt, depriving the holder of the high coupon. But in return for accepting such risks, investors are paid annual yields that recently exceeded yields on U.S. Treasury bonds by 7 percent.[2] Studies of the high-yield market that focus only on default rates, annual or cumulative, without considering returns on specific portfolios, are of little help in evaluating the attractiveness

---

1. High-yield bonds are usually defined as bonds rated less than Baa (Moody's) or BBB (Standard & Poor's) or securities of equivalent quality. Such bonds may be called "lower rated" or, more cavalierly, "junk."
2. *Salomon Brothers LT High Yield Index vs. Salomon Government Bonds,* October 1989.

of the market. Such analyses are like describing the risks of a professional football career without ever mentioning the players' salaries. The high-yield bond market studies that address return as well as risk, from the earliest to most recent, provide a strong rationale for high-yield bond investing.[3]

This chapter focuses on the game rules of successful high-yield investment. The ultimate objective is to achieve excess returns — largely in the form of a cash stream — for assuming risk and to compound the investment over time at attractive rates. The portfolio management process we will describe has evolved over more than a decade. It has been successful in creating superior results for mutual funds, but applies equally well to separate accounts management. We begin by examining portfolio objectives.

Definition of Portfolio Objective

Any portfolio management process is driven by the definition of portfolio objectives. High-yield bonds may be used as components of larger portfolios (for example, as a subset of bond portfolios to boost overall fixed income return) or as substitutes for common stock investments in equity portfolios. The approach we describe assumes a client who desires superior total return on a pure portfolio of lower rated debt. Inclusion of such a portfolio within a larger investment strategy is a separate and complex topic beyond the scope of this chapter. How should such a high-yield portfolio be managed? The first step is the definition of the available universe from which the portfolio can be assembled.

The High-Yield Universe:
New Issue versus Secondary Offerings

By definition, a portfolio can be assembled only from the universe of *buyable* securities. Although in excess of 900 issuers have used the market in the last decade, perhaps 125 to 150 issues normally trade in

---

3. See Chapter 4.

EXHIBIT 1 *Examples of Broadly Traded New Issues*

American Standard	FMC Corp.	PA Holdings
ARA Group	Forest Oil	Petrolane
Beatrice	Fort Howard Paper	Playtex Family Products
Burlington	Fruit of the Loom	Quantum Chemical
Cablevision	Gaylord Container	Ralph's Supermarket
Carter Hawley Hale	General Chemical	Reliance Electric
Chicago Northwestern	Harcourt Brace	RJ Reynolds
Coastal Corp.	Itel	Safeway Stores
Colt Industries	Jones Intercable	SCI (Storer Communication)
Comcast Cable	Kroger	Stop and Shop
Container Corp.	Macy Merger	Stone Container
Continental Cablevision	Mark IV Industries	Supermarkets General
Dr. Pepper/7-Up	McCaw Cellular	Sybron Acquisition
Duracell Holdings	Mitchell Energy	Turner Broadcasting
Eagle Industries	National Gypsum	US Gypsum
Eckerd Corp.	Owens-Corning Fiberglass	Viacom
First Brands	Owens-Illinois Corp.	Vons Supermarkets

the secondary market. (This number has been compressed in the recent market environment, which we review later.) The available universe is augmented by new issues. One evaluation a manager must make early on is to consider whether the new issue market is "cheap" or "rich" relative to the secondary market. That is, are new issues higher or lower in yield relative to risk than similar issues in the secondary market? Exhibit 1 provides some examples of broadly traded new issues.

After defining the array of possible holdings, the portfolio manager moves to create the portfolio. In order to make this process successful, experience teaches some "rules of the road," which we examine next.

Summary of High-Yield Investment Strategy

Low Cash Position

We manage high-yield portfolios on a fully invested basis; that is, cash positions are held below 10 percent of our portfolio. The cash versus market decision is a separate portfolio issue and departs from the most basic reason to own lower rated debt, which is to benefit from the positive net yield spread over reasonable holding periods. We believe that significantly raising or lowering cash within a high-yield portfolio, based on assertions that the high-yield market is cheap or rich relative to higher quality bonds, departs from this primary objective. Failing to be fully invested when the market rallies sharply, as for example after the 1987 stock market crash, can depress returns significantly.

Target Securities Rated Single or Double B

Our objective here is to purchase stable to improving credits in the middle range of the lower rated sector. These may be nonrated, but of comparable quality. Recent empirical results suggest that single and double B-rated portfolios have provided attractive net returns versus investment-grade bond portfolios over long holding periods. The annual realized return spread over government bonds for the period 1971 to 1987 averaged 4.09 percent for bonds rated single B at issuance and 3.05 percent for securities rated double B at issuance. Triple C securities dominate, but returns may be too volatile for many investors.

High Degree of Diversification

Diversification provides the primary method of risk management in the high-yield portfolio, as in any investment portfolio. Our portfolios typically hold 1–3 percent in a single issuer and never over 5 percent of total portfolio assets per issuer. All academic studies suggesting superior returns assume, in effect, a degree of diversification comparable to the market as a whole. Though we have demonstrated in our portfolios the added value of security selection over time, one large incorrect bet can damage results severely. The portfolio discipline should prevent such bets.

Investors may also want to think about percentage ownership of an issue — in the extreme case, the manager who owns an entire issue is not likely to find much of a trading market. Investors must balance the control that a large position provides in times of trouble with ongoing liquidity. We try to own less than 15 percent of any given issue, for example, no more than $15 million of a $100 million deal. Today, with liquidity at a premium, much smaller positions are the rule in our portfolios.

Diversification doesn't mean owning a sector of the high-yield market even if that sector has unattractive fundamentals in relation to high leverage or is unanalyzable. As part of our "critical factor" analysis, which we describe more fully later, we ask whether industry fundamentals are congenial to use of high-yield debt. For example, we have for many years sharply limited investments in airline issuers, believing that deregulation of the airlines and subsequent industry consolidation implies constant margin pressure and volatile cash flows, both broadly unfavorable conditions for high leverage. Further, we systematically avoided financial intermediaries (Southmark, Integrated Resources, savings and loans) because analysis of balance sheets appeared difficult if not impossible. Portfolio diversification should never force mechanical investment in unattractive industry sectors.

Intensive Fundamental and Credit Review of Each Issuer

Issuer analysis is worthy of a full-blown separate discussion and is discussed elsewhere in this book.[4] The following merely outlines important areas. The analysis should always focus on sources of *cash,* because cash is ultimately what pays debt service. Fundamental analysis of high-yield issuers begins with examination of an issuer's dominant lines of business and its position relative to competition, as well as industry trends and cyclicality. The seasonality, volatility, and profitability of operations are considered in light of the impact of these variables on operating cash flow before noncash charges, interest, and taxes, often referred to as EBDIT. This is cash flow available for interest, principal repayments, property and equipment expenditures, and working capital additions. EBDIT projection is the heart of high-yield bond analysis.

We prefer to invest in operating companies whose dominant products or services have proprietary or semiproprietary characteristics against an industry backdrop of high-capacity utilization, because these attributes favor stable pricing, higher margins, and more predictable cash

---

4. See Chapter 7.

flow. We also prefer issuers with strong brand names or product franchises for similar reasons (e.g., Duracell, American Standard, Colt, Conair).

Accounting practices are scrutinized. A smaller or less well known accounting firm is typically a flag for possible trouble. Similarly, a recent change in accountants should be questioned.

Balance-sheet analysis includes an evaluation of working capital requirements, estimated asset values, and the separability of assets or operations for sale. In effect, the analyst should ask: How much cash does this company need to invest in inventories, receivables, and other current assets to grow its business? What could it sell to raise cash if things go wrong? Would such sales be easy or difficult? If asset sales are built into the financing, as in RJR Nabisco, the realism of expectations about price and timing are crucial. Evaluation of intangibles like goodwill can lead to a more realistic view of the balance sheet.

Debt structure may include floating- versus fixed-rate debt, examination of the schedule of debt amortization, and contingencies affecting that schedule. Bank line availability and public marketability of the company's equity are considered. Here, the analyst should ask how appropriate the structure is to the company's business plan. Is too much debt repayable too soon? If zero-coupon bonds are used, what happens when they "go cash-pay"? How much does debt repayment depend on asset disposition instead of cash from the operating cycle? Can the company borrow more from its banks?

Also important are environmental and legal issues, union contracts (if applicable), and contingent liabilities, including self-insurance and underfunding of pension liabilities. The recent experience of Jim Walter shows the critical nature of good analysis of nonfinancial risk.

Overt judgments about management are of critical importance: character, experience, past performance, knowledge of the business, ability to state its business plan clearly, and degree of management equity ownership are evaluated. We like deals where management has significant personal wealth at stake below the subordinated debt.

Willingness to assume risk and ability to manage in financially risky circumstances are not always coupled. Management's motivation for underwriting a transaction should be examined. Is the deal "ego driven" or based on financial opportunity? The reader may wish to contrast the histories of Fruehauf and Cain Chemical transactions for further insights.[5] Is the business forecast on which the transaction is based realistic or "pie in the sky"?

These analytical elements form the backdrop for calculation of cash interest, total interest, and debt service coverages. Most of our holdings cover cash interest 1.3 to 1.5 times, when EBDIT — earnings before depreciation, interest, and taxes — is divided by annual charges. With such narrow margins, stability of cash flow is critical. Our forecasts have a time frame of no longer than two years. Experience teaches that outlooks beyond the two-year area are guesses, not analyses.

Market Analysis

Our objective here is to understand risks associated with indenture covenants; call, exchange, and sinking fund provisions; interest rate resets, and other elements of the issue's structure and provisions. In addition, the investment banker creating and distributing the deal should be examined both from the standpoint of (1) due diligence, and (2) sale/trading commitment and capability. Both issues deserve careful consideration. With newer forms of financing that include zero-coupon, pay-in-kind, and other deferred interest bonds (DIB), careful attention is paid to calculation of internal rate of return, security ranking, put characteristics, reset characteristics, and other structural elements.

Additionally and critically, market analysis also includes evaluation of the record of the underwriter, with attention to historical effectiveness of due diligence on past issues, support for issues in the secondary market, knowledge of investment bankers, responsibility for the issue, and overall corporate strategy of the underwriter toward the high-yield market. Federated Investors, Inc., has found specific consideration of these issues to be critical, as high-yield investment banking and trading performance varies sharply among firms and over time. A separate section discussing the analysis of investment bankers follows later.

Critical Factor Determination

The objective here is to identify those specific aspects of the deal that have the largest impact on risk and return. Results of sector, funda-

---

5. "The Best and Worst Deals of the '80s," *Business Week,* January 15, 1990.

mentals, and market analysis are evaluated to determine the *most important issues determining bond performance* (Critical Factor Identification). We have learned that in successful high-yield bond management, the ultimate challenge is to analyze what's *important* to an investment outcome, not every attribute of the issuer. This is the Pareto principle, or "80/20" rule, applied to high-yield analysis. For example, in the recent RJR deal, asset sales were initially most important to success. Now, with asset sales largely completed, tobacco operations, RJR's market share, domestic versus overseas performance, and cancer litigation will loom large in the future performance of RJR debt. No matter what the process is termed, we believe it is crucial to rank order analytical insights to focus attention on those that carry most weight for the issuer's performance. In the early 1980s, for many high-yield issuers, the critical factor was the trend in oil prices. Today, it may well be the impact of a recession on an issuer's major operations. Analyze the critical, not the trivial.

Simple Sell Disciplines

With this approach, we strive to sell issues when yields improve to an effective BB to BBB equivalent or when issuer fundamentals appear to be deteriorating. We strive to be early sellers: our rule is "first sale, best sale."

Analyzing the High-Yield Investment Banking Process

The investment banker is critically important in the creation of a successful high-yield issue. While issuer objectives for a high-yield transaction are important, it's the investment banker as intermediary who typically structures and engineers the transaction in its final form.

Ideally, the banker has performed extensive due diligence on the issuer, thought carefully about how the high-yield financing will fit the issuer's business and financing objectives, and helped the issuer plan the role of the deal in the issuer's overall strategy. What will the size of the issue be? What term will apply? Will the coupon be fixed, floating, adjustable, or increasing? Will the issue be a single financing or complex and multilayered (for example, the recent RJR Nabisco LBO financing)? Will the issue convert to common stock? Will warrants for common stock be attached, or is there some other form of equity kicker required to make the deal a success? What will the call and refunding provisions be? What covenants will be included in the indenture? Will the transaction be protected against event risk — that is, the releveraging of the enterprise at some later date with an adverse effect on current creditors? Will financing covenants be included? (For example, pledges as to minimum levels of interest coverage or net worth.) These examples are but a fraction of the issues the investment banker deals with when negotiating between high-yield buyers and the issuer.

The intelligent high-yield buyer will attempt to test the investment banking process within the analysis. Conversations with underwriters may cast light on the thoroughness of the due diligence. Questions to management may illuminate the appropriateness of the deal and its structure. For example, the high-yield buyer should ask whether the valuation process makes sense if assets are being acquired with bond proceeds: Have peak cycle operating earnings been discounted, with allowance for the down cycle? How does the equity market value similar businesses? Do competitors think the deal is fair, or is the issuer going to overpay? Such analysis led us to avoid the Federated-Allied deal at the outset. If cost savings will help repay the debt, are such savings realistic? Are capital expenditures being unrealistically reduced? A reasonable approach may be for the high-yield investor to stand in the shoes of the banker and then ask how he or she might have put the transaction together. Seen from the "sell side," the transaction may appear to change form. The presence of obscure covenants may become clear and the likelihood of developments adverse to the high-yield buyer may be clearly discerned. One additional rule of thumb: a thick, overly complex, poorly organized offering circular may signal an overly complex and poorly organized financing.

Evaluation of the deal and its structure is only part of the buyer's analysis. The buyer must also consider the history and reputation of the investment banker. Among questions the buyer should ask are: What continuing commitment, if any, will the banker have to the deal after it is placed? Does the investment banker have a record of supporting high-yield transactions in the secondary market — will it bid in the secondary market for its own deals? If a transaction runs into trouble, will the banker actively work to restructure the deal or will it leave this task to bondholders and their attorneys and advisors?

Perhaps more broadly, the high-yield buyer should consider what appear to be the investment banker's general objectives for its high-yield operation. To many observers, some Wall Street firms appear to participate in the market on a deal-by-deal basis. These firms appear to examine each transaction on its own merits without a sustained commitment to the market. Other firms appear to lack commitment to the high-yield market at the most senior level. High-yield market observers recognize that the policy toward lower rated debt at these firms has been a cause of much disagreement and rancor with high personnel turnover. Some firms have confined their high-yield efforts to a highly successful leveraging of their historical client base, focusing intelligently on industries with stable cash flow characteristics. Senior managers of one such firm have stated emphatically in recent years their intent to transact as principals, not on an agency basis, in their high-yield activities. Their well-articulated strategy focuses on diversified equity investment by the firm for its own account using high-yield bonds as one financing tool. This firm's high-yield debt issuance has been favorable for both buyers and sellers.

The successful high-yield manager will be both thoughtful regarding the difference between high-yield investment banks and knowledgeable about their track records in the market, since continuity and consistency have been scarce commodities in the 1980s.

In the current climate, the focus appears largely transactional. High-yield issuers switch investment bankers on a deal-by-deal basis. Corporate finance and sales and trading units swap personnel like professional sports franchises. These conditions have been exacerbated by the willingness of underwriters to commit significant percentages of their capital to so-called bridge transactions, though in recent months some such transactions are bridges to nowhere, as the high-yield market refuses to term out financing where buyers overpaid for operating assets. Several well-known high-yield broker/dealers have experienced severe illiquidity as a result of over-aggressiveness in such transactions. Finally, the recent collapse of Drexel Burnham Lambert has removed a once-dominant institution from the market altogether. All these factors have contributed to a sharp contraction in secondary market liquidity and falling high-yield prices in the second half of 1989 and the first quarter of 1990.

Thoughtful assessment of all of these issues as they bear on a specific purchase candidate is critical. Again, a useful analytical technique is to place oneself in the shoes of the issuer and its corporate finance advisor. Failure to address the history, intent, and objectives of the high-yield investment banker is a hallmark of incomplete analysis.

In the next section, we discuss issues concerning problem credits. Though it is certainly among the least attractive aspects of high-yield investments, an alert and aggressive approach to problem credits presents an area of added value provided by a high-yield manager.

Issues of Problem Credits

Most investors in high-yield bond portfolios will eventually encounter the complex problems of deteriorating credits. Various well-publicized studies of high-yield default experience suggest that between 1 percent and 2 percent of a representative high-yield portfolio will default in any given year. Several recent studies have looked at cumulative default experience for high-yield portfolios, and although the results may differ to some extent, all such studies show a tendency for high-yield issues to become more susceptible to credit problems with the passage of time. Hence, any effective approach to the management of lower rated bond portfolios must include a specific strategy for deteriorating and defaulted deals.

Early Detection and Sale Is the Best Defense

Our approach over the last 17 years has begun with the doctrine of "first sale, best sale." The mathematical advantage of taking a small loss on a position, selling that position with accrued interest, and reinvesting proceeds in a more attractive high-yield bond is instantly apparent when compared with holding a security through a work-out period of one to two years, during which the investment stops paying interest. Use of present value analysis in making the decision to exit a troubled issue at a loss is frequently helpful. Proceeds of a bond sale, even at a deep discount, can be reinvested at currently very high yields and immediately begin compensating for the difference between today's price and some hoped-for higher value in the future.

A full description of methods for detecting deteriorating credit worthiness is discussed in Chapter 7. However, several major causes of such deterioration follow:

Secular Deterioration in the Issuer's Principal Product or Service. Energy and energy services companies' inability to escape collapsing oil prices in the early 1980s provides a clear-cut example. Only a handful of such companies with high leverage could avoid debt service problems as oil prices plummeted from in excess of $30.00 per barrel to an eventual low of $7.00–$8.00 per barrel over the period 1981–1985. Early perception of the macro premise that the demand for hydrocarbons was elastic should have spurred high-yield managers to wholesale elimination of energy-related bonds from portfolios.

Inadequate Financing Controls. It is imperative for any issuer operating with high leverage to have a clear and timely way to monitor cash. Among the causes for the Chapter 11 filing of Revco Drug Stores were inadequate management accounting and inventory control systems. Rapid growth through acquisition by Northern Pacific similarly led to inventory management problems. This area should rank high among analyst concerns.

Initial or Second Stage Overleveraging. The problem of high-yield financings by Robert Campeau (Federated-Allied Stores) and by the Thompson family (Southland) are straightforward results of overpaying for operating assets. The early 1990s are likely to offer a powerful demonstration of the importance of skepticism and independent judgment where private market values supposedly justify high debt levels. Ray Lemanski of Prudential-Bache recently noted that debt amortization periods rise as a function of cash flow multiples more rapidly than many investors intuitively understand.

Given that perpetuals went out of style during Napoleon's time, one way to look at determining whether growth in earnings or cash flow and exit valuation are important in realizing the return on debt claim is to look at how long it would take to recover your investment from internally generated cash flow. The assumption here is that most lenders will not rent their money for longer than 20 or 30 years.

An example might clarify this. If you pay 5× cash flow for a company (as you may have in 1986), finance it with 95 percent debt at an average cost of 13 percent, and reinvest 10 percent of the cash flow back into the business, you could pay back all the debt without growth in 17 years (actually it would be a little faster than this). If you pay 8× cash flow (as you may have in 1988–89), finance it with only 80 percent debt at 13 percent, and reinvest the same amount as in the above case it would take about 94 years to pay off the debt. The risk in transaction two is one of continued or perhaps accelerated growth in cash flow and sustainability of the market multiples valuing that stream. Doesn't that sound like the risk you take in the stock market?[6]

Fraud and Criminal Activity by Management. The most difficult cause of a deteriorating credit to detect or avoid comes from malfeasance in the management of highly leveraged companies. Issuers like Saxon Industries, Flight Transportation, ZZZZ Best, and Wedtech are examples of high-yield transactions where managements systematically defrauded creditors while misleading investment bankers and accountants. The importance of thorough due diligence by high-yield underwriters cannot be overemphasized. Further, any suspicions by analysts or managers should be highlighted and discussed routinely. A sense of unease may provide the best signal to sell. Visits to production facilities and other operating assets financed by the issue should also be emphasized. A refusal by management to accommodate such visits is a danger signal.

Restructuring the Troubled Issuer

This section proposes a few summary observations derived from practical experience. The sharp rise in corporate debt use has been accompanied by deterioration in the rights and remedies of creditors. Recent changes in bankruptcy statutes provide growing flexibility for the troubled debtor. Leveraging of investment-grade bond issuers like R. J. Reynolds has incorporated the deliberate exploitation of weak inden-

---

6. Raymond J. Lemanski, Managing Director and Co-Head, High Yield Sales and Trading, Prudential Bache, in welcome address: 1989 Institutional Fixed Income Conference (unpublished).

ture covenants in older investment-grade bond offerings. High-yield borrowers have become, in the last 10 years, ever more ready to propose out-of-court exchanges of new securities for old, usually involving reductions in claims and attempted preservation of large equity stakes by underperforming managements or investors. Over the last several years these trends have been met by increased militancy on the part of high-yield bondholders. Some attributes of successful restructurings are set forth below; these appear to be increasingly embraced by high-yield creditors:

Out-of-Court Exchanges Must Be Guided by the Intent of the Bankruptcy Statutes.   In brief, this means that a company that fails to pay as agreed must sacrifice its equity to preserve creditor wealth. A high-yield company that cannot service its debt belongs to its senior and subordinated lenders. Restructurings that seek to escape this outcome are increasingly unsuccessful. Much time and energy can be saved in negotiations with issuers if all sides understand that an out-of-court proposal, which is inferior to the likely outcome of a court-supervised reorganization, is likely to be a nonstarter.

Aggressive, Concerted Action by Bondholders Is a Necessity.   The successful high-yield bond manager must be prepared to intervene early and forcefully in a deteriorating situation. Uncovering the list of issue holders and conferencing on the intent and objectives of the creditor group is paramount. Any negotiation with a troubled issuer is likely to be more efficient and successful when a large percentage of bondholders are negotiating within a united front. Knowledge of the general purpose and mechanisms of the bankruptcy laws and the ability by bondholders to retain top quality legal advisors are critical. The reader can immediately grasp the advantages of scale and institutional resources in a reorganization negotiation. The small-scale bondholder is disadvantaged compared to the institutional high-yield manager in a difficult negotiation with troubled issuers. Legal fees and travel expenses in a restructuring can mount quickly.

Further, the bondholder group must be alert to the prospect for restoring the investment through litigation, not only against the issuer, but also against parties involved in the initial transaction, such as managements and boards of directors, as well as individuals. The rise of lawsuits involving fraudulent conveyance is one example of a growing interest in a variety of litigation strategies. A recent seminar on this topic listed breach of covenant litigation, RICO liabilities, direct liability, and the class action lawsuit among important considerations for creditors.[7] The effective high-yield manager needs to understand such concepts as equitable subordination, constructive trust, and lender liability in order to successfully integrate with other bondholders and litigators. Note again the disadvantage suffered by the odd-lot bondholder and stand-alone money manager or investment advisor in this increasingly complex arena.

The importance of an aggressive and forceful approach in troubled negotiations, in or out of bankruptcy court, can be scarcely overemphasized. The insolvent or illiquid debtor is aided by the passage of time during which he is failing to pay debt service. Protracted negotiations over minor details and less important issues is an effective debtor strategy, as is dividing the creditor group and conducting separate negotiations with group members. Most effective resolutions are likely to result from the appointment of leadership among creditors and the delegation of authority to negotiate to those leaders.

The Importance of Not Liquidating at the Bottom

Given the complexity of troubled debt negotiations, along with the expense and time involved in moving such negotiations forward successfully, the student of high-yield management may wonder whether a quick sale of the defaulted issue may not prove the better alternative. While each investment must be individually analyzed, strong empirical evidence exists suggesting the perils of early sale of defaulted bonds. One of the most powerful conclusions from the Hickman study is the high return enjoyed by investors who purchased corporate bonds at deeply depressed levels in the trough of the Great Depression. Prices of high-yield bonds following the initial announcement of grave financial difficulties appear to overly discount the impact of such problems.

---

7. *High-Yield Bonds, Leveraged Buyouts, and Troubled Debt Financing Program,* November 13–14, 1989, New York City. Practicing Law Institute.

Exceptions to this rule exist of course, but such exceptions typically emanate from deals that financed assets of very limited economic usefulness (for example, the ultralarge and slow-steaming container ships of McLean Industries). Another exception is where the business is acquired for a price well in excess of the economic value of its operating units (e.g., Southland, Federated-Allied). But in many instances aggressive negotiations may be handsomely rewarded. A rule of thumb that has prevailed since the early years of this century is that the subordinated debt of troubled issuers ultimately provides a worth of approximately 40 cents on the dollar. This outcome is suggested in the Hickman report as well as in more recent studies by Edward Altman of New York University. Money managers use this benchmark to begin consideration of restructuring outcomes.[8]

Outlook for the High-Yield Market

As this discussion was written, the high-yield market in the second half of 1989 and early 1990 experienced a pronounced deterioration with sharp price declines, shrinking liquidity, and in rapid fire order, the defaults of Federated-Allied debt, the Jim Walter Chapter 11 filing, and the appointment of a receiver for the Allan Bond empire in Australia, all following earlier problems at Southmark, Integrated Resources, Resorts International, and Interco. This partial list does not include a host of smaller problem deals. Lastly, Drexel Burnham experienced critical financing problems and filed for Chapter 11 protection. What caused these problems? We list various factors below.

Inadequate Capital.   The high-yield market is suffering from diminished capital. No business can expand rapidly without increased capital, whether it is a manufacturer of machinery or high-yield bonds. We believe this condition was exacerbated in 1989 by problems at several firms that tied up capital in troubled deals, rendering such capital unavailable for making secondary markets in other bonds. Recent

---

8. An academic investigation of the apparent persistence of the "40 cents on the dollar" outcome across time and industry sector would be both useful and highly interesting.

recapitalizations by wealthy parents have mitigated such difficulties at some firms.

Correction of End-of-Cycle Excesses.   High-yield deals after 1986 included various over-aggressive financings that appeared primed for problems. In 1987–89, time ran out for Revco Drug Stores, Southmark, Integrated, Campeau (Federated-Allied), Bond Brewing, and Northern Pacific, all victims of asset overvaluation and leverage or control problems from too-rapid expansion. Such developments hailed the end of this debt cycle as they have in many previous cycles. Charles Kindleberger, in his excellent financial history *Manias, Panics and Crashes,* documents this process, or its parallels, going back to the 1600s.[9] A recession would exacerbate the problems of the market and default rates could rise. But the process is a predictable one, with straightforward precedents, and will likely run its course.

Competitive Reordering of the Debt Markets.   The demise of Drexel has created market share availability. Strong challenges have been mounted by Merrill Lynch, Donaldson Lufkin & Jenrette, and the money center banks Morgan Guaranty, Citicorp, and Bankers Trust. A host of smaller dealers like Alex Brown and Lazard Freres, Bear Stearns, Kidder Peabody, Morgan Stanley, and Prudential-Bache maintain constant presences. High spreads and underwriting fees will continue to attract these and other participants; however, the process of reordering the market is not instantaneous.

Usefulness of Historical Perspective

The reader should recall, however, that the modern high-yield market has survived and continued to prosper in the wake of the deep 1981–82 recession, with associated high default rates in steel- and oil-related issues and the 1987 stock market crash. The high-yield market remains open for business, somewhat diminished, in early 1990.

Further, lower rated debt and its ancestors have provided empirically demonstrable superior returns to the patient investor since before

---

9. Charles P. Kindleberger, *Manias, Panics and Crashes,* rev. ed. (Basic Books, 1989).

1900. Then, as now, common sense and diversification were well rewarded. In the last 90 years the lower rated debt market has survived two world wars, the Great Depression, and major changes in the trend of inflation and interest rates. Thus, the past offers some comfort for the future.

Finally, while defaults and illiquidity may continue to plague the high-yield market, particularly if the economy slows, the reader should recall one primary conclusion of the Hickman study—the attractive returns for those investors who bought lower rated debt in the early 1930s when fear was high and such assets were disdained.

A primary principle of successful investing is to purchase what is undervalued and out of favor. The high-yield market appears to offer just such an opportunity today, with risk spreads at decade-long highs. Defaults, though higher in recent years, are comparable to past experience.

We believe that current market conditions are explicable, not mysterious, and will eventually pass. Current yield spreads appear to discount all but a depression. Thus, the high-yield market, while held in the lowest regard of any time in the last decade, may paradoxically offer the greatest opportunity since 1981–82 to levelheaded investors.

11

The Management of High-Yield Bond Portfolios

Howard S. Marks, CFA
Managing Director
Trust Company of the West

Portfolio management consists of selecting individual securities and allocating differing amounts of investment capital to those securities. Quite aside from the isolated analysis of individual securities against some standard of acceptability, portfolio management consists of attempting to assemble a combination of securities, the holding of which will result in the attainment of the investor's objectives.

There are a number of questions that must be answered relating to managing portfolios of high-yield bonds. Some of the most important concern the *identification of acceptable classes of bonds, selection of individual securities, diversification versus concentration,* and *attitude toward turnover.* Perhaps the most important, however, is one that sets the scene for all the others: the matter of one's philosophy on *trying to be right versus avoiding being wrong* — toward winning versus not losing.

In discussing each of these subjects, I will attempt to describe the available alternatives. However, I have my own biases and I have made my choices. I am sure those biases will show through clearly. They will affect what I say here, and I will be much more articulate in defending my choices than in supporting the alternatives.

Before I discuss the choices, however, I wish to lay out the investment philosophy that guides my own high-yield bond management activities. I do so both to indicate my own predisposition and to provide an example of the type of personal philosophy necessary to undertake portfolio management in a rational manner.

I have elected to participate in high-yield bonds because of my conviction that these bonds suffer as a class from severe bias on the part of traditional investors. This bias causes the bonds to offer promised yields so high that they incorporate an excessive premium for risk-bearing relative to the actual risks I believe are involved. Since the principal attraction applies to the sector in general, and not just to a few bonds, it is my objective to participate in the sector in general, and to enjoy the excessive rewards, without bearing unnecessary risk.

The Basic Approach —
Offense or Defense?

In every investment decision, as in many other choices, we must decide whether to place primary emphasis on going aggressively for a win or on acting conservatively to avoid a loss. Approaching a water hazard on the golf course, you must decide between going over the water to try for a very good score or going safely around the water to avoid a bad score and a ruined round. Selecting such a "mind-set" is fundamental in the investment process and, because the conscious bearing of risk is at the core of high-yield bond investing, essential in the area of high-yield bonds.

The long-term return on any high-yield bond portfolio will be determined by a simple equation:

$$\text{Riskless return} + \text{yield spread} - \text{credit losses}$$

A riskless return such as the yield on Treasury bonds provides the foundation. We add to that the yield spread we are paid to bear credit risk, then we subtract the losses due to credit problems that we actually incur. When there are no credit problems, the yield spread is realized; only credit difficulties can keep us from receiving the contractual, promised return.

Anyone can achieve average performance simply by buying the same securities as everyone else — or some of each. The money manager who is forever average, however, adds no value. The task of assembling an average portfolio could easily be turned over to a computer, and thus the average manager does not deserve much compensation. Above-average performance must be the aim of active portfolio management and, given the above equation, there are two basic ways to achieve it: increase the yield spread or reduce the credit losses. The choice between the two hinges on whether one prefers to be very right or avoid being very wrong.

In a typical high-yield bond market like today's, the "promised yields" available on bonds of going concerns range from 12 percent to as high as 22 percent and more. However, if the market's operations are at all "efficient," the risk of default will rise along with the promised yields. (Otherwise, the buyers of the higher yielding bonds would be getting something—the additional yield—for nothing, a condition the market strives to prevent.)

Trying to increase returns by way of wider spreads raises the starting point—the promised yield—but also increases the risk that problems will be encountered. You must have access to credit research in order to be a high-yield bond investor, but the key question is: how much do you want to bet on being right in the more uncertain situations?

Choosing Between the High-Yield Bond Categories

Within the framework provided by investment objectives and personal philosophy regarding risk, a high-yield bond portfolio manager must decide which classes of bonds to purchase. This decision hinges largely on the above-mentioned attitude toward risk. First, do you wish to invest in the safer and lower yielding classes or in the riskier opportunities with their potential for top-of-the-chart returns? Second, do you wish to spread the risk by investing in many sectors? Or do you prefer to specialize in fewer sectors, attempting to add value by focusing your analytical efforts and acquiring above-average expertise, but also accepting the increased risk associated with concentration?

I have chosen to concentrate on what I consider to be the safer bonds selling near the bottom of the yield spectrum. Obviously, to the extent that I am able accurately to identify the less risky bonds, I can reduce the total risk in my portfolios (although at the cost of forgoing the higher available yields). I also feel that doing so permits me to develop a competitive knowledge advantage through concentrating my credit analysis. And, perhaps most importantly in my view, it allows me to avoid the need to make judgments on the hard-to-predict factors that will determine the survival or demise of issues in the more risky classes.

I feel the safest bonds are those of companies that

- Receive low ratings because of a lack of a record rather than a record of actual problems;
- Are riding positive fundamental trendlines rather than declining trends that must be arrested;
- Are likely to survive in their present form without having to pass any make-it-or-break-it trial; and
- Do not require unrealistic levels of prosperity and growth, major corporate restructurings, or successful turnarounds for survival.

To help sharpen my focus, I sorted the high-yield bond universe into four major types and developed a general view concerning each in the context of my investment approach. This enabled me to make a "first cut" on most high-yield bonds according to the safety standards listed above.

Fallen Angels

The initial decision concerned the "fallen angels," or former high-grade bonds that have experienced operating difficulties and thus fallen into the lower rated high-yield bond universe. The issuers of such bonds are prime examples of companies riding negative trends that will have to be reversed in order for them to survive and service their debt. I have not used them for this reason.

Emerging Credits

In contrast to fallen angels are the "emerging credits," the first companies to issue high-yield bonds receiving low credit ratings at the time of issue (rather than being downgraded to those ratings). I feel these bonds' low ratings stem from inexperience rather than poor experience — from a lack of years and "critical mass." I have chosen to invest in them, however, because of my conviction that most of them can look forward to stability, and perhaps improvement, and will survive in their present form.

Leveraged Buyouts and Recapitalizations

In the mid-1980s, major new groups of high-yield bond issuers appeared: the leveraged buyouts and recapitalizations. These companies often have decades-long histories and sales in the billions of dollars. On the other hand, they receive their low ratings because they have been leveraged up to extremely high debt/equity ratios and low and uncertain interest coverage ratios. In addition, they often depend heavily on restructuring and asset sales. The conclusion here is not black or white. I have chosen to invest in what I consider to be the best of these bonds, emphasizing those that have shown stable cash flow and that I feel can prosper essentially as they are, without benefit of massive managerial action or need for a uniformly favorable economic environment.

Divisional Divestitures

Lastly, I have found that the "divisional divestitures," which result primarily from the breakup of LBOs, have performance prospects similar to those of the emerging credits. These smaller units have to date been burdened with corporate overhead and bureaucracy and have often been lost as unrelated "orphan" businesses within corporate giants. Freed of these disadvantages and motivated through management ownership, in general they face excellent prospects and are low in risk.

For the above reasons, I have chosen to emphasize the emerging credits and divisional divestitures and to buy the best of the LBOs and recapitalizations. Other professional investors have chosen basic strategies quite different from that.

Some investors concentrate on the high end of the risk and yield spectrum, which is populated by bonds that scare away most investors and thus may languish at prices affording truly excessive promised yields. Prominent here are the less certain of the non-cash-paying bonds, the junior subordinated issues and the bonds of distressed and bankrupt companies. Other managers limit themselves to a small number of industries, bearing the risk of concentration in exchange for the chance to apply their specialized expertise and what they consider to be the strong outlook for these groups. Still others are willing to hold bonds in all categories and move from group to group as they perceive the shifts in relative value.

I feel strongly that none of these strategies is right or wrong. Any strategy can be viable if it is well thought-out, within the capabilities of the organization in terms of execution, and designed so that it fits the client's or employer's attitude toward risk and return. If so, it can satisfy investment objectives, which is the goal of portfolio management.

Selecting Individual Securities

Within the categories of bonds that have been chosen, a major task consists of selecting the individual securities that will go to make up the portfolio. Of course, the most important task is the approval or disapproval of companies for investment. It is also the subject about which I will say the least, hinging as it does on credit analysis, a subject on which other contributors will write extensively.

It is my view that the task of populating a high-yield bond portfolio with individual securities consists primarily of taking the credit analyst's reports and deciding whether the risk level indicated in each case is

1. Within the risk tolerance of the portfolio
2. Fully compensated by the promised yield

This is not something you can be told how to do. It requires experience, objectivity, cynicism, and judgments concerning both qualitative and quantitative factors. (It is to be hoped that the difficulty of passing on this skill will safeguard today's portfolio managers, including myself, from being entirely replaced by readers of books like this!) There are, however, certain topics under this broad heading about which a few pointers can be given.

Position in the Capital Structure

The accepted risk and the promised yield can be greatly influenced by the choice of location in the issuer's capital structure. "Priority" refers to the order of claim in case of bankruptcy, and the priority of unsecured creditors ranges from senior at the top, down through senior subordinated and subordinated, to junior subordinated. In the case of many companies, prospective bond buyers face a choice between various levels of priority; of course, each step upward in terms of priority brings with it a decrease in promised yield.

Two things must be borne in mind in this context. The first is that, except in those few cases where the market is making a glaring mistake, there is no single correct choice. The decision in each case will properly be a function of

- The ratio of yield forgone to priority gained;
- The relative riskiness of the issuer (that is, it seems illogical to give up yield to gain seniority in the case of a company perceived to be extremely creditworthy); and
- The attitude of the investor toward risk and return.

Second, note that high priority is not a substitute for creditworthiness. When a company defaults, it ceases to service *all* of its unsecured debt. Greater seniority will help to limit the losses, but not to avoid the problem.

Secured versus Unsecured

Analogously, it's possible to purchase debt securities that are secured by a lien against specific assets. In such cases, the investment is protected up to the value of those assets. Unlike unsecured debt, the law generally causes interest on secured debt to accrue after a bankruptcy petition has been entered, as long as the value of the collateral exceeds the amount of the debtholders' legal claim. Additionally, secured debtholders may enjoy the current payment of interest in bankruptcy or, less frequently, the compounding of interest on any unpaid interest.

The caveats regarding priority hold true here as well. Deciding between secured and unsecured debt will generally be a subjective matter, will hinge on the factors discussed under the topic of priority, and will not enable a creditor of a company falling into distress to avoid the associated travails.

Non-cash-paying Securities

Increasingly of late, and especially in connection with leveraged buy-outs and recapitalizations, non-cash-paying securities have come to make up a significant portion of the high-yield bond universe. They are often employed in highly leveraged transactions to bridge the funding gap when a company is incapable of paying cash interest on all of the debt being created. Companies issuing non-cash-paying securities plan to sell off assets or improve profitability and cash flow before zero-coupon, payment-in-kind, or deferred interest bonds mature (and before current interest payments come due on deferred interest bonds).

The choice here is also subjective and must be made on a case-by-case basis. Generally speaking, the compensation in terms of increased yield for accepting non-cash-paying securities is substantial. But the investor receives nothing as time passes, instead merely compounding the amount he is owed by the issuer. A holder of the current-pay bonds of a company that defaults in the fifth year will already have "taken a lot of cash off the table," but a zero-coupon bond holder will have taken none. I feel that a great deal of the attraction of high-yield bonds lies in the way substantial interest received today cushions against difficulties arising tomorrow. In non-cash-paying securities, the promise grows, but no cash is pocketed.

Covenants

The seeming attractiveness and subsequent performance of individual high-yield bonds can be greatly influenced by the covenants they bear. Rather than carrying the fiduciary duty they do to stockholders, with regard to bondholders managements can do almost anything they wish that is legal and not strictly prohibited in the indenture that serves as the contract between issuer and buyer. Thus, covenants are inserted by investment bankers during the issuance process to provide the buyer protections needed to make bonds salable.

Most of these covenants are designed to prevent the paying out of excess dividends, over-leveraging, and other actions on the part of management that would lead to the deterioration of credit quality. Bondholders have in recent years grown increasingly concerned about "event risk," the possibility that management will take voluntary actions that result in the transfer of wealth from bondholders to stockholders (perhaps including themselves). It is at event risk that most covenants are directed.

Covenants are not a solution to business difficulties, but they may help protect against actions that increase companies' susceptibility to problems or accentuate the impact on bondholders. In addition, tight covenants often prove to be of value to bondholders in that managements may later pay to have their restrictions lifted. Covenants constitute a specialized and somewhat esoteric aspect of high-yield bond portfolio management, but a very important one.

Overall, the great variety of securities and their features permits managers of high-yield bond portfolios to "dial their risk" according to risk/return attitudes and the peculiarities of individual securities. No one can be categorical about how best to do it, but I hope I have highlighted some of the important considerations.

How Much Diversification?

I have touched above on the trade-off between the risks and benefits to be derived from concentrating versus diversifying when deciding which bond classes to buy. Further consideration must be given to the same subject at the level of individual securities.

There is a principle in statistics called the "law of large numbers," which states that as the size of a sample increases, the likelihood decreases that the mean of the sample will vary greatly from the mean of the universe from which it is drawn. This principle is applied in investment management (sometimes unconsciously) in the form of something called diversification. Clearly, the larger number of securities a portfolio holds, everything else being equal, the higher the probability that the portfolio's return will resemble the return on the entire asset class.

At the lowest level, we can see that holding a portfolio consisting of only one security is very risky. First, the holder would be entirely exposed to individual events taking place at that one company or in the market for its securities. Second, there is a good possibility that because he holds only one security, the investor could miss out on a major move in the general market. In theoretical terms, the portfolio is overexposed to the nonsystematic, diversifiable risks attaching to the one security and underexposed to the nondiversifiable risk and general market dynamics that would attach to a portfolio more reflective of the broad universe of securities.

At the other extreme, however, it is equally clear that an active manager would not want to own everything. Doing so would ensure performance that is average, no more and no less. If the manager or the manager's organization possesses any superior insight concerning the outlook, its value will be fully diluted by the failure to act accordingly—that is, to eliminate some securities from the portfolio and emphasize others. Such totally diversified portfolios are called index funds. They offer a low-cost way to ensure "market performance" and total surrender on the subject of trying to add value and achieve above average performance.

Clearly, the answer for most portfolio management applications must lie somewhere between holding one security and holding every security. The question is where? The answer takes us back to the choice between trying to be right or avoiding being wrong.

Remember, it is my objective to enjoy the benefits of high-yield bond investing with strictly limited risk. I strive to employ the knowledge that results from credit analysis to avoid mistakes, not to try for a *tour de force*. That is, I want to have a high batting average and to avoid hitting into inning-ending double plays; I do not try to hit home runs.

I choose to hold a large number of bonds (70–100) in my portfolios, and the reasoning goes like this: There are 500 bonds out there with yields of 14 percent. I assemble 100 of them in a portfolio that then has an average promised yield of 14 percent. I normally expect on average to suffer a 1 percent default rate, with one of the 100 bonds defaulting each year, and to lose 60 percent of the amount I had invested in that one bond (or 0.6 percent of my total principal) in its default. Thus my net return (ignoring price fluctuations) will be 13.4 percent.

Suppose I choose instead to buy only 10 bonds. The fact that they are 14 percent bonds is unchanged, so the promised yield on the portfolio will still be 14 percent. However, if the one defaulting bond I bought in the 100-bond portfolio makes it through to the 10-bond portfolio, my default rate will be 10 percent. In such a case, I will lose 6 percent of my principal, and my net return will be only 8 percent.

Because of the way this example is constructed, concentration is shown to add to risk but not return. Obviously, however, those who concentrate do so in the belief that they can add to return in a way that more than offsets the increase in risk. That is, they view concentration as a chance to put their knowledge of credits to its best use.

This issue ultimately comes down to the reliability of opinions concerning future developments. Anyone who is sure he or she knows what lies ahead should put all of his or her capital into the one asset with the best outlook. While no professional investors hold only one security, those who feel they know a great deal about the future generally hold fewer securities (or should) than those who do not.

My portfolios are positioned toward the higher end of the diversification spectrum. Although I work hard through credit analysis to know as much as I can about each company's future, I remain concerned about the amount I cannot know. Going back to the example, I do not feel that I (or anyone else) can tell with a high degree of accuracy which of the 14 percent bonds will turn out to provide more than just the promised return (through capital gains) and which will depreciate or default. Clearly, there will be some of each, but which will be which usually comes as a surprise. From this stems my conviction that high diversification is an attractive way to increase safety and that concentration would not predictably increase my returns.

One last word on diversification: A large number of securities alone will not result in low risk. The key word is "covariance," and there should not be much of it. That is, the securities should not co-vary, or move together. A portfolio of 100 leveraged buyout bonds of wall-board companies should not be considered diversified. Instead, holdings should represent a variety of classes of bonds, broad economic sectors (such as heavy industry or consumer), industries, companies, and perhaps maturities. Only in this way can avoidable risk be reduced.

The Role of Trading

The last topic for consideration is that of turnover: how much to trade and when. This is yet another subject on which there is a difference of opinion. Some investors feel that superior knowledge of companies and the market can be used to reliably add a further component, short-term trading profits, to the formula for total return shown earlier.

My view, on the other hand, is that the principal purpose is to participate in the long-term, big-picture benefits afforded by the high-yield sector. Trading undertaken for short-term reasons might result in being either in or out of the market or an individual security at the wrong time. It might present an undesirable distraction from the major mission. And it might prove expensive, given the significant transaction costs and limitations on liquidity in the high-yield market.

On the subject of market timing, though it should be possible to gain an advantage through hard work in terms of knowledge of individual companies, it is less likely that anyone can do an above-average job of forecasting interest rates and broad bond market movements and thus of knowing when to be in or out of the market. For this reason, my portfolios are fully invested all of the time; the benefit in the long term comes from the bonds' high yields, and I live with what I consider to be the unpredictable and unavoidable short-term market fluctuations.

With regard to individual securities, rather than engage in short-term trading, which amounts to little more than a guess at the direction of the next fluctuation, I restrict sales to those that are fundamentally motivated.

1. If ongoing credit analysis indicates that a company is undergoing fundamental deterioration that threatens its survival, I will usually sell. This is doubly true if I feel the analysis is early, and thus the market has yet to get wind of the negative developments and reflect them in the bond's price.

2. If a company shows improvement in creditworthiness (or if improvement is perceived by the market), such that the price rises and the yield falls significantly, I will also sell. Though the bond has probably become a safer holding, it may fail to satisfy the portfolio's yield criterion.

3. Lastly, it is the portfolio manager's ultimate responsibility to examine each security's *balance between risk and return* (and its contribution to the overall portfolio in both regards). If these two elements get out of line—most importantly, if the risk is

perceived to rise relative to the prospective return — the holding should be reviewed for sale.

Overall, as was stated earlier, much of a manager's approach to portfolio management will depend on his or her fundamental stance regarding being right versus not being wrong, aggressiveness versus defensiveness. Aggressive portfolio managers might long for the opportunity to show how much they know about the future. Thus, they might concentrate their portfolios in a relatively small number of higher yielding (and riskier) bonds, and emphasize short-term trading, market timing, and/or movements from one sector to another.

More defensive managers would be more concerned about avoiding mistakes than about pulling off a major coup. They might tend to hold more diversified portfolios drawn from the less risky portion of the high-yield universe, and trade infrequently and only when demanded by significant changes in fundamentals or security prices.

It is most important to note, once again, that neither approach is right or wrong. The aggressive manager's actions might lead to excessive risks and losses. The cautious manager might either assume so little risk as to produce inadequate returns or be wrong in picking the low-risk bonds and walk into a minefield. Either strategy can produce above-average or below-average returns; either one can be executed well or poorly; and either can be appropriate or inappropriate depending on whose money is being managed.

Surviving Market Fluctuations

Finally, I want to touch on the subject of preparing for the regular fluctuations that are a normal part of every portfolio manager's existence. Much is expected of portfolio managers, especially in the area of knowing what the future holds, which I feel is unreasonable. There is one thing, however, that managers should be able to do for their clients: to stand against the extreme ebbs and flows of psychology. Put more simply, they should refuse to join the buyers who make the market's tops and the sellers who make its bottoms.

High-yield bonds are as attractive as they are, offering yield spreads that are excessive relative to the risks involved, primarily for one reason: They are controversial and less than fully understood. These same attributes, however, leave the market subject to significant fluctuations.

External developments have regularly buffeted this market. In addition, exaggerated fear of widespread recession-related defaults rears its head whenever a business cycle reaches old age. The sector finds few friends or defenders among nonparticipants, journalists, politicians, or regulators. Lastly, as an inefficient market, high-yield bonds are subject to fluctuation whenever most of the participants want to either buy or sell in amounts that exceed the market's liquidity.

The swirl of controversy and the excessively harsh reaction to adverse developments have from time to time produced significant price declines, such as when LTV went bankrupt, when Ivan Boesky was exposed, and when Campeau approached default. They also explain the enactment of a law prohibiting high-yield investment by savings and loan associations despite the total lack of loss experience to support such a ban. Finally, they explain the rash of press reports citing "crash" and "collapse" whenever high-yield bond prices drop more than a few percent — declines that are experienced often and greeted calmly in the stock and Treasury bond markets.

It is a fact of life in all markets that fluctuations come and go. They are regularly overblown in the controversial high-yield bond market, however, and they cause great concern. Every portfolio manager should be equipped with a well thought-out philosophy and strategy to stand by, should be backed by an organization with a strong execution capability, and should be operating under a game plan that incorporates the economic, psychological, and political realities of client or employer. If all of these requirements have been met, the portfolio and its manager should have the staying power needed to get through the rough spots. In the end, the generous returns in high-yield bonds should make all of the effort worthwhile.

12

Risk Control in High-Yield Portfolio Management

Paul T. Owens
Principal
Berkeley Capital Management, Inc.

Risk is one of the central issues in portfolio management. Although every portfolio manager is aware that high-yield fixed income investing entails risk, few really understand how much risk. This chapter is therefore not about portfolio management per se, but rather about risk management. Defining and controlling risk, more than any other single element, is the key to success in high-yield portfolio management.

Risk can be defined as the possibility that a class of securities will not achieve its expected return, principally because some of those securities may produce a negative return. The management of such loss is crucial to successful investing in high-yield portfolios because the securities in this sector have greatly varying characteristics.

The first step is to develop a set of criteria to determine the probability of loss in the portfolio and then to determine the consequences of loss to the portfolio's stated investment objectives.

The Decision-Making Process

Success in this endeavor will have its foundation in classical fundamental analysis and a sound decision-making process. Although portfolio management is an art rather than a science, all good portfolio managers share a discipline, fidelity, and consistency in application of fundamental analysis.

There are four general rules:

1. Consistently apply a stated investment philosophy that identifies the appropriate investment strategy. This step requires making decisions about the interrelationships of coupon income and total return, quality, maturity, and portfolio duration. These issues are typically specific to the client's stated objectives.

2. Clearly define a structured decision-making process via a set of procedural guidelines. This allows the discipline of analysis and management to be followed throughout and ensures consistency of application.

3. Articulate and implement a decision-making structure that determines when to sell those credits that no longer belong in the portfolio, regardless of whether the original investment decision was correct or incorrect. This ensures that you cut your losses from mistaken investments and sell those successful investments whose parameters no longer fit the investment objectives of the portfolio. Every credit, whether owned or not, must be evaluated as if the initial purchase decision were taking place. Every decision is, therefore, a buy or sell decision.

4. Keep score! Candidly reevaluate both incorrect as well as correct credit decisions *ex post*. Test to determine whether the philosophy, strategies, and decision-making structures are acting in concert.

The Separate Asset Class

Formally, if not always functionally, high-yield bonds are a proper subsector of the fixed income universe. The key question is how to measure risk in the high-yield asset class. The classical measure of investment risk is the beta coefficient, which measures the volatility of the individual investment compared to the market as a whole. The market by definition has a beta of one. If we assume that the market is defined as the universe of investment-grade bonds, the relationship between the two markets should be found in the correlation between the two. Although it covers only a short time, Salomon Brothers' study of this correlation from January 1985 to December 1988 is instructive.[1] The following correlation of monthly returns with various assets was found.

Long-Term High-Yield Index to
Treasuries	0.45
Investment-Grade Corporates	0.57
AA Corporates	0.56
S&P 500	0.63

Note that the high-yield market has the highest correlation to the S&P 500 and to corporate bonds rather than the U.S. Treasuries — a pure market instrument. This contrast is not surprising in an instrument that should trade on the basis of individual credit characteristics.

The same study also determined that the correlation between AA corporates and Treasuries is 0.93, meaning that 93 percent of AA corporate performance can be explained by Treasury bond prices.

Similarly the correlations above tell us that up to 55 percent of the high-yield market's return is not systematic but rather highly specific and not explained by factors relevant to the market fluctuations of the S&P 500 or the long U.S. Treasury bond. The relatively low correlation with the other asset classes underscores the point that high-yield bonds constitute a separate asset class distinct from high-grade bonds and equities, although they have many of the characteristics of both.

The conclusion we draw from this is that although high-yield credits may be influenced by the same types of factors that impact these other markets, specific credit analysis is the key to controlling risk.

Return Components

The performance component of high-yield bonds is like all fixed income securities found in the income stream. The above study of returns verifies that fact as well as the intriguing notion that some investors

---

1. Paul H. Ross et al., *High-Yield Corporate Bonds: An Asset Class For the Allocation Decision,* Salomon Brothers, February 1989.

may have substituted a discounted principal payment for a higher income stream.

Income Component of Total Return

Asset Class	1980–88
Long-Term High-Yield	109%
Investment-Grade Corporates	93%
S&P 500	31%

Coupon payment, and, to a lesser extent, principal return, is in a real sense a substitute for dividend payment on common stock. The substitution at the corporate level is not perfect, however, because the tax deductibility applies to coupon payments and not to common stock dividends. The difference is that the coupon payment is a "contractual dividend" and is nonnegotiable, apart from situations that indicate corporate distress, such as exchange offers and bankruptcy reorganization. This coupon payment and its similarity to common stock values may be found in the Graham and Dodd valuation formula:[2]

Valuation = Multiplier (Expected Dividend
+ One-third Expected Earnings)

Note that the dividend is valued at three times the retained earnings. This is because distributed earnings have a greater weight in determining market prices than do retained earnings.

Earnings are better retained if the reinvestment can earn a rate of return at least as large as the earnings yield on the common stock. In earlier times, shareholders were willing to leave retained earnings inside the corporation, with the complementary results of earning tax-advantaged capital gains and avoiding taxes on dividends.

High real interest rates make the task of earning high real returns on invested capital difficult. The high-yield analyst's task, to evaluate the firm's ability to generate those returns on invested capital to earnings, is highly specific to the company, which again explains the correlation results mentioned previously. The best approach is for the analyst to view coupons not merely as cash streams but as distributed

---

2. B. Graham, D. L. Dodd, and S. Cottle, *Security Analysis: Principles & Techniques* (New York: McGraw Hill, 1962), pp. 480–493.

earnings, and never as a substitute for the diminished likelihood of future principal returns.

Identifying the Risk

Modern portfolio theory tells us that risk, or volatility, is a measure of the dispersion about the mean of future returns. Financial risk is the variance or standard deviation of returns. The Capital Asset Pricing Model allows us to determine what part of a security's risk can be diversified away by optimizing the portfolio mix and what part cannot. Breaking down the risk of the high-yield bond into its subcategories, we find that the risk of this group versus high-grade securities is contained in the spread over high-grade securities. There are four components to that risk:

1. credit deterioration leading to the risk of default,
2. liquidity risk,
3. event risk unprotected by indenture covenants, and
4. early redemption.

Each of these risk components requires a separate, distinct analysis process.

The residual spread net of a premium is a statistical analysis calculated to compensate for liquidity risk and early redemption risk (assuming covenant protection). This is a statistical assessment of the probability of default for the credit being analyzed and of the loss if that default occurs. The product of these two factors is then compared to the basis point spread of that credit to the comparable credit-risk-free U.S. Treasury rate.

Controlling Risk by Optimization

Portfolio optimization is a technique used for generating returns and controlling risk. In its simplest form, optimization is achieved by diversification. There are two broad risk classifications: systematic and unsystematic.

- Systematic risk is that shared by all securities in the same asset class.
- Unsystematic risk is the exposure of a credit to events that affect it alone.

If securities trade together they are said to have a high degree of correlation. Diversification will always reduce the specific risk of a portfolio, the worst event being default. Systematic risk, however, cannot be eliminated by simple diversification.

The ideal path to portfolio diversification is to purchase securities that have a less than perfect correlation with each other. The less securities are correlated with each other, the greater the impact of diversification on the portfolio. Perfectly positively correlated securities move perfectly in tandem with one another, whereas negatively correlated securities move in opposite directions; securities that have no correlation may move in any direction.

What the high-yield manager attempts to capture is the yield advantage inherent in the high-yield security while minimizing specific security risk. With the vast number of issues in the high-yield market to choose from, the trick is deciding how broadly to diversify.

Wagner and Lau addressed the issue of diversification in randomly selected equity portfolios. They measured diversification versus R, the correlation coefficient of a basket of NYSE stocks.[3] A portfolio that correlates perfectly with the market will have an R of 1.0. A well-diversified portfolio will have an R of .80 or above, whereas a poorly diversified portfolio will have an R of .20 to .30.

Wagner and Lau found that diversification rapidly increased both R and the correlation coefficient squared (R^2) and that the volatility fell as the portfolio was diversified into 10 separate security holdings. They further determined that 40 percent of a single security's risk is eliminated by forming portfolios in which each holding averages no more than 5 percent of the total. Thus, a portfolio of 20 securities had a correlation with the market of .89. Additional diversification yielded rapidly diminishing reductions in risk.

However, Wagner and Lau observed that the highest quality issues achieved higher R^2 results with less diversification than the lower quality securities. This seems to indicate that lesser quality or "less well

---

3. W. H. Wagner and S. Lau, "The Effect of Diversification of Risk," *Financial Analysts Journal,* November–December 1971, pp. 2–7.

held" securities may mandate greater diversification. In the high-yield marketplace there are ancillary factors that may be additional elements of risk not found in equity investments. These factors include the broad category of covenant risk, specific releveraging risk, changing liquidity due to non-credit-specific factors, and early redemption risk.

Though it is difficult to quantify these additional elements, we have found empirically that 35–40 high-yield fixed income securities are the optimum diversification mix. Larger numbers of securities are counterproductive because such a number is usually beyond the span of control of an analytical staff. "Problem credits"—the result of poorer research—consume ever-increasing amounts of time. The end result is that the entire portfolio is less well managed than if it had contained fewer securities.

In addition, it does not appear appropriate to diversify a high-yield bond portfolio in the same manner as an equity portfolio. Although a bond purchased at par may lose 60 percent of principal, the same security is usually limited to a capital appreciation potential of no more than 10 points in the case of a successful investment. Control of the "downside" risk takes necessary precedence.

Diversification may reduce unsystematic risk, but it doesn't make the best use of correlation. We can best optimize by building a portfolio that offers the highest return for each level of risk. The task is to find those bonds that have the marginally highest expected returns.

It is seductively easy to over-diversify. The "have a hunch, buy a bunch" approach generally produces substandard results and multiple workout assignments, resulting in a higher level of risk without a higher return.

The goal is to combine sections of a portfolio into different groups. If, for example, we combine two credits with a correlation less than 1, the result will be an average of their expected returns, while the averaged risk will be less. Repeating this process offers the highest return for each risk. The major caveat is to recognize that even within industry groups there is considerable diversity.

Liquidity Risk and Trading

Liquidity in the high-yield market has been the subject of much generalization. In actual practice, high-yield bonds have varying degrees

EXHIBIT 1   *Liquidity Spectrum*

Rank	Sector
10	Futures, Options, U.S. Treasuries
9	GNMAs, Government Agencies
8 }	High-Grade Corporate Bonds
7 }	Medium-Grade Corporate, High-Yield Bonds
}	High-Yield Bonds
}	High-Yield Bonds
2 }	High-Yield Bonds
}	Private Placements
1 }	Venture Capital, etc.

of liquidity (see Exhibit 1). Grossman and Miller, in their study of markets and liquidity, noted that there are fewer market makers in less liquid issues because the cost of finding the ultimate buyer to a principal increases the risk of maintaining a market presence.[4] Smaller issues that were underwritten by a single dealer also increased the risk of buying with poor information. Dealer markets in less-liquid issues, whether they are in the high-yield market or NASDAQ, are more like postings or indications, with the ultimate transaction subject to negotiation.

Even in the more liquid issues the bid-asked spread is more a transaction fee than a charge for providing liquidity. Dealers in the high-yield market provide execution search rather than transaction upon demand.

Decisions to stay in more liquid issues mean those issues will be more actively traded. They are typically at the narrower end of the high-yield spread in compensation for that greater liquidity. The analyst should assign liquidity premium factors specific to each credit to establish the breakeven spread to the U.S. Treasury rate that is exclusive of credit-specific factors.

However, issues can change their liquidity characteristics over time. Markets are never static and can be unstable in response to new information. Careful monitoring of market activity and careful records on market spreads as well as the trading activity of the underlying equity are essential.

---

4. S. J. Grossman and M. H. Miller, "Liquidity and Market Structure," *The Journal of Finance,* July 1988, pp. 617–623.

It is also important to note that very narrow or very wide spreads give the issuer far more options to refinance the issue in the narrowest sense or restructure in the widest sense. The holder is protected by covenant in the former case if the analysis is correct. In the latter case, the company is strongly motivated to capture the discount from the original issue price for the sake of immediate earnings impact. Ironically, this discount is less valuable to the holder because its capture in the worst case will occur over the time to maturity.

Covenant Risk

Webster's Dictionary defines *covenant* as a "formal, solemn, and binding agreement." Prior to the mid-1980s, the covenants in bond indentures were taken at face value both formally and metaphorically. More recently, covenants have been evaded through loopholes of liberal interpretation. Although the directors of the corporation have a contractual obligation to the bondholders, they also have a fiduciary obligation to the shareholders. This may result in a conflict if the covenants appear to prevent maximizing equity value.

Because covenant interpretation is an evolving practice, the following list of covenants is not meant to be all-inclusive. It will help, however, to bear one firm rule in mind: Any event that may alter a credit's ability to meet its contractual obligation over the life of the bond or any covenant that may allow a material increase in leverage is cause for rejection of that credit as a portfolio investment.

There are five key covenant categories:

1. *Net Worth Test* — this covenant requires maintenance of tangible net worth above a threshold level.
2. *Restricted Payments Test* — this places a limitation on the upstreaming of dividends or other distributions to shareholders.
3. *Debt Incurrence Test* — this covenant places limitations on additional amounts of borrowing. "Carveouts" must be carefully appraised.
4. *Change of Control Provision* — this clause provides issue holders puts of redemption options if there is a change in the controlling equity stake in the company.

5. *Asset Sale Proceeds Restrictions*—this typically prevents the use of proceeds for purposes other than debt reduction.

The Risk of the Credit Cycle

The careful selection of credit to reduce unsystematic risk begins with the corporate credit cycle, which is an important model for developing the analysis. The effects of the various stages of the life cycle may impact on the company's ability to service debt. The familiar bell-shaped life cycle curve may be broken into four phases: developmental or investment, growth, maturity, and decline. In a simple financing the issue is straightforward. New financings tend to be produced by the first three areas while the latter phase is in the "fallen angel" or bankruptcy category.

Both the investment phase and the growth phase are characterized by low cash flows relative to debt service. Credits in these phases will show new investment exceeding depreciation and cash flow coverage. High margins as well as revenue growth will be imperative.

Growing companies also have real earnings and balance sheet values higher than those reported. Many outlays for growth, which tend to be expensed, are actually developmental in nature and end up understating the firm's earnings.

Finally, competitive growing companies may engage in fierce price competition at some cost to their own cash flows. Firms that compete aggressively may damage their income statements and balance sheets by attempting to buy market share. The risk is that the cash used may undermine the firm's ability to meet its obligations. High-yield investors are best compensated during this phase by investing in securities that have equity return characteristics either through warrants or deeply discounted features.

The maturation phase is characterized by more fully developed product lines and dominant market position. It is in this phase that we find restructured companies and leveraged buyouts. Strategies common to this phase are asset sales and cost reduction, which typify a business reorganizing itself to meet debt service. It is important for the analyst to be able independently to evaluate the assets by using objective comparisons; an experienced management team that can be viewed from a historical perspective is crucial to the formula. The risks here are clearly operating risks; the firm must remain free of new debt or an onerous amortization schedule.

Evaluation of the Individual Credit

It is important to understand a firm's ability to generate consistent future cash flows from its asset base, which will ensure future payments of interest and principal.

Despite their considerable value to the investor, Moody's and Standard and Poor's cannot provide the maximum advantage to high-yield managers because their credit judgments are based on historical financial information. High-yield managers must concentrate on the future perspective.

The rating services are "designed to provide a system ... by which relative investment qualities" may be measured (Moody's) and are a "current assessment of creditworthiness ... with respect to specific obligations" (S&P). Indeed, Moody's states that "ratings have no value in forecasting future trends in the marketplace."

Market Risk Characteristics

In the high-yield market, the systematic risk forces are the following.

1. Market risk, or the sensitivity of the security to market fluctuations. The more liquid securities may fluctuate more. However, a high-yield bond that exhibits less volatility may do so simply because of smaller issue size.
2. Economic environment risk, or the impact of a weak economic environment on revenue-generating activities.
3. Inflation risk, or the effect of rising costs on selling, general, and administrative expenses and the cost of goods sold.
4. Debt service risk, or the increase in variable debt service costs.
5. Market expectation risk, or diverse opinions about a credit that will contribute to its volatility.

Within this framework, the most important company characteristics to analyze are the following:

- Diversity of product lines
- Recession resistance
- Dominant, niche market positions
- High historical and projected operating margins
- Minimum capital requirements—investing less than core depreciation
- Strong cash flow
- Experienced company management
- Unexploited growth opportunities

Long-Term Evaluation

Because the high-yield investor's returns depend primarily on coupon income over an extended holding period and not on capital gains, the proper evaluation of the credit begins with the analysis of the company's ability to use its resources to generate cash flow stable enough to enable the company to meet future scheduled payments.

The ability of a firm to pay a coupon stream over the life of a bond and repay the invested principal is found in the operating and investing performance of the firm. Specifically, we assess the ability of the firm to earn a cash flow return on assets. (See Exhibit 2.) The cash flow return on assets is the cash flow margin multiplied by the asset turnover. Cash flow or EBITDA (earnings before interest, taxes, depreciation, and amortization or depletion) margin is the ability of the

EXHIBIT 2

	Historical Cash Flow Volatility	
	I	III
	High return	High return
	Low volatility	High volatility
Current Cash Flow Return on Assets		
	II	IV
	Low return	Low return
	Low volatility	High volatility

firm to generate cash flow from earnings before the noncash expenditures of depreciation, interest and taxes. (We will further refine the definition of cash flow later.)

Higher historical volatility of cash flow implies higher operating risk. Firms with high fixed costs will have greater volatility in cash flow as revenues fluctuate than firms that have lower levels of operating leverage. Indeed, Waite and Fridson determined that firms with low cash flow volatility relative to fixed-charge coverage were dominant in early LBO transactions.[5]

By way of contrast, firms that sell commodity-like products will typically be subject to competitive pressures and lower cash flow margins, which will put an upper limit on profits. As a result these firms will increase asset turnover more rapidly to address potential cash flow problems. Investors in these quadrant IV (see Exhibit 2) companies are more at risk to cyclicality.

Firms that have high entry barriers and economies of scale have high return on assets and low cash flow volatility and fit into quadrant I. They have dominant market share and high capital requirements. Firms that have low margins and low volatility are safe investments because — despite the fact that they usually have low entry barriers — they exhibit historical consistency.

The differences among industries and firms within those industries are often related to management's responses to the different phases of the corporate credit cycle and their needs to trade off profit margin against asset turnover.

Following Ongoing Performance

The determination of a nonvolatile cash flow stream is so important a tool to the analysis of risk that the correct definition of cash flow is essential. The scope should go beyond the classic EBITDA definition because we are trying to determine whether a company is a net provider or user of cash from its operations. The process amounts to adding credit changes in working capital accounts and subtracting debit changes.

---

5. S. R. Waite and M. S. Fridson, "Do Leveraged Buyouts Pose Major Credit Risks?" *Mergers & Acquisitions,* July–August 1989, pp. 18–21.

EXHIBIT 3

Source	Item
Statement of changes in financial position	Working capital provided by operations
	plus
Noncash changes in working capital accounts	Decrease in accounts receivable
	Decrease in inventory
	Increase in accounts payable
	minus
	Increase in accounts receivable
	Increase in inventories
	Decrease in accounts payable
	Decrease in accruals

As is shown in Exhibit 3, start with the statement of changes in financial position as the primary source and add noncash charges that decreased in current asset accounts and noncash increases in current liability accounts, and subtract changes in current asset accounts that increased and current liability accounts that decreased.

The Use of Ratios

The most effective use of ratios is in the development of a proprietary matrix of ratios. There is no "secret formula." The goal is to produce the strongest predictive powers for the life of the firm within the maturity boundaries of the security. The return generated by the firm and the volatility of return are the best predictors of that event. For example, research on the use of ratios has been used to determine failing corporate health. It is instructive to begin with those ratios that predict bankruptcy, because those ratios have been best tested.

Beaver did early work on the use of individual financial ratios to predict bankruptcy.[6] He made use of 14 ratios, of which he found 4 to be the most reliable:

---

6. W. Beaver, "Financial Ratios on Prediction of Failure," *Empirical Research in*

- EBITDA/total assets
- Net income/total assets
- Total debt/total assets
- EBITDA/total debt

Altman later used several ratios to measure corporate distress.[7] He found the following five variables to be most efficient in predicting bankruptcy.

- Working capital/total assets
- Retained earnings/total assets
- (EBIT)/total assets
- Equity market value/book value of total debt
- Sales revenue/total assets

Altman's work was the first to use ratios taken together rather than independently to assess the risk of credit deterioration.

Ratio work is indispensable to a correct model of the firm. Although they may be used as ends in themselves, their proper function should be to form the investment premise rather than the conclusion.

Measuring Return and Risk

Assessing portfolio risk versus the expected return is more manageable with a single return standard. In the high-yield universe this is made more difficult because of the diverse nature of the securities.

Investors have three sources of return:

1. the coupon payment stream,
2. interest on interest received, and
3. capital gains or losses incurred through portfolio transactions.

The commonly used measure for determining total return in fixed income portfolios traditionally has been the yield-to-maturity calculation.

Accounting: Selected Studies Supplement of the Journal of Accounting Research 5, 1961, pp. 71–111.
7. E. Altman, "Financial Ratios, Discriminant Analysis and the Prediction of Bankruptcy," *Journal of Finance,* September 1968, pp. 589–609.

The yield to maturity is the discount rate that equates the present value of the periodic payments and the principal repayment to the price.

The yield to maturity invests the periodic cash stream but reinvests those payments at the yield to maturity, which is assumed to remain constant throughout the life of the security. Because of this assumption, the yield to maturity is more of a hypothetical benchmark than a true return.

Homer and Liebowitz first suggested a formula for calculating the rate of return over some planned holding period called the realized compound yield.[8] Realized compound yield — now more popularly referred to as total, or horizon, return — first computes the future value of a bond investment. The total return is the interest rate that will make the dollars invested today grow to the future value of the bond investment at the end of the planned investment horizon.

The advantages of realized compound yield are as follows.

1. It allows for various reinvestment rates. This is particularly advantageous given that the high-yield portfolio may contain a variety of different securities, such as convertible securities and resets, as well as increasing-rate notes, "step-up" bonds, zero-coupon securities, and pay-in-kind (PIK) securities. All of these securities will have different rates of interest, and we may make different assumptions about their various maturities and repayment schemes.

2. It enables us to compare high-yield securities to other asset classes at various reinvestment rates.

3. It allows us to measure and draw comparisons of the future value from all sources of return.

4. Finally, we lose nothing by choosing this method over the yield-to-maturity calculation because it is directly comparable if we assume an identical rate of reinvestment.

Summary

It is an ancient paradox that the rules of nature are simple but the universe is complex. The world is populated by a rich variety of physical

---

8. S. Homer and M. L. Leibowitz, *Inside the Yield Book* (Englewood Cliffs, NJ: Prentice-Hall, 1972), pp. 169–187.

forms, but they are all governed by the same underlying laws. The means to understanding those laws and how they apply depend on the correct emphasis and focus. The art and science of portfolio management is little different. Applying the disciplines of fundamental analysis in an intelligent and proprietary format is the best means to control risk in high-yield portfolio management.

13

How to Hedge a High-Yield Bond Portfolio

Kenneth S. Choie, Ph.D.
Vice President
Chase Investors Management Corporation

The recent collapse in the high-yield bond market, capped by the demise of Drexel Burnham Lambert, may constitute a good opportunity to enter the market for some people and a trying time for those who are already in the market. For either group of investors, a reasonable hedging strategy for a high-yield bond portfolio can help protect their investment. This chapter demonstrates how to hedge the price risk of a high-yield bond portfolio, at least to a great extent.

For any hedging strategy to work, the objective must be clear. That is, it is necessary to define an appropriate performance benchmark for the portfolio to be hedged. Our hedging goal is to control the price risk caused by changes in the market assessment of credit risk associated with high-yield bonds. Accordingly, our hedged high-yield bond portfolio would be comparable to a long-term government/corporate bond index.[1]

Intertwined with the issue of setting an objective is the issue of the availability of hedging instruments, which may limit the attainable

---

1. Drexel Burnham Lambert had a hedging program whose goal was to transform a high-yield bond portfolio into a money market instrument with a big spread over U.S. Treasury bills.

goal. Our hedging tools are Treasury bond futures and municipal bond index futures, specifically, a spread position between the two (i.e., long in Treasury bond futures and short in municipal bond index futures).[2] As we shall see, a spread between equity futures (e.g., long in S&P 500 index futures and short in Value Line futures) is a potentially effective supplementary hedging instrument.

The Idea

For the sake of convenience, let us classify yields on a high-yield bond into three categories: the yield on a Treasury bond of similar tenor, the yield for the credit risk between Treasury bonds and A-rated bonds, and the yield for the credit risk between A-rated bonds and high-yield bonds.

Let us consider a portfolio consisting of a long position in high-yield bonds, a long position in Treasury bond futures, and a short position in municipal bond index futures. The municipal bond index consists of bonds rated A− or better by Standard & Poor's, or A or better by Moody's. Thus, a long position in Treasury bond futures and a short position in municipal bond futures has, loosely speaking, a net position that is short in the yield spread between Treasury bonds and A− or A-rated bonds. Suppose that the notional dollar amounts in each of the three positions are the same. The portfolio is then, in net, long in Treasury bonds and long in the yield spread between high-yield bonds and A-rated bonds. Such a portfolio reduces the price risk of a high-yield bond portfolio by eliminating the price sensitivity to changes in the yield spread between Treasury and A or A− rated bonds. This is the basic structure of our hedged portfolio.

We can augment this hedged portfolio with an equity spread position, for example, a long position in S&P 500 futures and a short position in Value Line futures. This equity position is equivalent to a net short position in small, low-capitalization stocks. The premise is that changes in the market price of the factors responsible for the

---

2. Drexel's hedging program calls for short positions in both Treasury note futures and S&P 500 index futures. Followed faithfully, this hedging program would have produced disastrous results in the last few years.

excess return of small, low-capitalization stocks over large-capitalization stocks are inversely related to changes in the yield spread between high-yield bonds and A-rated bonds.[3] This augmented hedge portfolio, however, may not be extensively implemented because of the low liquidity of Value Line index futures.

The Specifics of the Hedged Portfolio

The hedged portfolio, *H*, consists of a high-yield bond portfolio, *J*, a long position in Treasury bonds futures, *T*, and a short position in municipal bond index futures, *M*.

$$H = J + T - M$$

The yield on *J* consists of the yield on a comparable Treasury bond, the yield spread between the Treasury bond and a comparable A-rated bond, and the yield spread between the A-rated bond and *J*.

Suppose that for a given change in Treasury bond yield, the price sensitivity of the high-yield bond portfolio is the same as that of municipal bond index futures. If the notional dollar amounts for *J*, *T*, and *M* are the same, then the hedged portfolio will respond to changes in Treasury bond yield in the same way that Treasury bond futures would, and to changes in the yield spread between A-rated bonds and the high-yield bond portfolio in the same way that the high-yield bond portfolio would.[4] (The proof of this can be found in the appendix.) To the extent that the yield spread between A-rated bonds and the high-yield bond portfolio remains small, the impact of changes in the yield spread would also tend to be small. In this instance, an appropriate benchmark for the hedged portfolio might be an index such as the Shearson Government Corporate Long-Term Index.

---

3. Various studies have linked yield on corporate bonds with factors that determine stock market returns. One study measured the impact of equity components on the total return of a corporate bond. (See Richard Bookstaber and David Jacob, "The Composite Hedge: Controlling the Credit Risk of High Yield Bonds," *Financial Analysts Journal,* March-April 1986, pp. 25–36.)

In another study, the authors used positions in stock to control credit risk of high-yield bonds. (See Mark Weinstein, "The Equity Component of Corporate Bonds," *Journal of Portfolio Management,* Spring 1985, pp. 37–41.)

4. See equation (4) in the appendix.

An increase in the yield spread between the high-yield bond portfolio and A-rated bonds will require supplementary hedging. An equity spread consisting of a long position in S&P 500 index futures and a short position in Value Line index futures might be a good candidate for such a supplementary hedging strategy. The rationale is that the equity spread position is approximately equivalent to being short in the factors responsible for an increase in the yield spread between A-rated bonds and high-yield bonds. Hence, in a period of deteriorating high-yield bond quality, this augmented hedge portfolio may be more appropriately comparable to a long-term government/corporate index.

Empirical Test of the Hedged Portfolio

The first order of business is to validate the assumption that the price sensitivities of high-yield bond portfolios and municipal bond index futures are the same. Unfortunately, no historical data on the duration of municipal bond indexes are available to test the assumption. Nevertheless, it is possible to estimate the duration of municipal bond index futures using historical duration and yield data on the Shearson A-rated Bond Index, because the municipal bonds underlying municipal bond futures have an average rating of A or A−. The Salomon High Yield Bond Index provides historical duration data on high-yield bond portfolios. The price sensitivity relationship between municipal bond index futures and high-yield bond portfolios can then be estimated from these data.

Exhibit 1 shows monthly yield and duration data from the Shearson A-rated Bond Index for the period 1986 through 1989. It is possible to compute the time to maturity of a typical A-rated par bond using this data. Given the time to maturity of the typical bond, the duration of municipal bond index futures can be estimated using a certain fraction of the yield on the A-rated Bond Index as the yield on a typical par municipal bond. We use a marginal tax rate of 30 percent; thus the yield on A-rated municipal bonds is 70 percent of the yield on comparable A-rated bonds.

Exhibit 2 shows the estimated duration of municipal bond index futures and the duration of the Salomon High Yield Bond Index. For a given change in yield, columns (1) and (3) show the price sensitivities

EXHIBIT 1 *Shearson A-Rated Long Bond Index*

Year	Month	Yield	Duration
1986	1	10.73%	8.44
	2	10.69	8.40
	3	10.04	8.69
	4	9.81	8.78
	5	9.85	8.78
	6	10.09	8.70
	7	9.96	8.73
	8	9.99	8.70
	9	9.82	8.79
	10	9.90	8.76
	11	9.76	8.81
	12	9.64	8.84
1987	1	9.62	8.88
	2	9.36	9.00
	3	9.34	9.05
	4	9.46	8.98
	5	9.97	8.78
	6	10.11	8.70
	7	10.00	8.76
	8	10.17	8.63
	9	10.37	8.54
	10	10.97	8.27
	11	10.50	8.48
	12	10.39	8.54
1988	1	10.21	8.63
	2	9.73	8.84
	3	9.66	8.85
	4	9.95	8.71
	5	10.17	8.61
	6	10.38	8.51
	7	10.07	8.63
	8	10.24	8.54
	9	10.24	8.54
	10	10.03	8.63
	11	9.92	8.67
	12	10.15	8.56
1989	1	10.17	8.55
	2	10.04	8.56
	3	10.25	8.43
	4	10.32	8.38
	5	10.16	8.48
	6	9.85	8.61
	7	9.52	8.83
	8	9.40	8.86
	9	9.64	8.75
	10	9.66	8.73
	11	9.46	8.82
	12	9.48	8.81

EXHIBIT 2 *Durations: High Yield Bond vs. Municipal Bond Futures*

Year	Month	Salomon High Yield Bond Index (1)	Municipal Bond Index Futures (2)	(2) × 0.7 (3)	(1) ÷ (3) (4)
1986	1	5.89	10.53	7.37	0.80
	2	6.00	10.45	7.32	0.82
	3	5.97	10.16	7.11	0.84
	4	6.23	9.98	6.99	0.89
	5	6.20	9.95	6.96	0.89
	6	6.18	10.12	7.08	0.87
	7	6.16	10.05	7.03	0.88
	8	6.15	10.02	7.02	0.88
	9	6.02	9.97	6.98	0.86
	10	6.03	10.10	7.07	0.85
	11	6.01	10.02	7.02	0.86
	12	6.05	9.91	6.94	0.87
1987	1	6.04	9.93	6.95	0.87
	2	6.02	11.20	7.84	0.77
	3	6.13	11.22	7.85	0.78
	4	6.15	9.83	6.88	0.89
	5	6.05	10.04	7.03	0.86
	6	5.91	10.10	7.07	0.84
	7	5.88	10.01	7.01	0.84
	8	5.89	10.22	7.16	0.82
	9	5.83	10.20	7.14	0.82
	10	5.79	10.70	7.49	0.77
	11	5.62	10.38	7.26	0.77
	12	5.48	10.34	7.24	0.76
1988	1	5.56	10.19	7.13	0.78
	2	5.56	9.84	6.89	0.81
	3	5.62	9.90	6.93	0.81
	4	5.68	10.06	7.04	0.81
	5	5.65	10.22	7.16	0.79
	6	5.60	10.35	7.24	0.77
	7	5.59	10.14	7.10	0.79
	8	5.65	10.16	7.11	0.79
	9	5.63	10.16	7.11	0.79
	10	5.60	9.99	6.99	0.80
	11	5.60	10.08	7.06	0.79
	12	5.55	10.07	7.05	0.79

EXHIBIT 2 *Continued*

Year	Month	Salomon High Yield Bond Index (1)	Municipal Bond Index Futures (2)	$(2) \times 0.7$ (3)	$(1) \div (3)$ (4)
1989	1	5.52	10.22	7.16	0.77
	2	5.49	10.16	7.11	0.77
	3	5.50	10.15	7.10	0.77
	4	5.46	10.25	7.17	0.76
	5	5.52	10.06	7.04	0.78
	6	5.54	9.95	6.96	0.80
	7	5.57	9.79	6.85	0.81
	8	5.62	9.88	6.92	0.81
	9	5.60	9.91	6.94	0.81
	10	5.56	9.90	6.93	0.80
	11	5.52	9.83	6.88	0.80
	12	5.45	9.82	6.87	0.79

of the high-yield index and municipal bond index futures, respectively. Note that column (3) is the product of the duration of municipal index futures, column (2), and the marginal tax rate of 70 percent.

Our assumption that the price sensitivities of high-yield bond portfolios and municipal bond futures are the same must be modified in light of the data in Exhibit 2. Column (4) lists the ratios of the price sensitivity of the Salomon High Yield Bond Index to that of municipal bond index futures. These ratios serve as proxies for the price sensitivity relationship between high-yield bond portfolios and municipal bond index futures. If our assumption on the price sensitivities were valid, the ratios in column (4) would all be equal to one. Because they are not, we must revise the equation above for H. That is, for equation (4) in the appendix to be valid, the notional amount invested in municipal bond index futures must be a fraction, indicated by the ratio in column (4), of the equal notional amounts invested in the high-yield bond portfolio and in Treasury bond futures.

Exhibit 3 shows the historical simulation results of hedging a high-yield bond portfolio, represented by the Salomon High Yield Bond Index, with a long position in Treasury bond futures and a short position

EXHIBIT 3 *Unhedged vs. Hedged Salomon High Yield Bond Index Returns*

Year	Month	Salomon High Yield Bond Index (1)	Treasury Bond Futures (2)	Municipal Bond Futures (3)	Municipal Bond Adjustor (4)	Futures (2) − [(3) × (4)] (5)	Hedged Salomon High Yield Bond Index (6)	Shearson Government/ Corporate Bond Index (7)
1986	1	1.44%	−0.07%	1.42%	0.80	−1.20%	0.24%	0.46%
	2	4.80	11.34	5.73	0.82	6.64	11.44	8.56
	3	2.70	8.84	2.99	0.84	6.34	9.04	5.55
	4	1.52	−1.53	−4.80	0.89	2.75	4.27	−0.02
	5	0.81	−6.82	−5.20	0.89	−2.20	−1.39	−3.74
	6	0.70	6.95	3.92	0.87	3.53	4.23	4.16
	7	−1.76	−1.76	−1.31	0.88	−0.61	−2.37	−0.15
	8	1.68	4.70	6.95	0.88	−1.39	0.29	3.50
	9	1.42	−5.07	−3.90	0.86	−1.71	−0.29	−2.20
	10	1.70	1.59	2.57	0.85	−0.60	1.10	1.80
	11	−0.27	1.56	1.84	0.86	−0.01	−0.28	1.83
	12	0.76	−0.51	−0.57	0.87	−0.01	0.75	0.43
Annual Return		16.50	19.10	9.11		11.58	29.43	21.42
1987	1	4.12	1.53	1.93	0.87	−0.15	3.97	2.17
	2	1.94	1.75	1.24	0.77	0.80	2.74	0.99
	3	0.43	−1.96	−2.32	0.78	−0.15	0.28	−1.30
	4	−3.00	−5.49	−8.63	0.89	2.22	−0.78	−4.58
	5	−0.02	−1.07	−1.42	0.86	0.15	0.13	−0.93
	6	1.85	0.48	0.46	0.84	0.09	1.94	1.32
	7	0.53	−2.19	0.32	0.84	−2.45	−1.92	−1.32
	8	0.76	−2.23	0.85	0.82	−2.94	−2.18	−1.30
	9	−3.32	−5.60	−8.22	0.82	1.11	−2.21	−4.24

10	-3.29	7.19	5.39	0.77	3.02	-0.27	6.03
11	2.54	0.11	0.22	0.77	-0.07	2.47	0.62
12	2.27	1.41	3.11	0.76	-0.95	1.32	2.15
Annual Return	4.57	-6.53	-7.75		0.54	5.41	-0.85
1988							
1	3.71	6.75	6.17	0.78	1.94	5.65	5.59
2	3.84	0.80	1.18	0.81	-0.15	3.69	1.24
3	-0.65	-3.80	-3.61	0.81	-0.88	-1.53	-2.40
4	0.29	-2.39	-0.55	0.81	-1.95	-1.66	-1.58
5	0.83	-2.38	1.72	0.79	-3.74	-2.91	-1.23
6	2.01	4.53	3.19	0.77	2.06	4.07	3.88
7	0.69	-2.89	0.90	0.79	-3.60	-2.91	-1.43
8	0.06	-0.15	1.00	0.79	-0.94	-0.88	0.51
9	1.75	3.80	3.40	0.79	1.11	2.86	3.24
10	1.03	2.99	2.97	0.80	0.61	1.64	2.73
11	0.08	-3.21	-2.65	0.79	-1.11	-1.03	-1.76
12	0.73	1.17	3.26	0.79	-1.40	-0.67	0.91
Annual Return	15.23	4.65	17.89		-7.94	6.02	9.75
1989							
1	1.90	1.89	0.82	0.77	1.26	3.16	1.96
2	0.35	-2.99	-1.91	0.77	-1.52	-1.17	-1.53
3	-0.08	0.25	-0.14	0.77	0.36	0.28	0.77
4	0.69	2.02	3.20	0.76	-0.42	0.27	2.39
5	1.74	3.19	1.63	0.78	1.91	3.65	3.53
6	1.64	5.31	2.43	0.80	3.38	5.02	4.89
7	0.44	1.85	0.63	0.81	1.34	1.78	2.13
8	-0.43	-3.51	-2.91	0.81	-1.14	-1.57	-2.11
9	-1.80	-0.39	-0.41	0.81	-0.06	-1.86	0.37
10	-2.84	3.65	0.92	0.80	2.91	0.07	3.42
11	0.14	0.13	1.38	0.80	-0.98	-0.84	0.80
12	0.18	-0.82	-0.83	0.79	-0.16	0.02	-0.11
Annual Return	1.84	10.68	4.74		6.94	8.88	17.55

in municipal bond index futures. Column (1) shows unhedged Salomon High Yield Bond Index returns, whereas column (6) shows hedged
returns of the index. The hedged return is the sum of the return on the
unhedged Salomon index, column (1), and the return on the two futures positions, column (5). Note that column (5) is the sum of the
Treasury bond futures position, column (2), and the municipal bond
index futures position, which in turn is the product of columns (3)
and (4). The performance benchmark for the hedged Salomon High
Yield Bond Index is the Shearson Government/Corporate Bond Index, listed in column (7).

Overall, Exhibit 3 indicates that the index portfolio, under the proposed hedging strategy, yields returns roughly comparable to the benchmark index returns. An exception occurs in 1989 and to a lesser extent
in 1988. However, a reasonable explanation for the large performance
lags in those two years is readily available. The portfolio would be
comparable to an index similar to the Shearson Government/Corpo-
rate Bond Index as long as the yield spread between A-rated bonds
and high-yield bonds remains small. However, since October 1988,
the credit quality of the Salomon High Yield Bond Index has been
down-graded from an average B+ rating to B. This deterioration of
credit rating implies that changes in the yield spread between A-rated
bonds and high-yield bonds are larger than before. Thus, the performance lags in 1988 and 1989 are due to this change in credit quality.

A more thorough hedging strategy would call for a supplementary
hedging position to counter the changes in the yield spread between
A-rated bonds and high-yield bonds. An equity spread position, consisting of a long position in S&P 500 index futures and a short position in Value Line futures, appears to offer such a supplementary
position.

Exhibit 4 shows the impact of the equity spread. Column (2) lists
the returns on the Salomon High Yield Bond Index hedged with the
interest-rate futures spread. Column (6) shows monthly returns from
the equity spread. Column (7) indicates the returns on the hedged
portfolio supplemented with the equity spread. Note that the notional
amounts of the long S&P 500 futures position and the short Value
Line futures position are the same as that of the high-yield bond position. Also note that the equity spread is added on to the high-yield

bond portfolio hedged with the interest-rate futures spread when the rating of Salomon High Yield Bond Index is B rather than B+. Columns (7) and (8) show that the return pattern of the hedged portfolio with the supplementary equity spread does become comparable to that of the Shearson Government/Corporate Bond Index. Unfortunately, we must reiterate that the equity spread may not be implemented in any meaningful size because of the lack of liquidity in Value Line futures contracts, however effective the equity spread theoretically may be.

Conclusions

In this chapter, we proposed and tested a hedging strategy for a high-yield bond portfolio. The basic premise for our hedging strategy is that an interest-rate futures spread, a long position in Treasury bond futures, and a short position in municipal bond index futures can make a high-yield bond portfolio comparable to a long-term government/corporate index. The results of our empirical test indicate that the hedged Salomon High Yield Bond Index is roughly comparable to the Shearson Government/Corporate Bond Index.

Our second premise was that an equity futures spread, a long position in S&P 500 index futures, and a short position in Value Line futures was equivalent to being short in the factors responsible for the yield spread corresponding to the credit risk of high-yield bonds. The test results strongly support this premise. Furthermore, the results show that the Salomon High Yield Bond Index hedged with both the interest-rate futures spread and the equity futures spread is very similar to the Shearson Government/Corporate Bond Index.

Appendix

Recall that the hedged portfolio, H, consists of a high-yield bond portfolio, J, a long position in Treasury bond futures, T, and a short position in municipal bond index futures, M:

$$H = J + T - M \tag{1}$$

EXHIBIT 4   *Hedged Salomon High Yield Bond Index with Supplementary Equity Spread*

Year	Month	Salomon High Yield Bond Index (1)	Hedged Salomon High Yield Bond Index (2)	Rating of Salomon High Yield Bond Index (3)	Value-Line Futures (4)	S&P 500 Futures (5)	Equity Spread (5)−(4) (6)	Hedged Index with Equity Spread (2)+(6) (7)	Shearson Government/ Corporate Bond Index (8)
1986	1	1.44%	0.24%	B+				0.24%	0.46%
	2	4.80	11.44	B+				11.44	8.56
	3	2.70	9.04	B+				9.04	5.55
	4	1.52	4.27	B+				4.27	−0.02
	5	0.81	−1.39	B+				−1.39	−3.74
	6	0.70	4.23	B+				4.23	4.16
	7	−1.76	−2.37	B+				−2.37	−0.15
	8	1.68	0.29	B+				0.29	3.50
	9	1.42	−0.29	B+				−0.29	−2.20
	10	1.70	1.10	B+				1.10	1.80
	11	−0.27	−0.28	B+				−0.28	1.83
	12	0.76	0.75	B+				0.75	0.43
Annual Return		16.50	29.43					29.43	21.42
1987	1	4.12	3.97	B+				3.97	2.17
	2	1.94	2.74	B+				2.74	0.99
	3	0.43	0.28	B+				0.28	−1.30
	4	−3.00	−0.78	B+				−0.78	−4.58
	5	−0.02	0.13	B+				0.13	−0.93
	6	1.85	1.94	B+				1.94	1.32
	7	0.53	−1.92	B+				−1.92	−1.32
	8	0.76	−2.18	B+				−2.18	−1.30
	9	−3.32	−2.21	B+				−2.21	−4.24

			Rating					
10	−3.29	−0.27	B+	−0.97	1.81	2.78	−0.27	6.03
11	2.54	2.47	B+	−3.18	−2.17	1.01	2.47	0.62
12	2.27	1.32	B+	3.30	1.61	−1.69	1.32	2.15
Annual Return	4.57	5.41					5.41	−0.85
1988								
1	3.71	5.65	B+				5.65	5.59
2	3.84	3.69	B+				3.69	1.24
3	−0.65	−1.53	B+				−1.53	−2.40
4	0.29	−1.66	B+				−1.66	−1.58
5	0.83	−2.91	B+				−2.91	−1.23
6	2.01	4.07	B+				4.07	3.88
7	0.69	−2.91	B+				−2.91	−1.43
8	0.06	−0.88	B+				−0.88	0.51
9	1.75	2.86	B+				2.86	3.24
10	1.03	1.64	B				4.42	2.73
11	0.08	−1.03	B				−0.02	−1.76
12	0.73	−0.67	B				−2.36	0.91
Annual Return	15.23	6.02					8.17	9.75
1989								
1	1.90	3.16	B	5.51	6.54	1.04	4.20	1.96
2	0.35	−1.17	B	−1.05	−3.05	−2.00	−3.17	−1.53
3	−0.08	0.28	B	1.21	1.53	0.32	0.60	0.77
4	0.69	0.27	B	3.75	4.60	0.85	1.13	2.39
5	1.74	3.65	B	3.21	3.18	−0.04	3.61	3.53
6	1.64	5.02	B	−0.75	−1.44	−0.69	4.32	4.89
7	0.44	1.78	B	5.43	8.44	3.01	4.79	2.13
8	−0.43	−1.57	B	1.58	1.00	−0.58	−2.15	−2.11
9	−1.80	−1.86	B	−0.92	−1.05	−0.13	−1.99	0.37
10	−2.84	0.07	B	−5.72	−2.68	3.04	3.12	3.42
11	0.14	−0.84	B	0.00	1.27	1.27	0.43	0.80
12	0.18	0.02	B	0.55	1.25	0.70	0.72	−0.11
Annual Return	1.84	8.88					16.29	17.55

Let

a = the yield on a comparable Treasury bond

b = the yield spread between the Treasury bond and a comparable A-rated bond

c = the yield spread between the A-rated bond and the high-yield bond portfolio

g = marginal tax rate

The change in the value of the hedged portfolio can be approximated as follows:

$$dH = \left[\frac{\partial J}{\partial a} + \frac{\partial T}{\partial a} - \frac{\partial M}{\partial a}(1-g)\right]da$$
$$+ \left[\frac{\partial J}{\partial b} - \frac{\partial M}{\partial b}(1-g)\right]db$$
$$+ \left[\frac{\partial J}{\partial c}\right]dc \tag{2}$$

From the definition of duration,[5] it follows that

$$dH = [-D_j(J) - D_t(T) + D_m(M)(1-g)]da$$
$$+ [-D_j(J) + D_m(M)(1-g)]db$$
$$+ [-D_j(J)]dc \tag{3}$$

where D_j, D_t, and D_m are the duration of the high-yield bond portfolio, Treasury bond, and municipal bond index futures, respectively.

Suppose that for a given change in yield, the price sensitivity of the high-yield portfolio is the same as that of the municipal bond index futures [i.e., $D_j = D_m(1-g)$]. If the notional dollar amounts for J, T, and M are the same, then

$$dH = -D_t(T)da - D_j(T)dc \tag{4}$$

---

5. That is, $(dX/X)dr = -D_X$ and $dX/dr = -D_X(X)$.

14

High-Yield Investments for Insurance Companies

Mamak Shahbazi
Vice President
First Boston Asset Management Corporation

This chapter outlines the overall investment objectives and the role of high-yield investments for both property and casualty insurance companies and life insurance companies, with emphasis on life insurance companies. It also contains information regarding the guidelines and regulatory requirements for high-yield investing, as well as a general guide to managing high-yield investments for insurance companies.

Overall Investment Objectives for Insurance Companies

An insurance company's investment objective is to create ample financial reserves in order to provide a comfortable safety margin to protect first its policyholders and also its stockholders. Theoretically, the strongest protection would be provided by a company that has all of its assets in cash. At the opposite extreme, a company that backs all of its liabilities and capital funds with equities would provide the least protection for its policyholders, because of the volatility and uncertainty of returns from this asset class. Government securities and high-grade corporate bonds are generally regarded as providing protective features similar to those provided by cash instruments, but with higher income that can be divided between stockholders and policyholders. Insurance company investments must first provide a reserve cushion for policyholders; after such reserve requirements have been satisfied, excess funds may be invested in securities that provide a higher risk-adjusted return for the company's stockholders.

Property and casualty companies balance the liabilities created by their policies with "liquid assets" (cash and receivables), in addition to government, municipal, and other high-grade bonds. After business liabilities are covered, a certain amount of higher-return assets such as high-yield, equity, and related investments are used for added income and appreciation. The degree of flexibility permitted is a function of the surplus after liabilities are covered with liquid assets, which varies with the company's insurance exposure. A company that continually operates at a loss and writes business several times its surplus cannot adopt a more aggressive investment course than a company with a long-term profitability record.

Life insurance companies' liabilities primarily stem from underwriting policies over various term periods. These companies must accept and accurately estimate mortality risk, often on a long-term basis. The typical insurance company also underwrites disability, annuity, health, and other long-term obligations that, from an accounting standpoint, have many of the same characteristics of mortality risk. Because it is difficult to predict mortality risks on a long-term basis, there is a need to secure adequate reserves to meet future obligations. The types of life insurance policies underwritten influence the formulation of investment policy by management. The liabilities of a life insurance company are covered by the reserves established to stand behind its insurance and annuity products. Approximately 80 percent to 90 percent of life insurance liabilities are long-term, fixed-rate obligations. Therefore, the corresponding assets should be invested in long-term, fixed-rate obligations with a yield at least equal to, and ideally greater than, the interest rate guaranteed in the outstanding contracts. Although some attention is given to the distribution of maturities, the basic objective is to acquire the longest maturities with the risk, yield, and liquidity considerations associated with a company's current investment strategy. However, recent shorter term annuities have had the effect of shortening the maturity profile of some insurance companies.

Liquidity historically has been of less importance for life insurance companies. During the 1980s the life insurance industry introduced more complex, higher yielding annuity and variable life products. Such products directed some insurance companies toward sacrificing some safety of principal through the acquisition of investments with higher risk but relatively higher yields. This reflects more sophisticated investment planning among life insurance companies. Competitive yield is increasingly important; balancing the relative safety of principal with maximizing portfolio yield is the current challenge in investment policies of most life insurance companies.

Investments of insurance companies, both property and casualty and life, are heavily regulated through the National Association of Insurance Commissioners (NAIC) and individual state laws. The NAIC annually promulgates guidelines for the valuation of assets for annual statement purposes. In addition to such regulatory constraints, insurance companies must also follow surplus restrictions and provide adequate risk-based reserves for their investment portfolios. Bonds, mortgages, and preferred stocks are generally known as *admitted assets* for insurance companies. Admitted assets are those assets allowed by law or insurance department ruling to be shown on the company's balance sheet. Such investments are usually valued on an amortized basis, which often differs from market value.

The Role of High-Yield Investments in Insurance Company Investments

Property and Casualty

The recent price discounting on property and casualty products has caused a significant downturn in these companies' profits. High-yield investments may offset some of these bottom line losses and may boost policyholders' surplus and net income. High-yield investments may additionally provide some pricing flexibility on the various property and casualty products. The property and casualty industry, however, because of its short-term liability structure and greater liquidity needs, is not and cannot be heavily involved in long-term high-yield investments.

Life, Health, and Annuity

New life insurance products such as annuities, universal and variable life, and guaranteed investment contracts depend on their rate of return to attract and hold customers. The use of high-yield bonds in life insurance investments is driven by such high-return products; therefore, the demand for high-yield bonds is liability driven by the products insurance companies offer to their customers. Life insurance companies today also face problems resulting from whole-life policies previously issued and the investments that were assumed to finance them. Such problems include high lapse rates for policies, low revenue growth, increased demand for policy loans, and low returns on prior investments.

High-yield bonds have become more important to life insurance companies. Investing in these securities is cost efficient, and high-yield bonds provide a competitive advantage by increasing profit margins and improving the ability to match assets and liabilities. According to NAIC records, in 1987 approximately 11.4 percent of the insurers' bond portfolios were invested in high-yield securities. Some life insurance companies have invested heavily in high-yield bonds and have reaped the benefits of higher yields during the past years. In addition, high-yield investments outperformed all other investment vehicles from 1980 to 1988. In 1989 returns were weaker than most other markets, but over larger time periods high-yield investments have outperformed most other asset classes.

Regulation of Investments

As mentioned earlier, investment activities of insurance companies, specifically life insurance companies, are conducted within limitations prescribed by state insurance regulators. The NAIC provides some uniformity in the formulation of investment regulations throughout different states. Nevertheless, individual state statutes and regulations vary widely in the allowed percentage of allocation for different investments, including high-yield bonds. In general, state laws provide limitations aimed at preserving the safety of assets standing behind policyholders' reserves and preventing undue control of the life insurer through disproportionately large investments of one type.

Valuation of Assets

Although there are no legal requirements for the valuation of insurance company assets, the NAIC and the codes of various states as they relate to the valuation of assets serve to encourage investments of higher quality assets. The NAIC has supplied specific criteria, contained in two tests, for determining the eligibility of various classes of bonds for amortization.

The first test incorporates higher credit and financial standards and lower Mandatory Securities Valuation Reserve (MSVR) requirements. The MSVR was introduced in 1951 to deal with the problem of valuing securities. The mandated reserve is used primarily as a means of preventing undue surplus changes arising from fluctuations in the market value of securities owned. The MSVR absorbs, within certain limits, fluctuations in surplus caused by increases and decreases arising from realized capital gains and losses. The amount of the MSVR is a function of a company's preceding year's balance sheet and capital gains less capital losses for the current year.

The second test relates to bond ratings given by reputable rating agencies, fixed-charge coverage ratios, and the long-term debt to total capitalization ratios. The NAIC, through its Securities Valuation Office (SVO), presently defines high-yield bonds in a slightly different way than the rating agencies. It has therefore created its own system for rating private placement bonds, as well as publicly rated high-yield bonds.[1] In the NAIC's rating system, YES bonds are considered investment-grade securities with the lowest MSVR requirement. YES bonds can be rated below investment grade (BBB or lower) by rating agencies such as Standard & Poor's or Moody's Investors. Only higher quality high-yield credits are included in the NAIC's high-grade rating. These issues are generally ranked BB or split BB by other rating agencies; however, some strong B-rated credits also appear in the NAIC's YES list. The NAIC further breaks down its lower grade rating to medium-risk and high-risk. The rating categories are given in Exhibit 1.

---

1. The NAIC recently (June 1990) proposed a complete change from its traditional YES/NO rating system to the rating agencies' system for determining reserve requirements on high-yield bonds. The proposed reserve requirements are higher than the traditional YES/NO standards.

EXHIBIT 1   *NAIC Bond Rating System*

NAIC Category	Meaning	MSVR Requirement	Reserve Accumulation Period	Annual Reserve Accumulation
Yes	Investment-Grade	2.0%	20 years	0.10%
No*	Medium-Risk	10.0%		0.50%
No**	High-Risk	20.0%	10 years	2.00%

The investment-grade profile consists of a rather stringent set of objective criteria and subjective judgments that tend to favor larger capitalized, mature, successful companies that have well-diversified stakes in stable businesses. Faster growing companies with thinner capitalizations generally fall under the No* category, which would normally receive a single B or lower rating by the larger rating agencies.

Most of the corporate bonds in insurance companies' investment portfolios are carried at the amortized value, and market value swings are not recorded on the surplus and reserve requirements. If a bond defaults — and SVO has its own definition of default — then it must be valued at its fair market value and adequate reserves must be assigned to the loss. SVO defines default in such a broad way that any breach or potential breach of contractual terms or significant covenants of a loan agreement is grounds for default for the outstanding bonds.

Specific Regulations for High-Yield Investing

There are several restrictions in insurance company high-yield investing that need to be explored. The following gives an outline of them.

Allocation Restrictions.   Most states provide a maximum allowable allocation for high-yield bonds. California does not have a maximum limit on high-yield participation for life insurance companies; however, some other states, such as New York and Arizona, recently announced a maximum of 20 percent of assets allowable for investment in high-yield bonds. The recent controversy in high-yield bond investing has prompted state regulators to impose more stringent limitations on high-yield investments. In order to determine what percentage of assets should be invested in high-yield bonds, certain variables such as capital, surplus, MSVR, cash flow, liquidity, and quality and mix of other assets must be considered.

Such factors should be considered in addition to individual state regulation restrictions on high-yield bond investments. On average, conservatively managed life insurance companies invest only 5 to 10 percent of their assets in high-yield securities. Though most of the larger life insurance companies have investments in high-yield securities, many smaller companies have not yet explored these investments.

Mandatory Securities Valuation Reserve (MSVR). Any insurance company involved in high-yield investing must have adequate capital, surplus, and MSVR cushion. MSVR is constructed in a way that shifts large aggregate sums from surplus to MSVR for any company that actively engages in high-yield bond investing. MSVR requirements for different classes of bonds are outlined in Exhibit 1. The maximum reserve for a high-risk bond (NO**) is 20 percent accumulated over a 10-year accumulation period; low-risk (YES) bonds require only 2 percent over a 20-year accumulation period. These transfers of surplus to MSVR may exceed a company's net operating gain, causing a reduction in surplus, which may necessitate a need to raise additional statutory surplus. Exhibits 2 and 3 show selected MSVR of some larger insurance companies involved in high-yield investing.

Surplus Restrictions. Insurance companies involved in the high-yield market must determine whether their surplus cushion is adequate for such investments. As discussed earlier, the MSVR may require large sums of surplus in the presence of low-grade bond investments. By

EXHIBIT 2 *300 Largest U.S. Life Insurers*

	Ratio of Junk Bonds to		Ratio of MSVR to	
Year	Invested Assets	Total Surplus	Invested Assets	Statutory Surplus
1986	4.35%	47.44%	1.95%	27.02%
1987	5.32%	61.83%	1.82%	26.88%

Source: Frederick Townsend, "Junk Bonds Can Devour A Life Insurance's Surplus," *National Underwriter,* March 6, 1989.

EXHIBIT 3   *1987 Bond and Preferred Stock Components of the Mandatory Securities Valuation Reserve (Data in Millions)*

	First Executive Corp.			First Capital		
	Executive Life, Cal.	Executive Life, N.Y.	First Stratford	First Capital	Fidelity Bankers	Guaranteed Security Life Ins.
Junk bonds as % of Invested Assets	55.0%	53.1%	67.0%	26.1%	32.3%	61.4%
Maximum MSVR	1,129	372	81	150	71	114
Asset Value	9,424	3,360	595	1,982	802	882
Maximum/Assets	12.0%	11.1%	13.6%	7.6%	8.9%	12.9%
Jan. 1 MSVR	406	174	49	36	7	15
MSVR/Maximum	36.0%	46.8%	60.5%	24.0%	9.9%	13.2%
Dec. 1 MSVR	547	225	57	90	27	31
MSVR/Maximum	48.4%	60.5%	70.4%	60.0%	38.0%	27.2%
Annual Increment	101	33	8	13	6	10
Multiplier	2.0	1.0	1.0	1.0	2.0	2.0
Annual Accum.	202	33	8	13	12	20
Dec. 31 Surplus	203	83	27	74	37	23
Annual Accum.	202	33	8	13	12	20
Accum./Surplus	99.5%	39.8%	29.6%	17.6%	32.4%	87.0%

Source: Frederick Townsend, "Junk Bonds Can Devour A Life Insurance's Surplus," *National Underwriter,* March 6, 1989.

comparing the expected amount of defaults (2 percent annually has been used historically, however we suggest a higher annual loss rate of 2.5 percent) and comparing this to available surplus, a company can get a good idea of whether the cushion is sufficient over an extended time period. Regulators check companies' default records to determine whether a 2 percent annual rate is sufficient.

It is important to emphasize the role of the MSVR in high-yield investments for life insurance companies. Any medium- to high-risk investment has an MSVR requirement of 10 percent to 20 percent, while low-risk bonds are mandated at 2 percent. MSVR was introduced in 1951 for high-grade corporate bonds; long-term MSVR requirements for high-yield investments have not been tested. In 1988, the Securities Valuation Office announced that it will reevaluate the MSVR requirements for low-grade investments. We expect such requirements to change throughout the maturity process of high-yield bonds.

Holding		Six Largest U.S. Life Insurance Companies Ranked by Assets					
Presidential Life Ins.	United Pacific Life Ins.	Prudential Insurance	Metropolitan	Equitable Life, N.Y.	Aetna Life Ins.	Teachers Insurance & Ann.	New York Life Ins.
35.9%	28.3%	7.6%	2.1%	4.2%	3.7%	5.4%	0.0%
96	163	1,984	917	758	470	570	428
1,063	2,433	40,681	34,024	14,143	14,386	15,560	15,973
9.2%	6.7%	4.9%	2.7%	5.4%	3.3%	3.7%	2.7%
35	82	738	797	201	422	481	278
35.7%	50.3%	37.2%	86.9%	26.5%	89.8%	84.4%	65.0%
40	89	1,366	917	329	378	570	343
40.8%	54.6%	68.9%	100.0%	43.4%	80.4%	100.0%	80.1%
8	13	152	55	62	31	39	26
2.0	1.0	1.0	0.5	2.0	0.5	0.5	0.5
16	13	152	28	124	16	20	13
56	92	3,469	3,009	1,250	1,158	1,374	1,854
16	13	152	28	124	16	20	13
28.6%	14.1%	4.4%	0.9%	9.9%	1.3%	1.4%	0.7%

As explained in Chapter 4, the high-yield bond default experience has been measured by many research analysts. One of these studies, by Edward Altman, found an annual average 2 percent default rate in the high-yield market.[2] The actual loss rate was lower than 2 percent because defaulted bonds have some residual value after default. Such a default rate, however, has been experienced during a time of economic expansion. A slowdown in economic growth or a mild to severe recession may produce higher than historical default rates in the high-yield universe. Default rates by rating category over 3-, 5-, 7-, and 10-year periods are shown in Exhibit 4.

The NAIC's Securities Valuation Office recognizes these possibilities and expects to review such default rates in conjunction with new

---

2. Edward I. Altman, "Measuring Corporate Bond Mortality and Performance," *Journal of Finance* (September 1989), pp. 909–923.

EXHIBIT 4   *Adjusted Mortality Rates by Original S&P*
Bond Rating Covering Defaults and Issues, 1971–1988

Original Rating	Years after Issuance			
	3	5	7	10
AAA	0.00%	0.00%	0.21%	0.21%
AA	1.39	0.71	0.93	2.42
A	0.71	0.71	0.93	1.13
BBB	0.35	1.00	1.14	2.13
BB	1.07	1.86	7.48	10.70
B	4.72	11.54	20.31	30.88
CCC	8.01	24.64	N/A	N/A

Source: Edward I. Altman, "Research Update: Mortality Rates and Losses, Bond Rating Drift," unpublished study prepared for a workshop sponsored by Merrill Lynch Merchant Banking Group, High Yield Sales and Trading, 1989.

MSVR rates. As concerns increase regarding rising default rates in high-yield investments, only the larger surplus cushion companies will be able to become involved in higher risk investments. It is also noteworthy that at least 10 percent of the low-risk (YES) bond category is rated below investment-grade by rating agencies such as Moody's and Standard & Poor's. Some higher quality single B–rated companies have been categorized as YES bonds, which provide relatively higher yields with the lowest MSVR in insurance company bond portfolios.

Insurance company regulators look at the loss to capital account, including the high-yield portion of the MSVR, which may render a company insolvent, impaired, or in need of regulatory attention because of failed financial tests.

Managing a High-Yield Portfolio for Life Insurance Companies

High-yield bonds require intensive credit analysis to achieve proper risk balance and diversification. Insurance companies should have a fully staffed in-house research team or a professional money manager to perform this function. In addition, it is not recommended that high-yield portfolios be bought and put in a vault. They should be constantly monitored. William Smythe, Executive Director of the NAIC Securities Valuation Office, stresses the importance of a good in-house or outside manager, research, and trading staff.[3] As adverse credit developments occur in high-yield bonds, early sale of these securities can prevent large losses in market value. Smythe also stresses the need for intensive research and proactive management of such portfolios.

Though no consensus exists on the diversification of high-yield portfolios, a minimum of 30 issuers in at least 10 different industries is suggested, with no more than a 10 percent concentration in any one industry and with no more than 30 percent of a high-yield portfolio invested in CCC/Caa (NO** by SVO) issues. It is also recommended that at least 15 to 20 percent of a life insurance company's high-yield portfolio be in cash and short-term liquid securities. Although the NAIC's rating process is valuable in categorizing high-yield securities, additional credit research and trading capabilities are essential to maintaining a healthy portfolio. YES bonds are rated investment-grade by the NAIC's standards; however, other rating agencies may rate such bonds as low as single B. YES bonds are not disaster-proof. Focus on forward-looking rather than historical perspectives and quarterly financial monitoring are important to eliminate potential problems. It is also important to note that the NAIC updates its ratings only once a year and if adverse conditions develop with a particular credit, the rating may not immediately reflect the problems. Several YES bonds currently in default or trading at extremely distressed trading levels include Southmark Corporation, Nortek Corporation, and Jim Walter Corporation.

The most reasonable approach to managing high-yield portfolios requires a heavy dependence on a solid, experienced research staff. Obviously, diversification of issuers and industries further reduces risk of defaults in a high-yield portfolio. Industry analysis should be especially emphasized in order to monitor the cyclical issues within the portfolio. With cyclical industries appropriate caution should be

---

3. William Smythe, "Insurance Investments in Junk or Below-Investment Grade Bonds: Some Questions and Answers for Regulators," *Journal of Insurance Regulation* (September 1987), p. 4.

exercised, because the volatility risks are greater; however, high-yield managers can take advantage of upside potential in certain cyclical industries. Some of the most important areas for high-yield research are

1. industry fundamentals and sensitivity to changes in the operating environment
2. cash flow and operating income projections
3. financial flexibility, such as available lines of credit, ability to raise new equity capital, and possession of liquid assets
4. asset values, either whole or broken up
5. covenant packages and the amount of protection provided through debt restrictions, change of control provisions, net worth requirements, dividend limitations, merger and asset sales restrictions, and other covenants
6. equity components, on- and off-balance sheet liability valuation, and a company's accounting practices

We estimate that credit research constitutes over 85 percent of the total asset management process. Such research includes initial coverage of new issues and ongoing fundamental analysis of the portfolio holdings. Quarterly financial analysis is highly recommended for all of the issues within a high-yield portfolio. Early-warning indicators can be detected by analysts and managers through this process, helping to avoid large losses.

High-yield portfolios should also take advantage of market swings. It is important to be able to trade high-yield issues at advantageous periods in the market. A high-yield portfolio manager may take advantage of a security's spread relationship to Treasury securities, its rating, or industry peer group.

Successful, research-driven portfolio management of high-yield securities offers insurance companies higher current income and better long-term performance potential. We believe that insurance companies with well-managed high-yield portfolios are likely to grow more quickly and become more profitable over the longer term than companies that ignore this important asset class. Though debate will undoubtedly continue regarding the appropriate degree of exposure, many insurance companies are still avoiding the market entirely.

15

Performance Measurement

Martin S. Fridson, CFA
Managing Director*
Merrill Lynch Capital Markets

Measuring the performance of investment managers is a time-honored
tradition. A parable in the New Testament (Luke 19:11–27) tells of a
nobleman embarking on a journey who entrusts one mina (unit of
money) to each of his 10 servants, telling them, "Trade with these till
I come." In his absence, three of the servants earn profits of 1,000%,
500%, and 0%, respectively. Sounding a strikingly modern note, the
text further relates that as a penalty for his comparatively poor showing, the third servant's assets are transferred to the manager reporting
the best results.[1]

Two millennia have passed since that story was first told, yet financial theory still has not solved certain fundamental problems of

---

*This chapter is derived from research that the author conducted while employed at
Morgan Stanley & Co., Incorporated. He was assisted by Kevin M. Fitzpatrick and
James E. Lucas.
1. We cannot claim to be the first to comment on the New Testament's discussion of
performance measurement. For example, in *The Law and the Lore of Endowment
Funds,* published by the Ford Foundation in 1969, William L. Cary and Craig B.
Bright allude to the parable of the talents. This story, told in Matthew 25:14–30,
closely resembles the parable in Luke, but differs in certain details. In Matthew's version, the man who leaves on a journey divides his funds among just three servants
and in proportion to their abilities, rather than equally. The poorest faring servant,
however, suffers the same punishment meted out in Luke.

performance measurement. Although conceptually simple, the process of quantifying returns and evaluating managers proves extraordinarily difficult in practice. As we shall see, some of the difficulties that complicate the measurement of equity and investment-grade bond performance are especially acute in the high-yield area.

Absolute Ambiguity

At its simplest, most literal level, the phrase "performance measurement" means determining the absolute rate of return on a portfolio over a specified period. Relative return, a refinement discussed below, is to some investors' way of thinking a sham; they say they are interested in making money, not in losing less than others do.

Straightforward as the objective of measuring performance seems, the execution requires careful thought about reinvestment of coupons and the treatment of intraperiod contributions and withdrawals. More fundamentally, unless the entire portfolio is acquired on the first day of the measurement period and liquidated on the terminal date, return measurement depends on price indications, not actual transaction prices. In a highly liquid, central-exchange-oriented market such as large-capitalization U.S. equities, there is relatively little chance for distortion of returns through price quotations that vary from the true values of the securities. On the other hand, in over-the-counter markets in which two-sided quotations are provided only irregularly for many issues, pricing-related measurement problems can be meaningful.

An Indictment of Indexes

Assuming that pricing-related obstacles can be overcome—if not entirely, then at least to the investor's satisfaction—the next major challenge involves normalizing absolute returns for general market movements and for risk. Although a 20 percent rate of return may exceed an investor's long-run requirements, it is not a strong recommendation for hiring a manager if achieved during a period in which the high-yield sector as a whole returned 25 percent or if it was accomplished by incurring extraordinarily high risk during a period that happened to reward risk taking.

As with determining absolute returns, normalizing them seems to be a simple undertaking. Judging by the common practice, normalizing for the general market trend merely requires selecting an index that represents the total market in which one is investing and comparing the return on that index with the return on the portfolio being evaluated. This procedure ought to work well so long as the riskiness of the portfolio under consideration is equivalent to the riskiness of the index. If not, one has merely to compare index risk with specific portfolio risk, locate the specific portfolio on the risk axis of Exhibit 1 and determine whether its return places it above or below the Capital Market Line. A manager who achieves an above-market rate of return with the same level of risk as the Market Portfolio (i.e., the aggregate of all available assets) is deemed superior; below-market returns with market-level risk constitute inferior performance.

EXHIBIT 1   *Risk and Return in an Efficient Market*

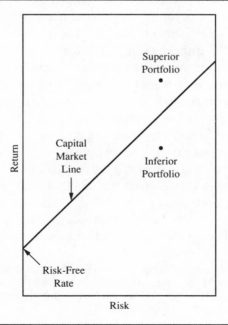

Real life, unfortunately, is not so simple. The analytical framework depicted in Exhibit 1 represents an ideal beyond the reach of practitioners.

Richard Roll, professor of finance at UCLA's Anderson Graduate School of Management, has argued that the commonly used (and in some cases almost universally accepted) performance benchmarks, including the Standard & Poor's 500 common stock index, are not equivalents of the market portfolio.[2] In technical terms, they all fail the test of mean/variance efficiency. (Simply stated, an index is not "optimal" in this sense if there exist securities not included in the index that, if added to the index portfolio, would reduce its risk — defined as volatility — without lowering its return.) Viewed in this light, the various efficient-market anomalies that have been documented over the years — low P/E stocks, small-capitalization stocks, stocks exhibiting relative strength, and so on — do not constitute genuine evidence of superior risk-adjusted performance by certain classes of securities. Rather, they demonstrate that the commonly employed proxies for the market are themselves inefficient because they are not "the market" but imperfectly representative subsets of it.

An important implication of the "benchmark error" phenomenon is that managers may be able to "game" the index by adopting strategies that exploit its imperfections. As Roll puts it, "Given that the market index is not an optimized portfolio, any of these [strategies] will consistently produce 'superior' results. Of course, this appearance is completely illusory, is due to benchmark error, and is not an indication of the portfolio manager's true ability."[3] In other words, the return achieved in this way does not exceed the return one would expect in light of an accurate assessment of the portfolio's true risk.

Based on an empirical test of his thesis, Roll finds that, "On average, then, even with an eight-stock portfolio, a manager could appear to outperform the S&P 500 by over 5% per annum simply because of benchmark errors. Undoubtedly, this apparent performance could be and probably has been improved upon by managers using more refined

---

2. Richard Roll, "Performance Evaluation and Benchmark Errors (I)," *The Journal of Portfolio Management* (Summer 1980), pp. 5–12, and "Performance Evaluation and Benchmark Errors (II)," *The Journal of Portfolio Management* (Winter 1981), pp. 17–22, hereinafter referred to as "Errors (I)" and "Errors (II)," respectively.
3. "Errors (I)," p. 9.

methods (such as choosing small firms and not correcting for non-synchronous trading)."[4] Note that pseudo-superior returns arising from benchmark errors are not simply random instances in which managers achieve above-average returns through luck. Variances of that sort will be statistically eliminated through repeated observations, but "repeated evaluations will not eliminate error in estimating the expected return, since the error will be present in the difference between the true performance and the estimated performance in *every one* of the evaluation periods."[5]

Discussing his work with us in connection with the present chapter, Roll confirms that his proposition is generalizable, applying to fixed income as well as to equities. If anything, he suggests, the nonoptimal index problem may be even more acute in high-yield bonds than in the stock market, given pricing-related questions of the variety discussed above. The high-yield universe is less broadly diversified and has fewer issues with long price histories than the equity universe.[6] Calculating an accurate mean, and therefore constructing an optimal index, is consequently more problematic. Attempts to measure high-yield managers' performance in a rigorous, risk-adjusted fashion will consequently require more effort than the reader might suppose. The problems are not so severe as to make it unwise to allocate a portion of one's assets to noninvestment-grade bonds, but they do underscore the fact that selecting a manager is not a matter of merely measuring performance relative to a universally recognized index.

Risk and Volatility

Since the publication of Roll's seminal articles on benchmark errors, many scholars have studied the degree of inefficiency in commonly used benchmarks. At the same time, some investment managers have argued that indicators such as the S&P 500 are, practically speaking,

---

4. "Errors (II)," p. 20.
5. "Errors (I)," p. 6. Italics appear in original.
6. Positively, the high-yield universe has become better distributed among industries over the past several years. See Martin S. Fridson, Steven B. Jones, and Fritz Wahl, "Anatomy of the High Yield Debt Market: 1988 Update," *High Performance* (February 1989), pp. 8–9.

satisfactory proxies for the idealized market envisioned by the Capital Asset Pricing Model. Notwithstanding the above-mentioned mechanical problems inherent in their construction, existing high-yield indexes might likewise be judged by practitioners to lie within acceptable tolerances. Even so, the measurement-versus-benchmark approach is vulnerable to attack on grounds altogether different from Roll's. Both Roll and the model he criticizes define "risk" as equivalent to volatility. In the high-yield market, investors may not be willing to accept this definition as comprehensive.

To understand why equating risk with volatility is not a satisfactory approach to analyzing high-yield securities, consider the two portfolios in Exhibit 2. Viewed in a mean/variance framework, the manager of the Low-Volatility Portfolio beat the High-Volatility Portfolio hands down in the performance game. The winning manager achieved a higher mean monthly total return (1.10 percent versus 0.94 percent) over the measurement period with less volatility (1.28 versus 2.47). Upon closer examination, however, it is not so clear that the "winner's" superior return was obtained with lower — or even equivalent — risk.

Several points of comparison complicate the risk adjustment process.

Liquidity. The average amount outstanding of the 10 issues in the Low-Volatility Portfolio is only $31.9 million. To put this figure in perspective, note that the average size of high-yield new issues in 1988 was $196.4 million. In today's market, a float in the $15 to $60 million range represented in Portfolio A is not sufficient to attract regular market makers other than the underwriter. Even the underwriter is likely to find it difficult to make a tight, two-sided market when called upon, because potential buyers will not have the benefit of regular research coverage by disinterested parties. (The rating agencies and investment banks tend to focus their analytical resources on the issues that trade with reasonable frequency.) Because of the small average issue size of his holdings, the manager of the Low-Volatility Portfolio would almost certainly incur higher transaction costs in a sudden, forced liquidation than his competitor who is running the High-Volatility Portfolio. The latter owns issues with an average outstanding amount of $240 million, including several "go-gos" that are

EXHIBIT 2   *Which is Truly the Lower Risk Portfolio?*[a]

Issuer	Coupon	Maturity	Price[b]	Amount Outstanding[b] ($ Million)	S&P Rating[b]	Direction of Last Rating Change in Measurement Period	Seniority[c]	Price Volatility[d]
				Low-Volatility Portfolio				
Arrow Electronics	12%	6/1/98	88.62	17.0	B–		Sub.	2.136
Banner Industries	12¼%	3/15/96	93.12	60.0	B–		Sr. Sub.	2.454
Fairfield Communities	14¼%	12/31/89	98.00	35.0	CCC+	–	Sub.	2.329
General Host	11⅞%	12/15/93	98.62	40.0	B		Sr. Sub.	2.526
Genesco	14¼%	12/15/94	103.37	16.6	B	+	Sr.	1.718
Horn & Hardart	11%	10/15/91	96.25	15.6	B–	–	Sub.	1.956
Kerr Glass	13%	12/15/96	99.62	40.0	B–		Sub.	2.372
Nortek	11½%	5/1/94	93.37	50.0	B–	–	Sr. Sub.	2.417
Orion Capital	12½%	12/1/97	101.25	20.0	B		Sub.	2.208
Standard-Pacific	12¾%	6/15/99	96.87	25.0	B	+	Sub.	2.336
			Average					
			97.19	31.9	B–	Upgrades: 2	Senior	10%
						Downgrades: 3	Subordinated	90%

Summary Portfolio Statistics
Average Monthly Total Return: 1.10%
Volatility of Return:[e] 1.28
Duration:[b] 4.35

EXHIBIT 2 *Continued*

Issuer	Coupon	Maturity	Price[b]	Amount Outstanding[b] ($ Million)	S&P Rating[b]	Direction of Last Rating Change in Measurement Period	Seniority[c]	Price Volatility[d]
High-Volatility Portfolio								
Colt Industries	10⅛%	12/1/95	95.37	150.0	B		Sr.	3.725
Continental Group	12.30%	5/1/05	98.00	75.0	BB−		Sr.	3.495
Eckerd Holdings	11⅛%	5/1/01	89.50	291.0	B−		Sub.	4.017
Heritage Communications	11½%	7/15/97	94.50	100.0	BB−	+	Sr.	3.711
MCI Communications	10%	4/1/11	90.25	575.0	BB+	+	Sub.	3.778
Mesa Capital	12%	8/1/96	97.50	300.0	BB+		Sub.	3.871
Middle South Energy	11%	5/1/00	100.75	300.0	BB	+	FMB	8.508
Philadelphia Electric	11%	4/1/11	100.37	350.0	BB+		Sr. Unsec.	4.481
Storer Communications	10%	5/15/03	78.12	139.0	B−	+	Sub.	4.357
Tesoro Petroleum	12¾%	3/15/01	87.00	120.0	B		Sub.	4.204
Average			93.14	240.0	BB−			
						Upgrades: 4	Senior	50%
						Downgrades: 0	Subordinated	50%

Summary Portfolio Statistics
Average Monthly Total Return: 0.94%
Volatility of Return:[e] 2.47
Duration:[b] 6.94

a. Measurement period: January 1, 1987 – May 31, 1989.
b. As of May 31, 1989.
c. FMB = First Mortgage Bond; Sr. = Senior; Sr. Unsec. = Senior Unsecured; Sr. Sub. = Senior Subordinated; Sub. = Subordinated.
d. Standard deviation of monthly price quotations.
e. Standard deviation of monthly returns for the entire portfolio. Note that this does not equate to an average of the price volatility of the constituent issues.
Source: Standard & Poor's.

traded daily by competing market makers and followed intensively by high-yield analysts.

Validity of Price Quotations. In all probability, the low volatility exhibited in the "winning" portfolio is illusory. When dealing with small issues that trade irregularly, pricing services (Standard & Poor's in our study) must rely heavily on "matrix" evaluations derived from actual transactions in other, ostensibly comparable issues. These somewhat hypothetical prices may not reflect the ups and downs of larger issues, such as those in the High-Volatility Portfolio, which trade frequently and therefore fully reflect general market fluctuations. The price variability observed in the go-gos pales in comparison with the potential declines in a sloppy market for small, illiquid issues that trade only on a workout basis.

Credit Quality. The Low-Volatility Portfolio has an average rating of B−, versus BB− for the High-Volatility Portfolio. Analysts may quibble about the accuracy of individual ratings, but it is a safe bet that in aggregate the lower rated portfolio would suffer a larger increase in its credit risk premium than the higher rated portfolio in the event of a more severe economic decline than has characterized this study's measurement period. In an especially severe crunch, the lower rated portfolio would probably suffer more of the drastic price declines that ordinarily accompany defaults.

Lest the reader imagine that the picture is distorted by rating changes that occurred during the measurement period, we have included in Exhibit 2 data on upgrades and downgrades. The data show that the Low-Volatility Portfolio not only ended the period with lower ratings but also deteriorated on balance (three downgrades versus two upgrades), while the High-Volatility Portfolio improved in quality (four upgrades and no downgrades). Incidentally, the fact that ratings changed on 50 percent of the Low-Volatility Portfolio during the 29-month measurement period argues against the otherwise plausible hypothesis that its small, inactive issues were underrated as a result of neglect by Standard & Poor's.

Seniority. Only 10 percent of the bonds in the Low-Volatility Portfolio have senior status in bankruptcy, versus 50 percent of the issues in the High-Volatility Portfolio. Holders of senior securities (whether secured or unsecured) generally recover a larger percentage of their principal value in the event of bankruptcy than do the holders of subordinated issues. Accordingly, by this measure, the High-Volatility Portfolio is superior in terms of capital preservation and hence less risky than the Low-Volatility Portfolio.

Dollar Price.   Besides seniority, another factor that influences recovery in bankruptcy is the dollar price paid for the security. In liquidation or in reorganization proceedings, the holder of a bond with $1,000 principal value has a claim of $1,000, regardless of whether she paid $1,100 or $500 for the security. Therefore, holders of two different *pari passu* issues may have the same downside (say, to 40 cents on the dollar). That downside, however, represents a larger potential percentage loss for the investor who bought an issue trading at 90 prior to default than for the investor who bought another security trading at 70.

On this basis, the Low-Volatility Portfolio, with an average dollar price of 97.19, is slightly riskier than the High-Volatility Portfolio, with an average price of 93.14. The High-Volatility Portfolio's lower average dollar price also constitutes an added measure of insulation against the risk of early redemption.

Duration.   Unlike the other measures we have mentioned, duration indicates lower risk for the Low-Volatility Portfolio. At 4.35, it is less sensitive to interest rate fluctuations than the High-Volatility Portfolio at 6.94. Given the overall trend of rising interest rates during the measurement period, the Low-Volatility Portfolio's lesser sensitivity was a benefit. The difference in duration also means that an increase in credit risk premium of a given number of basis points will cause a smaller price decline in the Low-Volatility Portfolio than in the High-Volatility Portfolio. By definition, however, a propensity for smaller price swings is what gives the Low-Volatility Portfolio its name. Accordingly, shorter duration, rather than being a risk-reducing benefit distinct from lower volatility, is to a great extent subsumed by it.

The lesson of this exercise is that a money manager can beat a system based on defining risk as volatility, simply by taking other risks not considered in the analysis. By buying illiquid issues that confound the pricing systems, a manager can create the illusion of low risk while simultaneously exposing the client to comparatively high probabilities of default and early redemption, as well as the risk of a comparatively large principal decline in the event of default.

Unfortunately, there is no established method for combining volatility with all of the other factors discussed here to form a single risk measure. Consequently, manager selection necessitates a thorough analysis of the candidates' past performance, rather than reliance on a single, overly simplistic method such as using volatility to gauge risk.

Peer Group Pressures

The difficulties of assessing overall risk, extensive though they are, do not mark the end of the problems encountered in comparing the performance records of high-yield managers. As we shall see, ranking managers within a peer group is a reasonable alternative to using an index to assess performance, but it does not eliminate the complications brought on by risk adjustment.

Indeed, even comparing raw, non-risk-adjusted returns of competing managers is far from a straight up-and-down exercise. Simply ranking managers on the basis of the most recent year's performance is an unsatisfactory approach. A poor judge of credits may post superb numbers during a 12-month stretch of low interest rates and booming GNP, but investors are more interested in knowing how his style has fared over several years. The longer the measurement period, the better, but might it not be unfair to compare one management firm's 10-year record against the (total) history of 3 years of another firm? Also, managers have a bad habit of changing firms — voluntarily or otherwise. Do managers take their track records with them when they leave, or are those records at least partially attributable to resources that may not be transportable? (These might include in-house research support and the ability to command "first call" coverage from Wall Street by virtue of controlling large asset bases.)

Any number of solutions can be devised for the dual problems of developing comparable return figures and adjusting for risk. Unfortunately, it appears that to date no one has come up with a theoretically well-supported method of unifying the two strands of analysis.

Consequently, the decision rules applied in peer group rankings — number of years of return considered, relative weighting of most recent versus longer term returns, definition of risk, and so on — are inevitably somewhat arbitrary. Many particular systems look fair on the surface, but the rankings they generate prove quite sensitive to the specific ranking method that is chosen. The investor who uses such ranking schemes to select a manager consequently finds that they offer contradictory advice and, to make matters worse, he cannot identify the "best" ranking system on the basis of any well-established theory.

As with a lot of other analytical issues, the complexities of performance ranking can most readily be illustrated in the mutual fund sector, where the data availability is greatest. For many readers of this chapter, the ranking of investment advisors is more relevant — they are either competitors in this segment or potential selectors of managers — but examining the question in the mutual fund realm brings out all of the important issues of ranking, regardless of sector.

A number of organizations publish mutual fund performance rankings, ranging from specialized consulting firms to business periodicals to consumer organizations. In some cases, the consultants' work is purchased and repackaged by the other purveyors of surveys, but even so, mutual fund buyers are presented with numerous competing formulas for assessing return and risk. The following survey of mutual fund surveys does not purport to be comprehensive, but includes enough examples to document the sensitivity of rankings to the methodology employed.

For the purposes of our analysis we concentrated on five surveys published within a few months of one another, thereby minimizing ranking differences related solely to timing differences. Brief discussions of these surveys follow.

Business Week, **February 27, 1989**

Separate from its equity fund survey, *Business Week* ranks taxable bond mutual funds within a single peer group that includes corporate, government, international, convertible, and closed-end funds. Observe that high-yield funds are ranked not just among themselves, but within a larger universe of fixed income funds.

Business Week utilizes data provided by Morningstar (discussed later). The overall ranking is based on three-year total return (adjusted for "load," i.e., sales charges) minus the risk-of-loss factor, which essentially is the Morningstar method of average shortfall versus Treasury bills, also calculated over three years. Within the peer group the resulting figures are plugged into a normal distribution to allow classification within the following categories:

↑↑↑	superior performance
↑↑	very good performance
↑	above-average performance
AVG	average performance
↓	below-average performance
↓↓	poor performance
↓↓↓	very poor performance

Among the other data reported but not explicitly reflected in *Business Week*'s rankings are asset size and growth, one-year total return, yield, average maturity, and a three-year analysis of performance by quartile.

Financial World, May 2, 1989

Utilizing data provided by Schabacker Investment Management, *Financial World* assigns rankings within a broad peer group that includes stock, corporate bond, government bond, municipal bond, balanced international, and gold funds. A Composite Performance Rating weights short-, intermediate-, and long-term past performance (adjusted for load), with an A+ rating placing a fund among the best performers and a D rating placing it among the worst. Rather than incorporating its Risk Rating into an overall ranking, *Financial World* lists it separately for each fund. The Risk Rating ranks the fund's volatility within the entire peer group (i.e., stock, bond, and other funds), with 1 representing the least risk and 5 the greatest risk.

As shown in Exhibit 2, the better performing high-yield funds tend to fall into *Financial World*'s B− Composite Performance Rating category and its 2 Risk Rating category. In one case we have not shown, however, a high-yield fund received a D (lowest ranking for performance) and a 1 (lowest risk). A result of this type reiterates the point made above that volatility is not a comprehensive measure of risk in high yield. Low but stable returns, as implied by D/1 ratings, may be the result of a perennially poor choice of credits, leading to a high incidence of default. If this is the case (which would require additional analysis to verify in the specific instance), characterizing the funds as low risk is absurd.[7] Although the purchase of exceptionally risky credits can stabilize returns by providing a high current yield, the strategy also maximizes the danger of principal loss in the event of a severe recession, which is closer to the average investor's notion of the risk in a noninvestment-grade bond fund.

Additional facts reported in the *Financial World* survey include asset size, net asset value, yield, and year-to-date and three-year performance and ranking.

Forbes, September 5, 1988

Forbes ranks a peer group consisting of a wide variety of domestic bond (both taxable and tax-exempt) and preferred stock funds. Its survey reports total returns for the last 12 months and for the period 1980 through 1988, on an average annual basis, using data provided by CDA Investment Technologies for the open-end fund figures. Load is reported separately. *Forbes* does not combine long- and short-term returns into an overall rating, instead focusing for ranking purposes on each fund's relative performance (vis-à-vis the Merrill Lynch corporate/government bond index) in up and down markets. (The up market and down market ratings are separate and not combined by *Forbes* into a single measure.) Letter ratings are distributed as follows within the bond/preferred peer group:

Rating	Percentile
A+	96–100
A	81–95
B	56–80
C	31–55
D	6–30
F	1–5

---

7. This same fund was rated low-return, high-risk under the Morningstar system described below, underscoring the sensitivity of rankings to the methodology employed.

Nonrating factors that *Forbes* reports include yield, asset size, and asset growth.

Morningstar, February 10, 1989

Chicago-based Morningstar publishes a biweekly subscription service entitled *Mutual Fund Values,* which ranks equity, fixed-income, and hybrid funds within 22 specific peer groups. The high-yield bond peer group contains 33 funds. Morningstar assigns its overall rankings (MFV ratings) according to the following scale:

*****	Buy
****	Above-Average
***	Neutral
**	Below-Average
*	Avoid

A fund's *MFV* rating represents an equal weighting of two scores:

Return Score. Total return, weighted according to the length of the available history, for example:

	Years of Return History Available		
	Ten	*Five*	*Three*
10-Year History	50%	—	—
5-Year History	30%	60%	—
3-Year History	20%	40%	100%
Total Weighting:	100%	100%	100%

(Load is reflected in the *MFV* ratings but not in the separately listed returns for each fund.)

Risk Score. The sum of monthly shortfalls versus the Treasury bill rate, divided by the number of months recorded, produces the average loss statistic. Funds are then ranked according to the following scale to produce the risk rating.

Risk Rating	*Percentile*
High Risk	90.1–100.0
Above-Average Risk	67.6–90.0
Average Risk	32.6–67.5
Below-Average Risk	10.1–32.5
Low Risk	0.1–10.0

Mutual Fund Values provides a full-page report on each fund, which includes (among other data) net asset value; a breakdown of total return by income and capital gains; yield; average weighted maturity, coupon, and price; number of issues; distribution of assets by rating; total returns; comparisons versus the Shearson-Lehman government/ corporate index; rankings within peer group and within the universe of all funds over 3-month, 6-month, 1-year, 3-year, 5-year, and 10-year periods; a list of the fund's 12 largest holdings; and a discussion of the portfolio manager's strategy and performance.

U.S. News & World Report, **February 6, 1989**

With data provided by Kanon Bloch Carre & Company, *U.S. News & World Report* ranks high-yield funds within a peer group that includes some tax-exempt and convertible funds. Its February 6, 1989, survey does not report scores for all funds, but instead lists the 10 best performers over the long term and (separately) for 1988 only. The long-run Overall Performance Index (OPI), a zero-to-100 ranking, is the one we employ in the following analysis. It reflects consistency of relative performance (versus all taxable bond funds in the case of taxable high-yield funds) over periods of 1, 3, 5, and 10 years. Longer term performance is weighted more heavily than shorter term performance, and an adjustment is made for performance during the past six bear markets. *U.S. News & World Report* does not adjust returns for load but provides for each fund a designation of "Load," "Low Load," "No Load," or "Deferred Load." The survey also reports asset size and breaks out the components of the OPI, that is, periodic returns and bear market performance grades.

Analysis of Surveys

While the mutual fund surveys described above generate data sufficient to support many pages of worthwhile analysis, we have limited our scope to the study of differences in the overall rankings of funds. This approach keeps our focus on our central point, namely, the sensitivity of results to the choice of methodology, a choice that is necessarily subjective. Because it is not our objective to recommend particular funds—especially not if the basis of selection is fallible—we

EXHIBIT 3 *High-Yield Mutual Fund Rankings in Selected Surveys*

| Fund | U.S. News & World Report | Morning-star | Forbes[a] | | Business Week | Financial World | |
			(Up Market/ Down Market)			Composite Performance Rating	Risk Rating
A	1	2	2	(B/A+)	↑↑↑	B−	2
B	2	5	3	(B/A)	↑↑↑	B−	2
C	3	4	4	(C/B)	↑↑↑	B−	2
D	4	3	1	(A/A)	↑↑	B−	2
E	5	1	5	(C/C)	↑	B−	2

a. Numerical ranking inferred by author from *Forbes* up market/down market ratings (see text).

have not listed the funds by name. (In any case, our survey of surveys does not present a fair basis for choosing a fund, because as we have already noted it does not purport to include all available mutual fund surveys.)

Exhibit 3 summarizes ranking data from the five surveys included in our study. Because *U.S. News & World Report* lists only the top performers, we have concentrated on the five funds that appeared both in the *U.S. News* survey and in each of the other four surveys. Other worthwhile findings would undoubtedly emerge from analysis of a broader spectrum of funds, but our limited analysis suffices to establish our basic point.

Note that to extract an overall ranking from the *Forbes* data we had to perform a transformation not sanctioned by the authors of that survey. *Forbes* suggests that a buyer may select a fund on the basis of an outlook on the market and that some funds will look more attractive under bullish assumptions while others will look better under bearish assumptions. We in turn have assumed that an investor who has no strong conviction either way will choose the fund most likely to perform best on average, no matter which direction the market may go. Accordingly, we have averaged each fund's up market and down market scores (counting A+ as 0.67, A as 1.00, A− as 1.33, B+ as 1.67, etc.) to determine an overall ranking.

The key implication of Exhibit 3 is that different methodologies employed in performance evaluation tend to rank managers similarly with respect to broad tiers, but not in terms of fine-tuned comparisons. For example, all five funds (which, remember, were drawn from *U.S. News & World Report*'s top performers) received identical B— (performance) and 2 (risk) ratings from *Financial World*. Since certain other high-yield funds received much different ratings in the latter survey, it appears that the *Financial World* method succeeded in classifying the best performers in one broad category that distinguished them from lesser performers. When it came to differentiating within a tier, however, the pecking order depended heavily on the specifics of the ranking scheme. For instance, Fund E, which by Morningstar's reckoning placed first among the five-member elite peer group, ranked fifth in the *U.S. News & World Report* and *Forbes* systems and received only the third-best performance ranking from *Business Week*. Similarly, Fund B received numerical rankings ranging from 2 to 5 and the top rating from *Business Week*. Fund D, which received perfect A/A ratings from *Forbes,* ranked fourth in the *U.S. News* survey and received only the second-best rating from *Business Week*. Only Fund A (1, 2, 2, *Business Week* top rating) may be said to have been ranked in almost perfectly consistent fashion among its peers.

Implications

As we have already argued, these findings derived from surveys aimed at mutual fund buyers have relevance as well to anybody charged with selecting an investment advisor. Instead of load one is considering fees, but otherwise the basic performance measurement issues are the same: What is the proper historical measurement period? Which managers belong in the peer group? Most important of all, how does one adjust for risk?

On the last point, none of the conductors of surveys discussed above can claim to have discovered the unquestionably correct approach to risk-adjusted performance measurement in high yield. Volatility, preferred by *Financial World,* is the criterion most strongly supported in the financial literature, but as we have seen, it can understate the risk incurred by managers who emphasize small, illiquid issues or who consistently select weak credits. Morningstar's method (also used in a variant form by *Business Week*) of quantifying the frequency with which a portfolio underperforms Treasury bills can perhaps claim the most ancient antecedents. In the New Testament parable discussed above, the nobleman criticizes his servant not only for earning 0 percent but also for not having at least put the money in the bank and paid his master the interest. His performance benchmark, in other words, is the epoch's closest equivalent to the risk-free rate. However intuitively appealing it may be, though, the T-bill shortfall method runs smack into the same problem that plagues all evaluation of historical returns, namely, identifying a suitable measurement period. Despite the similarities of their methodology, Morningstar ranks Fund B fifth while *Business Week* assigns it a top rating. Likewise, Morningstar's version of the T-bill method (weighted 3-, 5-, and 10-year measurement periods) puts Fund D in first place while *Business Week*'s (3-year period) assigns it a third-best rating. Which method is superior? No one can say. Likewise, the bull and bear market methods of *Forbes* and *U.S. News* (which are described only in general terms) have not yet been validated by rigorous academic research.

If the various performance measurement approaches currently in use produce different conclusions and no approach is indisputably the correct one, an investor seeking to select a high-yield manager cannot rely entirely on quantitative evaluations. Instead, performance rankings, adjusted for risk on whatever theory may be applied, should be used to identify the managers who do fairly well under everybody's system and to eliminate those on which the verdict is uniformly negative. Beyond that, a prudent investor has no choice but to dig in and subjectively evaluate the organizations under consideration.

The criteria for such evaluation are numerous. In a talk entitled "You Need More than Numbers to Measure Performance,"[8] Robert G. Kirby stressed the importance of personnel continuity in selecting an investment manager: "I would satisfy myself that the organization provided an environment in which it was rewarding to work so that good people would stay." Eileen Lynch of Wilshire Associates emphasizes the need for a fit between the endowment funds her firm advises and the managers it recommends. Compared to pension fund sponsors, endowment funds tend to be more yield- than total return–oriented and to require a lot of client contact. The ability to satisfy these

---

8. Presented at a seminar sponsored by The Institute of Chartered Financial Analysts and The Financial Analysts Research Foundation, Chicago, Illinois (April 2, 1976).

needs may be a decisive element when choosing a manager from among several with similarly strong performance records. Lynch also lists as a qualitative consideration the potential for disruption if a management organization takes on a new client that is inordinately large relative to its existing base. By the same token, a firm that is overly dependent on the fees generated by one existing client could suffer demoralization and resignations of key people if that one client were lost. A. Michael Lipper and Alling Woodruff of Lipper Analytical Services add the following advice:

> For most investors a fund that follows consistent basic policies in respect to portfolio structure and turnover rate is likely to produce a more predictable result than one that shifts policy frequently and rapidly, even if the more changeable fund occasionally produces a better result ... [A] fund that demonstrates more flexibility is likely to change policy after a new trend has already gotten underway, and thus will be playing catch-up ball. On the other hand, a fund that has a consistent policy that has recently had a period of poor relative performance is probably much closer to the point in time when it will have relatively good performance, unless it changes its policy.[9]

Kirby states the case for long-term consistency of approach even more emphatically:

> For some reason that I never will understand, it seems that no one involved in investment management and performance measurement has ever studied the history of the several large portfolios, with published data available, that have had outstanding records over periods of 25 or 30 years or more. Almost without exception, no matter how good the overall long-term record has been, the performance includes a couple intervals of from one-and-one-half to three years where the results were terrible.[10]

The pressure to change course at the wrong time is only one of several undesirable effects of misapplied performance evaluation. To the

---

9. A. Michael Lipper and Alling Woodruff, "Performance and Portfolio Analysis of Fixed Income Funds," in *The Handbook of Fixed Income Securities,* Second Edition, edited by Frank J. Fabozzi and Irving M. Pollack (Homewood, IL: Dow Jones-Irwin, 1987), p. 449.
10. Kirby, op. cit.

extent that contemporary investors are shifting managers more frequently on the basis of short-term performance and to the extent that
they are opting for incentive-based fee structures, they are increasing
the temptation of managers to game the index. Managers who sincerely
want to do what is best for their clients may not be able to afford re-
jecting strategies based on creating an illusion of outperforming without increasing risk. In short, by putting excessive faith in performance
numbers that are inevitably somewhat arbitrary, an investor may encourage his managers to act contrary to his interests.

Conclusion

Among our quoted sources for this chapter are articles dealing with
performance measurement problems in equities and investment-grade
bonds. The similarities between those markets and the high-yield market underscore the fact that a perfect measurement system is no prereq-
uisite to prudent investment. Nobody refuses to buy common stocks
because the S&P 500 fails to match a theoretical abstraction of the
Capital Asset Pricing Model. Similarly, the problems of performance
measurement should not deter anyone from investing in speculative-
grade bonds. True, it takes time and effort, rather than a simple measurement system, to scrutinize reported returns and purported risks.
An investor or fiduciary who makes the commitment, however, will
find that the better high-yield managers' portfolios rest comfortably
in the zone of satisfactory risk-adjusted performance.

SECTION IV

Investing in
Distressed Companies

16

Investing in
Chapter 11 Companies

Jane Tripp Howe, CFA
Senior Credit Analyst
Pacific Investment Management Company

The *Random House Dictionary* of the English language defines bankruptcy as "utter ruin, failure, depletion, or the like." No one would want to invest in a company that fits this description. On the other hand, many companies use the bankruptcy process to reorganize; this reorganization process often gives companies a new start that can provide rewarding investment opportunities. The key to success is to distinguish between the companies that are truly depleted and those that will reorganize successfully.

Historically, most investors who owned companies in bankruptcy did so by default. Today, however, many investors actively invest in companies in reorganization. These investors attempt to profit by taking advantage of the substantial inefficiencies in this market. This chapter gives the investor an understanding of the bankruptcy process and outlines a method for evaluating securities in bankruptcy.

Importance of Basic Understanding

Most investors believe that they will never have to deal with a company that has filed for protection under the Bankruptcy Code. Although

I wish to thank George Putnam III, publisher of Bankruptcy DataSource, for his helpful comments and suggestions.

this may be true for the majority of investors, as long as publicly traded companies go bankrupt, there will be investors who own the securities of the bankrupt companies. The possibility of owning the securities of one of these companies is increasing, as the number of companies filing for protection under the Bankruptcy Code has been increasing in recent years. A basic understanding of bankruptcy analysis is important for investors who find themselves in such a situation and also for investors who want to evaluate the potential rewards of this market.

Bankruptcy Process

Overview of Bankruptcy

There are two types of investors who deal with the securities of companies in bankruptcy. The first is the investor who owns the security by default. This type of investor purchases the security with the intention of profiting from a healthy company. The second type of investor buys the securities of bankrupt companies after the companies have filed for protection. Regardless of how the investor came to own the security, the analysis of the holdings is basically the same.

Investors who analyze their investment holdings carefully are unlikely to be surprised if one of their investments declares bankruptcy. The decline of a company into bankruptcy generally takes place over several years and is often the result of illiquidity and deteriorating operating performance. Although most bankruptcies can be predicted in advance through sound credit analysis, financially sound companies may also file for protection. For example, Johns Manville was profitable when it declared bankruptcy in August of 1982. Manville filed for bankruptcy because of the contingent liabilities arising from claims of individuals suffering from asbestos-related diseases, as well as from claims from property owners who incurred costs for the removal of asbestos materials from their property. Although bankruptcy filings for nonfinancial reasons are less easy to predict, they should not be complete surprises. For example, sometime in the future, tobacco companies could be faced with a similar situation regarding their contingent liabilities for illnesses caused by smoking.

All companies that file for bankruptcy are governed by the Bankruptcy Reform Act of 1978, which was signed into law by President Carter on November 6, 1978. The act became law on October 1, 1979. The purpose of the law is to provide a consistent procedure for the companies filing for protection under the law and to provide a framework under which a company can either reorganize or liquidate in an orderly fashion. Perhaps the most important facet of bankruptcy law is the protection it affords companies in distress. Filing for protection triggers the automatic stay provisions of the code. This provision precludes attempts by creditors to collect pre-petition claims from the debtor or otherwise interfere with its property or business. This provision gives the debtor breathing room to formulate a plan either of reorganization or orderly liquidation. Creditors are necessarily discouraged from racing to the court to dismember the debtor.

The current Bankruptcy Code consists of 15 chapters. Each chapter deals with a different facet or type of bankruptcy. For most investors, an understanding of chapters 7 and 11 is sufficient; these deal with corporate liquidation and corporate reorganization, respectively.

When a Company Files for Protection

When a company files for protection under the bankruptcy law it can do so either voluntarily or involuntarily. A voluntary petition is filed by the company declaring bankruptcy; in an involuntary bankruptcy, the petition is filed by the company's creditors.

When a company files for bankruptcy, it files in the appropriate circuit and the appropriate district within that circuit. (There are 11 circuits and 93 districts.) The appropriate court is not necessarily predictable. "Appropriate" can mean the court having jurisdiction over the company's headquarters location or perhaps the court having jurisdiction over its principal place of business. Companies have some flexibility in their choice of geographic location for filing. Eastern Airlines, for instance, filed in New York, even though its corporate headquarters is Miami. The company stated it filed in New York because it has substantial operations in New York, and its financial efforts and lawyers are there. Many of Eastern's creditors are also in New York, which will facilitate meetings.

When a company petitions for protection, its petition is accompanied by several items, including basic administrative information and a list of the twenty largest creditors. These creditors will be contacted by the court and called for a meeting. Other financial information is required within 15 days of filing. Sometimes, the financial information accompanies the filing; other times, it is delayed. Included in this financial information is a list of assets and liabilities as of the petition date. This list presents the company's best estimate of its assets and liabilities.

Significant adjustments are often made to the assets and liabilities by the time a company completes its reorganization process. The value of Eastern Airline's shuttle exemplifies how the value of assets can change. In the fall of 1988, Donald Trump was negotiating to purchase Eastern's shuttle operation for approximately $365 million. The negotiations were not completed when Eastern filed for protection in March 1989. Shortly after the filing, Trump stated that the shuttle's value had declined by perhaps as much as $125 million and that he wanted to renegotiate the deal. On March 31, 1989, Trump announced that he had reached an agreement with Texas Air to buy the shuttle for the original price of $365 million. However, the number of planes in the deal had been increased from seventeen to twenty-one.

These adjustments are also noticeable when the asset values are compared to estimates of the liquidation value of the assets. This is principally because the values are based on the company as an ongoing business. Although the assets and liabilities are not precise, they are useful in that they give an indication of the overall picture of the company. For example, when Manville filed for protection in 1982, it had more assets than liabilities and was a profitable company. On the other hand, when Worlds of Wonder filed on December 22, 1987, it listed $271.6 million in debts and $222.1 million in assets.

Once a company files for protection under the Bankruptcy Code it becomes a debtor-in-possession. As such, the company continues to operate its business under the supervision of the court. Usually, the debtor-in-possession needs to obtain court approval only for major items. Generally, the U.S. Trustee for the particular district is assigned to the proceeding. The trustee's duties are essentially administrative. The appointment of the U.S. Trustee has become fairly standard.

The increasing complexity of bankruptcies has resulted in the increased frequency of a second appointment to a bankruptcy case. This appointment is usually an examiner but can also be a trustee. The requirements for the appointment of an examiner are fairly broad. An examiner can be appointed if the appointment serves the interests of creditors, equity holders, or other interests. For example, an examiner was appointed in the case of A. H. Robbins because management had shown an inability to follow the bankruptcy rules. An examiner was also appointed in the case of Eastern Airlines, whose slide into bankruptcy was at least partially caused by striking unions. Shortly after Eastern Airlines filed for protection, the unions petitioned the court to have a trustee appointed to run the Company. Eastern management petitioned the court to have an examiner appointed rather than a trustee, so that it would have more flexibility in running its business. The federal bankruptcy judge in the Eastern case initially ordered the appointment of a "powerful" examiner who was given a broad mandate to end the strike. Later in the bankruptcy proceedings, the judge appointed a trustee. Sometimes, if there are allegations of negligence or mismanagement, an examiner will be appointed to investigate the allegations and report to the court. Occasionally, a trustee will be appointed by the court to take control of the business if there is gross negligence or mismanagement. This is relatively unusual. A recent case where a trustee was appointed was Sharon Steel, where there were allegations of fraud.

Proceeding toward a Plan

The purpose in filing for protection under the Bankruptcy Code is to give the debtor time to decide whether it should reorganize or liquidate and to formulate a plan for the chosen action. The intent generally is to reorganize successfully. The first step in formulating a reorganization plan is the appointment of committees. Generally, only a committee of unsecured creditors is appointed by the U.S. Trustee. Frequently, this committee is an elected subcommittee of the twenty largest creditors. The committee functions as a representative of the various classes of claimants. Its principal function is to help formulate a plan of reorganization that is equitable to all classes and that will be confirmed (approved) by the court and the claimants.

Although only one committee is usual, there has been a growing incidence of multiple committees, each representing a different class of creditors. For example, in the Manville bankruptcy, there were four committees, the Asbestos Litigants Committee, the Co-Defendants Committee, the Equity Holders Committee, and the Unsecured Creditors Committee. Often, the existence of multiple committees slows the bankruptcy process, as factions can develop that undermine the spirit of cooperation necessary to formulate a plan. Cooperation is necessary because plans of reorganization rarely work under a premise of absolute priority under which the most senior classes are paid in full before a less senior class receives anything. The negotiation process inherent in a reorganization generally grants all classes some token distribution in order to obtain their acceptance of the plan. This is the reason why shareholders often receive some percent of the equity of the reorganized company. (The percentage distributed to equity holders varies considerably, however. In recent proposed plans of reorganization, equity holders of Po Folks are to receive 0 percent, while equity holders of Allis Chalmers are to receive 19 percent.)

After the committee of unsecured creditors has been appointed, the debtor generally makes specific decisions about whether to assume or reject its executory contracts (contractual commitments for the provision of future goods or services entered prior to bankruptcy). In many bankruptcies, the rejection of high-priced contracts has been beneficial to the debtor. For example, when LTV declared bankruptcy, it was enabled to reject several high-priced contracts for raw materials. Several debtors have also rejected high-priced labor contracts. For example, in 1984, a bankruptcy judge upheld Continental Airline's decision to break its labor agreements with its pilots' union. The laws have changed for the rejection of labor contracts, however. Currently, collective bargaining agreements cannot be rejected so easily.

Formulation of a Plan

Once the committee or committees are in place, the formulation of a plan begins. The debtor has the exclusive right to file a plan of reorganization for 120 days. The length of the exclusive period is determined by the court and can be extended or shortened. (Generally, the exclusive period tends to be longer than 120 days.) No other plan from interested parties can be filed during this period. If filed, the debtor receives an additional 60 days to solicit acceptances of the plan.

However, this exclusive period does not stop other parties from formulating plans. In the case of Allegheny International, the unsecured creditors formulated a plan during the exclusive period (which had been repeatedly extended) because of their frustration with a perceived lack of progress. The first plan of reorganization often is not the final plan. It is common to see the first amended and second amended plans of reorganization. (During the spring of 1989, All Season's Resorts, Inc., was seeking approval of its fourth amended plan dated September 8, 1988.) Sometimes, even the debtor knows that its first formulation of a plan will not be its final formulation. This fact was evidenced by Allegheny actually labeling its August 30, 1988, Disclosure Statement "Preliminary." It is important to be mindful of the fact that at least one amendment to a plan is common before the plan is confirmed. Because amendments can entail significant changes in distributions to classes, it is important to ensure that the potential investor is working with the most recent plan of reorganization.

There are several ways to ensure that the investor is working with the most recent plan. One way is to keep in contact with the debtor. A second way is to keep in contact with the court in which the petition was filed. A third way is to subscribe to a bankruptcy service such as Bankruptcy DataSource in Boston, which has the advantages of being up to date and convenient.

In filing a plan of reorganization, a debtor with one or more subsidiaries must decide whether the plan will incorporate substantive consolidation of the subsidiaries. Under substantive consolidation, all of the assets and liabilities of the entities in question are pooled and used collectively to pay debts. Substantive consolidation must be approved by the court. The approval is not granted lightly. In order for substantive consolidation to be granted, proponents must prove that the parent and the subsidiaries in question operated as a single unit. This can be proved by means of such things as intercompany guarantees and transfers of assets. The issue of substantive consolidation can have important ramifications for the investor. For example, in the case of LTV, the aerospace/defense subsidiary was profitable and had assets in excess of its liabilities. On the other hand, the steel subsidiary was unprofitable at the time of filing and had liabilities significantly in excess of its assets. If LTV is reorganized without substantive consolidation, investors owning the securities guaranteed by the aerospace/

defense subsidiary will receive generous distributions. If substantive consolidation is granted, however, the distributions to these investors will be decreased, as the assets of the aerospace/defense subsidiary will be pooled to pay the debts of the entire corporation.

Disclosure Statement

Once a plan of reorganization has been finalized (and generally received the informal approval of the major creditors), the debtor produces and files a disclosure statement with the court for approval. A disclosure statement contains more detailed financial information about the debtor and the plan of reorganization, including reasons for filing. It also contains the comany's five-year pro forma statements, which are required by statute, and liquidation analysis of the company that supports the company's contention that creditors will receive a higher distribution under the plan than they would if the debtor were to be liquidated. Importantly, the disclosure statement is supposed to be more understandable and readable than the legal plan. Before approving the disclosure statement, the court must be satisfied that the information presented is accurate and provides sufficient information for the impaired classes to make a decision about whether to vote for the plan.

If the court approves the disclosure statement, the plan and the disclosure statement are mailed to the impaired classes for approval. Holders of claims that are not impaired — either the claims are paid in full or the interests they represent are not adversely affected by the proceeding — are not entitled to vote. This is because unimpaired classes are conclusively presumed to have accepted the plan. Classes that are entitled to vote are generally given 30 days to vote on the plan.

In order for a plan to be accepted, more than one-half of the number of eligible claims in each impaired class, comprising at least two-thirds of the amount of the eligible claims, and at least two-thirds of the outstanding shares of each class of interests must accept the plan. If the plan is approved by the voting classes, it is sent to the court for confirmation. When the court confirms the plan, it approves the transactions specified in the plan and approves a date for the reorganization to take effect.

Cramdown

It is interesting to note that a plan can be confirmed under the cramdown provisions even if the required number of creditors do not approve the plan. The confirmation of a plan under the cramdown provisions must meet several specific requirements. The plan must be shown not to discriminate unfairly with respect to any impaired class. Such a determination includes the requirement that no class receive more than 100 percent of the amount of its claim. In addition, each dissenting class must receive as much as it would be entitled to under liquidation. Often, plans state that the bankruptcy court will confirm the plan under the cramdown provision if all the requirements for confirmation are met except for the requirement that each class has accepted the plan.

Analysis of Companies in Reorganization

There are several different approaches that can be used to invest in the bankruptcy market. Large and aggressive investors buy a large block of the debtor's bonds and try to become a significant factor in the reorganization plan. Often these investors pool their resources in "vulture funds," which invest in the securities of bankrupt companies. Equities Strategies Fund, which invests heavily in the securities of bankrupt companies, exemplifies how this strategy can work. Equities Strategies Fund purchased a secured class of debt from the bankers of Anglo Energy, a Chapter 11 company. In the process, Equities was able to help design a reorganization plan that was favorable to the class of debt.

Not all such maneuvers are profitable. The Balfour Group, which also invests heavily in Chapter 11 companies, had hoped to profit in the Global Marine reorganization. The Balfour Group acquired a significant percentage of Global Marine's subordinated debentures, which it hoped it would be able to swap for a controlling interest in the reorganized company. Unfortunately for Balfour, the subordinated debenture holders received only a nominal stake in the company. Under Global's plan of reorganization, more than 90 percent of the equity in the reorganized company was distributed to the holders of secured debt.

Investing in Individual Securities

Another approach to investing in Chapter 11 companies, more suited to individual investors, is to buy specific securities in a bankrupt company. This approach has the advantage of not requiring a huge investment and thereby allows the investor to diversify his or her investments. It does require a significant commitment to analysis of the company, but it has the potential of being extremely profitable.

In buying the securities of a bankrupt company, the investor has the choice of investing for a general improvement in the overall condition of the company or of investing in situations (such as secured bonds) where the return is more quantifiable because of the assets. Itel and Charter exemplify investing in a company for a general improvement. In late 1981, investors could have purchased the common stock of Itel Corporation for $.25 ($2.875 on an adjusted basis) and sold it in the summer of 1987 at over $26 per share. In a similar manner, investors could have purchased the common stock of Charter Company at $1 per share in early 1985 and enjoyed an appreciation to $5 by the time Charter emerged from bankruptcy.

Penn Central's Series B preferred exemplifies the second type of investing. The Series B preferred was issued by Penn Central pursuant to the reorganization. The issue had a contingent payment feature. When Penn Central's rail operations were transferred to Conrail in 1976, a large disputed claim against the government resulted. The Series B preferred was to be paid off with the proceeds of this dispute, if any. Investors who purchased the Series B preferred at $4.125 received $20.00 per share less than one year later.[1]

Selecting the Universe

Investing in bankrupt securities starts with the selection of a universe of potential acquisition candidates. According to *The Broken Bench*

---

1. George Putnam III, *The Ten Largest Bankruptcies — And Their Lessons for Investors* (Boston, MA: New Generation Investments, 1987).

Review,[2] thousands of corporations each year file Chapter 11 petitions (16,620 filed for Chapter 11 in the 12 months ended June 30, 1988). However, many of these filings are made by corporations whose securities are not publicly traded or by very small corporations. In these cases, the individual investor could have difficulty obtaining sufficient financial information for analysis or difficulty purchasing the securities if analysis could be accomplished. Individual investors are well advised to confine their universe to companies that are publicly traded and that have assets of at least $25 million. Candidates fitting this description can be collected from a variety of sources. An individual investor will probably find a sufficient universe from which to select simply by consulting the business section of newspapers. All listed bankruptcies are identified by a symbol. All bankruptcies listed on the New York, American, and National Association of Securities Dealers Automated Quotations system's over-the-counter exchanges have a "vj" preceding the name of the stock. For example, BASIX Corp. was listed on the New York Stock Exchange Composite Transactions as of April 6, 1989, as "vjBASIX." The NASDAQ National Market Issues listings include an additional indication of bankruptcy. These listings are identified by a four or five letter symbol. The fifth letter indicates the issues that are subject to restrictions or special conditions. Securities that are in bankruptcy have a "Q" as the fifth letter of their symbol. For example, American Carriers was listed on the NASDAQ National Market Issues as of April 6, 1989, as "vjAmCarriersACIXQ." A reading of the business section of a major newspaper should keep investors current on recent bankruptcy listings.

Obtaining Financial Information

Perhaps the most difficult aspect of investing in Chapter 11 companies is obtaining financial information. Trading in the securities of small companies that have filed for bankruptcy can present problems if the companies are delisted. (If a company is delisted, its price can often be found on the National Daily Quotation Service "Pink Sheets," published by the National Quotation Bureau.) More importantly, financial information can be difficult to obtain after filing. Although SEC

---

2. *Broken Bench Review,* Vol. 7, No. 1, 1989, p. 9.

filing requirements are not suspended in bankruptcy, they are often neither strictly observed nor enforced. In addition, the financial statements that are filed with the bankruptcy court often contain minimal information. Therefore, a potential investor may want to limit her universe of candidates for investment to those Chapter 11 companies whose filings are current. This is not always necessary, however, if the investor uses other sources of information and invests only in those securities that are clearly undervalued using alternative methods of evaluation.

Once a list of candidates has been selected, the collection of financial information should begin. For each company, the investor should obtain the most recent annual report, 10-K, and quarterly report. In addition, the investor should obtain the 8-K, which reports on the bankruptcy, as this document may have useful facts about the filing. These documents will give the investor some indication of how the company has performed historically and perhaps why it declared bankruptcy. The investor should also collect information on the company's publicly traded securities. For stock, such data would include current shares outstanding and current price. The information that should be acquired for bonds is more substantial. For bonds, such data should include a complete description of the bond, the amount of bonds outstanding, price, and security (i.e., the specific assets supporting the bond). If the value of the security is known or can be estimated, this should also be listed. All bonds should be listed in order of seniority. Sometimes the securities data are found in the 10-K; more often the investor needs to consult the appropriate Moody's Manual (industrial, public utility, etc.). These are found in most libraries. It is also important to keep current on the news items that affect each of the companies being considered. The easiest way to do this is to use a computer news retrieval service such as the Dow Jones News Service (the Broad Tape), *The Wall Street Journal,* and *Barron's.* Finally, one should attempt to be placed on the mailing list of the companies being considered. This is sometimes difficult, particularly for those who do not own any securities.

Investing without a Plan of Reorganization

Perhaps the most important documents for the analysis of bankrupt securities are the most recent plan of reorganization and the accompanying disclosure statement. These documents give the investor the specifics of what each class of claimants (including each class of security holders) will receive upon reorganization. Without a plan of reorganization, investors must speculate on what most classes of security holders will receive. Investing without a plan of reorganization is not generally recommended for the individual investor, as it does not lend itself to thorough analysis. This inability to analyze thoroughly is particularly troublesome in the area of common stock. If one were to analyze distributions for numerous bankruptcies one would quickly observe the large variance of distributions for similar classes of claimants. This is most noticeable in the distributions made to common shareholders, who have received from 0 percent to a major portion of the equity in reorganized companies. Investors can, however, make intelligent decisions regarding some of the more senior debt of the debtor.

The valuation of the securities of a debtor that has not filed a plan of reorganization is similar to a liquidation analysis with one important exception: The company is assumed to be an ongoing business, therefore no substantial discount is applied to the value of its assets. Under this approach, the assets of the company are totaled and the liabilities are systematically subtracted from this total to give an approximation of how many assets are available to repay each class of claimants. Each class is subtracted in order of seniority. For example, the fully secured claims will be among the first to be subtracted. This approach has the advantage of being a quick valuation technique but has the drawback of imprecision. It can, however, be used even with somewhat dated financials. A useful extension of this methodology would be to apply the technique to both a full as well as a liquidation value of the company. This application would serve to bracket the value of the company with a worst case (liquidation value), as well as an optimistic case (full valuation). The application of this technique is outlined in Exhibit 1.

This approach is generally not applicable to the valuation of common stock simply because the assets are depleted before the common stock holders are eligible for a distribution. In order to estimate a value for common stock holders, one must make assumptions regarding a plan of reorganization and what percentage of the reorganized company's equity the old shareholders will receive. If this approach is used, the valuation of the common stock should follow the methodology presented later ("Investing with a Plan of Reorganization").

EXHIBIT 1 *Estimated Valuations of Securities*

Total assets	$xxx
Less collateralized debt	
Banks	xxx
Other	xxx
Amount remaining for distribution to other creditors	xxx
Other creditors in order of seniority	xxx

Secured Bonds

A major exception to the premise that investors should generally wait until a plan of reorganization is filed relates to secured bonds. When a company petitions for protection, it is subject to the automatic stay provisions of the Bankruptcy Code. These provisions generally disallow the accrual of interest during bankruptcy, but there is a major exception to this. Secured claims are allowed to accrue post-petition interest during bankruptcy to the extent of the value of the collateral. (Although post-petition interest is accrued, the code does not generally require that it be paid.) Given these provisions of the code, an astute investor could conceivably purchase a secured bond whose collateral exceeds the principal amount of the bond at a substantial discount to par, knowing that the bond eventually will be either reinstated or paid off at par plus post-petition interest. An example of how this provision of the Bankruptcy Code could have been beneficial to investors is provided by the LTV bankruptcy. When LTV filed for bankruptcy on July 1, 1986, all of its securities declined significantly. The overall decline overlooked the intrinsic value of the Youngstown Sheet & Tube First Mortgage Bonds, whose collateral exceeded the value of the bonds. These bonds, therefore, were entitled to the continuation of their interest.

An additional exception to the rule that investing without a plan is highly speculative relates to certain equipment trust financing. Much airline equipment debt and railroad equipment debt is exempt from the automatic stay provisions of the code and from the power of the court to repossess the equipment, due to sections 1110 and 1168 of the Bankruptcy Code, respectively. Instead, the court gives the debtor 60 days to reaffirm the lease on the equipment or return the equipment to the lessor. The debtor is unlikely to cancel the lease as the equipment leased constitutes the operating assets of the company, without which the company cannot operate. Airlines cannot operate without airplanes! Generally, in cases of Section 1110 equipment trusts, the debtor assumes the lease and resumes current interest payments, including interest payable during the 60-day period. Recent examples of Section 1110 equipment trusts are Eastern Air Lines' 16.125 percent Secured Equipment Trust Certificates, due 10/15/02, and Eastern's 17.5 percent Secured Equipment Certificates, Series A, due 1/1/98, and Series B, due 7/1/97. The fact that a particular equipment certificate is covered under Section 1110 is not part of the general description of the certificate. The investor must refer to the "Events of Default, Notice, and Waiver" section of the prospectus or indenture covering a given issue.

Investing with a Plan of Reorganization

The analysis of companies in bankruptcy that have filed plans of reorganization should be approached in the same systematic way that the analysis of any security is approached. However, there are two important differences. First, the analyst must place more emphasis on pro formas and less emphasis on historical results, because a reorganized company is generally significantly different from the company that filed for protection. Second, the analyst must be a combination equity/fixed income securities analyst. It is not always clear which of the securities of the reorganized debtor are the most attractive. Often, the relative rates of return among old securities are substantially reordered under the plan. The analyst must therefore be willing to value all securities of the debtor and purchase those that offer the highest potential returns.

Evaluation of the Plan

The first step in analyzing a company in reorganization that has filed a plan is to read the plan carefully and determine the distribution each class will receive upon reorganization. This effort should be conducted on a per share or per bond basis. Terms of new securities that are to be issued under the plan should be examined for incorporation into their valuation. For example, the dividends on the new preferred stock issue that was proposed in Coleco's January 1989 plan of reorganization can be paid in kind for the first two years, at the option of Coleco. Generally, pay-in-kind securities are discounted because of this feature. In valuing these securities, the analyst must be aware of this provision to accurately value the preferred.

The analysis of a plan should begin with a list of each class of creditor, the amount of the claim, the proposed distribution, the proposed distribution per security (where applicable), and the value of the distribution. For the hypothetical XYZ, Incorporated, this part of the analysis could take the form shown in Exhibit 2.

Frequently, there is only a total of 6 to 12 classes of creditors. These can be individually listed. Sometimes, as in the case of Allegheny, there are over 50. In these instances, it is wise to itemize only the relevant classes. The classes that should be listed are those classes containing publicly traded securities or classes receiving securities that will be publicly traded. By consolidating the proposed distribution in this manner, the investor can easily focus on the relevant securities.

It is also advisable at this point to chart the proposed equity ownership per class. This chart allows the investor to quickly convert changes

EXHIBIT 2   *Plan of Reorganization — XYZ, Incorporated*

Class	Amount of Claim	Total Distribution	Distribution per Security	Valuation per Security
1st Mortgage bonds	$100 million	$100 million plus accrued interest in cash	100%	100%
Debentures	$100 million	$100 million face value of debentures of reorganized debtor	100%	90%[a]

a. The amount of discount attributable to the new debentures is a function of coupon, credit considerations, etc.

EXHIBIT 3   *Proposed Equity Ownership of Wheeling-Pittsburgh*

Class	Number of Shares	Percent of Common
Secured claims under the bank mortgage	10,000,000	50.0
General unsecured claims	7,500,000	37.5
Preferred stock (five series combined)	1,000,000	5.0
Common stock	1,500,000	7.5

Source: Wheeling-Pittsburgh's Initial Plan of Reorganization, dated December 29, 1988, Bankruptcy DataSource, Boston.

in the valuation of the company into tangible values. A chart of equity ownership could take the form shown in Exhibit 3.

Wheeling-Pittsburgh's proposed equity ownership is fairly straightforward. Frequently, plans of reorganization also include warrants and options that can be exercised to acquire common stock. The chart of proposed equity ownership must include such potential dilution, as it is a significant factor in the valuation of the debtor's securities. The following chart of Coleco's proposed equity ownership exemplifies how significant dilution can be. Although Coleco's common shareholders are initially given 11.1 percent of the common stock of the reorganized company, this share can be potentially diluted to 3.9 percent (see Exhibit 4).

Determining a Price per Share for the Debtor

Once the specifics of the plan of reorganization are known, including potential dilution, the traditional analysis of the company should be performed. The analysis of the company should begin with the debtor's pro forma income statements, balance sheets, and cash flow statements, which are provided in the disclosure statement. Care should be taken to evaluate the debtor's assumptions in formulating these pro formas. Modifications should be made to the pro formas where the assumptions look doubtful. After the pro formas have been adjusted, an estimate of the company's value (in terms of price per share) should be calculated. One way of approaching this task is to apply

EXHIBIT 4   *Proposed Equity Ownership of Coleco*

	Number of Shares	Percent of Common	Fully Diluted Number of Shares	Percent of Common
Existing lenders	33,000 Pfd.	0.0%	27,500,000	43.0%
Unsecured claims	18,000,000 Common 11,500,000 Warrants	80.0	29,500,000	46.1
Preferred and common shareholders	2,500,000 Common	11.1	2,500,000	3.9
Management	2,000,000 Common 2,500,000 Warrants	8.9	4,500,000	7.0

Source: Coleco's Consolidated Plan of Reorganization, dated January 26, 1989, Bankruptcy DataSource, Boston.

valuation multiples. The analyst should estimate what range of multiples the stock should command in terms of earnings, sales, book value, and cash. The analyst can use the traditional approach of averaging the appropriate multiples of comparable companies and then applying these multiples to the company being analyzed.

In the case of Coleco, the analyst must first determine the market multiples of the toy industry. To estimate toy industry multiples, one should first select an industry sample of companies. In this example, Hasbro, Mattel, Tonka, and Tyco are used as the representative sample. These four companies were selected in part because they are all followed by Value Line, and therefore consistent projections of earnings, sales, book value, and cash flow were readily available. Once the sample was selected, Value Line's estimates for 1991–1993 for each of the companies were listed. These estimates are listed in Exhibit 5.

Once the estimates of these values have been logged, the range of valuations relative to price/share can be calculated for each of the sample companies by dividing the estimated prices by each estimate. As Value Line gives a range for estimated prices, it is necessary to divide the appropriate per share figure by both the high and the low price

EXHIBIT 5 *Toy Industry, 1991–1993 Value
Line Estimates*

	Price Range	Sales/ Share	BV/ Share	EPS	Cash/ Share
Coleco[a]		.38	3.70	.48	1.05
Hasbro	15–25	28.80	18.90	2.10	2.95
Mattel	8–14	24.50	6.90	1.10	1.75
Tonka	10–20	137.50	15.00	1.95	7.20
Tyco Toys	20–30	64.30	23.55	3.55	4.55

a. Company estimates from disclosure statement.

EXHIBIT 6 *Range of Valuations*

Price	Range
Sales/Share	.31 to .52
BV/Share	.87 to 1.49
EPS	6.29 to 10.84
Cash/Share	3.86 to 6.46

estimates. Once these calculations are made, the numbers should be averaged to generate an average range of valuations for the industry (see Exhibit 6).

To arrive at an estimated value for Coleco's common stock, one must multiply the above multiples (or more realistically, some discount of the multiples, to reflect the problems associated with the debtor) by the appropriate variable for Coleco. When these valuations are multiplied by the pro forma estimates of Coleco's sales/share, book value/share, EPS, and cash/share, the result is an estimated value of $2.60 to $4.42 per share. This looked attractive versus a March, 1989, price of $1.25. However, this price assumes that each old share of Coleco will own the same proportionate share of the new company. In fact, Coleco's January 1989 plan of reorganization provides that each old share will receive the equivalent of .14 new shares. Therefore, these prices must be discounted to reflect that a share purchased at current prices may only be worth .14 shares if the plan is confirmed. When the estimated valuation is discounted by 86 percent, as required, the estimated value declines to $.36 to $.62. At these levels, the stock is overvalued. It becomes even more overvalued when the potential dilution is considered.

Although the common stock of Coleco is overvalued, the analysis is not complete. The analyst should proceed to investigate the other securities of the debtor, if any. Sometimes, even if the common stock is overvalued, the debtor's bonds present a buying opportunity. In order to determine whether the bonds are undervalued or overvalued, the relationship between the current price of each bond and the valuation of its proposed distribution must be compared. Frequently, this is where value is found. In the case of Coleco, debenture holders are proposed to receive 43.17 shares and 27.58 warrants per $1000 of face value of debenture. The analyst must value these distributions to see whether the debentures reflect an undervalued situation. If the valuation of Coleco common stock outlined above is used, then the debentures are also overvalued at their March 1989 price of $11.00 ($110 per bond).

Although the above analysis of Coleco indicates that its securities are currently overvalued, it does not conclude that the securities should be forgotten. After completing the analysis, the analyst should maintain a list of valuations of each of the securities. These should be periodically compared to market prices. The securities should be purchased if they become undervalued. Importantly, new plans of reorganization should be screened to determine whether distributions have been changed. For example, if a new plan were to be proposed that eliminated the warrants and maintained Coleco's old shareholders' stake in the company, the common stock could become a candidate for purchase.

Conclusion

The analysis of bankrupt securities is multifaceted. The investor must analyze both the plan of reorganization and the debtor. The analysis should not stop once these two analyses are complete, however. Both the plan of reorganization and company prospects can change quickly and significantly when a company is in reorganization. The likelihood of these changes occurring must be factored into the analysis. These changes also signal the need for diversification in bankruptcy investing. The time element must also be factored into the analysis. Most bankrupt securities do not accrue interest during reorganization. Therefore, the investor must estimate when the company will emerge from bankruptcy to fully estimate values. As most bankrupt companies take at least a year to reorganize, and some have taken over seven years (Manville), the time element can be significant. In order to compensate for the time factor, the estimated recovery must be discounted.

17

Strategies for Investing in Distressed Securities

George Putnam III
President
New Generation Investments, Inc.
Boston, Massachusetts

The securities of companies in distress present opportunities for substantial returns, but they also present substantial challenges for prospective investors. The distressed securities market may be an inefficient niche, but it is inefficient for good reasons. Information about troubled companies is hard to come by and hard to analyze. And even after fully analyzing all the information available on a particular distressed situation, the investor is still faced with a large degree of uncertainty.

The world of distressed securities can be particularly perplexing to fixed income analysts. Most of the usual fixed income analytical tools are not available: bond ratings are often meaningless; there is no longer any yield; there probably are no earnings; and cash flow may be significantly negative. Moreover, the company that emerges out of the bankruptcy or restructuring process may look very different from the one that went in. In other words, historical financial information may have little or no value.

Even though the instruments you are buying may be called "bonds," they resemble equity securities in many ways. First, investors in troubled securities are almost always looking for capital appreciation rather than current return. Second, the analysis of troubled securities involves trying to predict the future prospects of the company. Finally, distressed securities always involve a substantial amount of downside risk, much like a stock.

There are three principal elements to any decision to invest in distressed securities: (1) choosing the companies in which to invest; (2) deciding which security (in terms of seniority) to purchase; and (3) determining the best time to buy.

Choosing the Companies

The following discussion sets forth broad strategies for selecting troubled companies in which to invest. Chapter 16 describes specific techniques for valuing distressed companies.

For a distressed security to be worth anything, there has to be some value in the company. The value can be in the form of substantial assets that can be liquidated to pay off creditors, or it can be in the form of a viable business that will generate earnings and cash flow in the future.

Assets

If you are looking to the assets to provide your return, you must find a situation where the true market value of the assets is not reflected in the security price. This undervaluation may be the result of security-holders overreacting to bad news about the company, or it may result from the market not realizing that certain assets may have much more value than is shown on the balance sheet.

An example of the first type of undervaluation can be seen in the period just before Public Service of New Hampshire filed for bankruptcy in January 1988. Bad news about the Seabrook nuclear plant drove down the prices of the company's mortgage bonds. After the bankruptcy filing, people began to look at the real value of PSNH's assets, and they realized that the company had plenty of assets to secure the bonds, regardless of what happened to Seabrook. Secured bonds that traded at $75 (per $100 of face value) in early January 1988 bounced back to $105 by June.

"Hidden" assets can provide even larger price appreciation. When the Penn Central and other eastern railroads went into bankruptcy in the 1970s, most people focused on the companies' troubled rail operations. They overlooked the fact that most of these companies owned very valuable real estate and other assets that were reflected on the balance sheet at minuscule historical costs. In many of the railroads these overlooked assets not only covered the bonds but also provided substantial value to the stockholders.

Going Concern Value

As pointed out in Chapter 16, it is very difficult to put a specific value on a bankrupt company until it distributes a plan of reorganization and disclosure statement. Until that time, it is usually more fruitful to look for broad indications of likely value rather than to try to calculate precise numbers. The following are some of these key indicators.

Core Business. The most important characteristic to look for in a troubled company is a solid core business. If a company is going to successfully reorganize, it must have at least one line of business that will provide both immediate cash flow and the opportunity for future growth.

The company's chance for survival may be further enhanced if it has some assets that can be sold off to raise cash without destroying the core business. These assets may be whole lines of business or just assets that are not essential to the core business. The cash raised can be used to pay off creditors and to bolster the company's core business.

This ability to sell assets or ancillary businesses favors large, multi-line companies, and historically they have fared the best in bankruptcy or restructuring proceedings. Smaller, single-business companies have nothing to fall back on or sell when they get into trouble. They often end up being liquidated or sold, with little or no return to the securityholders.

The core business on which a company bases its survival need not be its biggest or best-known line of business. For example, Interstate Stores entered bankruptcy as a chain of full-line department stores and emerged a few years later as Toys R Us, a toy discounter. Similarly, Itel Corporation was best known in the late 1970s as a computer and high-tech leasing company. It went into bankruptcy in 1981 and emerged in 1983 as a lessor of railroad equipment and shipping containers. These comparatively mundane businesses were overshadowed by Itel's computer business in its high-flying days, but they provided the foundation on which Itel reorganized. Itel has since continued to prosper by going into other low-technology businesses such as dredging.

Ability to Satisfy Obligations.　Most companies get into trouble because they are unable to generate enough cash to satisfy their financial obligations. Therefore, if a company is going to successfully reorganize, it must somehow get its cash inflows and outflows back into balance. It can either increase cash inflows or decrease its obligations.

Usually, by the time a company is in distress, it has exhausted its means of increasing revenues. This means that it must be able to reduce either its operating costs or its financial costs. On the operating side, a troubled company will close facilities, lay off workers, and sometimes even reduce management salaries.

On the financial side, the company can sell off assets and use the proceeds to pay down its debt. If it is unable to raise cash to pay creditors, the company must persuade its creditors to accept less than the full amount they are owed (which often means accepting stock in lieu of debt). This last approach is likely to cause the securityholders some pain, and so it is desirable to find companies that can still cut costs or sell assets to raise cash.

It is interesting to note that the steps that a distressed company takes to raise cash are very similar to the steps that new management usually takes after a leveraged buyout of a healthy company — cut overhead to the bone and sell off all ancillary assets. This means that when a post-LBO company gets into trouble, its only remaining course of action is to restructure its debts, usually to the severe detriment of its securityholders.

New Management.　More often than not, the management team that led a company into trouble is not going to be able to lead the company back to health. Sometimes it is poor management that led to the problems. Sometimes old management has lost the confidence of the creditors. And sometimes special turnaround expertise is needed to get the company back on its feet. At any rate, a change in top management is usually desirable at a troubled company.

Special Problems. Sometimes a basically healthy company will be in distress because of one particular problem. This often takes the form of a large legal liability. For example, Manville (asbestos liability), A. H. Robins (Dalkon Shield product liability), and Texaco (Pennzoil judgment) all were forced to file for bankruptcy to deal with special legal problems. If the special problem can be isolated and resolved, the company will return to health.

In many of these special situations, the securities of the troubled company will be undervalued because of uncertainty over whether the liability can be resolved. For example, Robins stock dropped as low as $8 per share in the early stages of its bankruptcy before recovering to over $30 per share. Similarly, Texaco's stock and bonds all had nice gains during its bankruptcy.

Not every security fares well in these special situations, however. Sometimes value must be taken away from securityholders to compensate the claimants in the lawsuits. For example, Manville's common stockholders saw the value of their shares drop steadily throughout the bankruptcy proceedings, from $16 per share a few months before the filing to less than $1 per share when the company emerged from bankruptcy.

Industry-wide Distress. Where an entire industry is suffering, you may be able to find good companies whose securities are temporarily trading at distressed prices. When industry conditions improve, or at least stabilize, the securities of the stronger companies can appreciate sharply.

This happened in recent years in the U.S. energy industry. The securities of the companies that survived the turmoil in the mid-1980s showed good gains in the last year or two of the decade. However, it can be important to identify the companies that are likely to avoid bankruptcy. Securityholders fared badly in most of the energy companies that went into Chapter 11.

Big Players. Finally, it can sometimes be profitable to follow in the footsteps of a large investor that specializes in distressed companies. Such an investor will usually take a significant position in one class of a company's securities and play an active role in the restructuring. If the large investor succeeds in influencing the outcome to its advantage, other investors that hold the same securities will also benefit.

Choosing the Securities

It is important not only to pick good companies, but also to pick the right classes of securities to fit your objectives. The different levels of securities in a distressed company can have very different risk/return characteristics.

The leveraging of corporate America in the 1980s has created a number of troubled companies with very complex capital structures. For example, LTV Corporation, which filed for bankruptcy in 1986 (and is still in bankruptcy as this is being written), has more than 30 different classes of publicly traded securities. Although each security has its own unique characteristics, the LTV public securities can be broken down into at least nine different categories that are likely to be treated quite differently in the reorganization: (1) mortgage bonds secured by LTV's more modern plants; (2) mortgage bonds secured by the older plants; (3) parent company senior unsecured bonds; (4) steel subsidiary senior unsecured bonds; (5) parent company subordinated bonds; (6) steel subsidiary unsecured bonds; (7) aerospace subsidiary unsecured bonds; (8) preferred stock; and (9) common stock.

The risk/return characteristics of these various classes are ultimately derived from their claims on the assets of the company if it is liquidated. At least in theory, in a liquidation each class must be paid off in full in order of seniority before the classes below it can receive anything. In a bankruptcy reorganization this rule of "absolute priority" may not always be strictly followed, but it at least provides the basic framework for distributions to different classes.

Except as noted below in the discussion on secured bonds, coupon rates on bonds usually do not play a major role in determining return once the issuer goes into bankruptcy. Also, maturity date is usually irrelevant once a company files for bankruptcy.

In general, the securities of distressed companies follow the basic risk/return rule: the higher the risk (i.e., the greater the uncertainty), the higher the possible return. The following discussion considers the principal features of different security classes and their implications for potential risk and return. It also looks at the possible significance of different legal issuers, such as parent and subsidiary, and discusses the consequences of buying private versus public debt obligations.

Secured Debt

Secured debt generally has the lowest level of risk, but both the risk and the ultimate return from secured debt depend on the value of the assets securing the debt. Obviously, if the liquidation value of the assets is less than the principal amount of the debt, the holders of the debt will not be paid off in full if the company is liquidated. However, the value of the assets also can affect the securityholder's return in other ways.

First, if a debt is adequately secured at the commencement of a bankruptcy proceeding, the holder of the debt is entitled to have interest continue to accrue during the bankruptcy. Absent full security, a debt holder is entitled to claim only unpaid interest that accrued prior to the bankruptcy filing—known as pre-petition interest—and not interest accruing after the filing—post-petition interest. If the bankruptcy court can be convinced of the adequacy of the asset coverage, it may even allow allow interest to be paid currently during the bankruptcy proceedings. For example, Public Service of New Hampshire's first and second mortgage bonds have been paying interest throughout the bankruptcy proceedings.

Unfortunately, the adequacy of the asset coverage may be in dispute right up to the end of the bankruptcy proceedings. Any uncertainty about asset coverage can have a substantial impact on the market price of "secured" bonds. For example, LTV Corporation has two groups of secured bonds outstanding. They are both first mortgage bonds secured by steel-making facilities. One group is secured by the facilities of the former Youngstown Sheet & Tube Co., and the other is secured by plants of the former Jones & Laughlin Steel Co. The Youngstown facilities are considered to be very modern and to provide adequate security for the applicable bonds; the value of the Jones & Laughlin facilities are more questionable. As a result, throughout LTV's bankruptcy the Youngstown bonds have traded from 30 percent to 100 percent above the Jones & Laughlin bonds with almost identical coupons.

Also, where asset coverage is clearly inadequate, secured bondholders may face the unfortunate prospect of being given priority over other claimants only to the extent of the value of the underlying assets. The balance of their claim may be treated as a general unsecured claim. For example, where a court found that the assets securing a certain bond issue were worth only 40 cents for each $1 principal amount of bond, the bondholders would be given priority treatment for only 40 percent of their debt, with the other 60 percent being treated on a par with trade debt, unsecured debt, or other seemingly junior securities.

Potential returns on distressed secured bonds depend on how quickly and accurately the market values the underlying assets. At one end of the spectrum, the Youngstown Sheet & Tube bonds mentioned previously have roughly doubled in price over the nearly four years since LTV filed for bankruptcy. At the other end of the spectrum, investors were well aware of the value of aircraft securing some of Eastern Air Lines' bonds, and so the bond prices barely budged when the company filed for bankruptcy.

Unsecured Bonds

The term "unsecured bonds" can cover a variety of debt instruments, ranging from senior debt that comes ahead of everything but secured obligations to junior subordinated debt that comes behind everything except the equity interests. Thus, the first step in analyzing an unsecured bond is to determine exactly where it ranks among the company's obligations. This depends on the covenants in the indenture under which the bond was issued.

The next step is to try to estimate how much value is likely to be distributed to the holders of the bond in question. To figure the minimum amount that should be received by the bondholders, you can take the liquidation value of the company and assume that all securities senior to yours will be paid off in full (following the "absolute priority" rule mentioned above). Whatever value is left would be available for distribution to your class.

Unfortunately, the foregoing analysis is not always very helpful, for several reasons. First, in a complex bankruptcy, even the liquidation value of the company may be hard to determine. Second, the going concern value of the company may be substantially higher than the liquidation value and will therefore ultimately determine the value of the bonds. Finally, the reorganization plan is likely to deviate from the absolute priority rule.

Although the absolute priority rule always applies in theory, every bankruptcy or other restructuring is in fact a negotiation process. In a vigorously negotiated bankruptcy, various parties may decide it is in their best interest to compromise some of their rights. For example, senior bondholders may be willing to let more value flow down to the junior bondholders in order to expedite the reorganization. Though the senior bondholders might ultimately prevail if they insisted on absolute priority, the junior securityholders could perhaps tie up the proceedings for years with various motions and appeals.

As a result, any valuation process other than liquidation value based on absolute priority is tenuous at best. The investor must try to predict what the company will look like when the reorganization is complete, how much the new company will be worth, and how that value will be divided among various classes of creditors.

In general, the more junior the security, the greater the uncertainty surrounding its ultimate value. This greater level of uncertainty, of course, also leads to greater appreciation potential. It is not unusual to see junior bonds double or triple in value during a bankruptcy. Unfortunately, it is also not uncommon to see junior bonds receive only a few cents on the dollar for their claims.

Securities Issued by Different Entities

In some situations, particularly those involving large companies, there technically may be more than one issuer of the securities involved. For example, in the LTV case, some of the unsecured bonds were originally issued by the parent company, some were issued by the steel-making subsidiaries, and others were issued by the aerospace subsidiary.

In some such situations, the bankruptcy cases may be "substantively consolidated" and the various issuers treated identically. In other cases, however, the court will decide that different corporate entities should be treated differently. This is likely to happen where one entity is viewed as having more value than others and where it has historically been treated separately from the rest of the corporate family.

In addition to the LTV case, where it is not yet clear how the consolidation question will be resolved, the significance of the issue can be seen in the case of Allegheny International. While the company has not yet emerged from bankruptcy, the parties have apparently agreed to different treatment for various Allegheny subsidiaries. Under the company's reorganization plan, bonds issued by Allegheny International are expected to be exchanged for mostly stock and are trading for $25, while bonds of comparable seniority issued by Allegheny's Chemetron and Sunbeam subsidiaries are expected to receive cash and new notes; they are trading at $71 and $87, respectively.

Nonpublic Claims

In recent years, a number of investment firms have begun investing in, and even trading, bankruptcy debt obligations other than public securities. These private debt obligations include the claims of creditors such as bank lenders, trade suppliers, and industrial revenue bondholders. These claims can vary in their level of seniority, depending on the nature of the underlying debt of the company.

The advantage of buying private claims is that they can often be obtained at a lower price than comparable public securities. The holders of the private claims may be willing to sell their claims at substantial discounts because they need liquidity or because they just do not want to be involved in the bankruptcy proceeding.

The disadvantage of private claims is that they are less liquid and involve more paperwork than public securities. Although some securities firms are beginning to make markets in private claims, the buyer of a private claim should probably expect to hold it for the duration of the bankruptcy. Also, all transfers of private claims must be approved by the bankruptcy court. Some judges are beginning to question the process of trading private claims, and in a few cases they are even imposing requirements that buyers provide certain disclosures to the sellers of the claims.

Equity Securities

When a company goes into bankruptcy, its equity securities (common and preferred stock) are treated basically like very junior bonds, and they should be analyzed in much the same way. The equity holders are entitled to whatever value is left in the company after all of the other creditors have been satisfied.

Preferred stock is theoretically entitled to its liquidation preference before any distribution is made to the common stock. This is rarely the case in actual practice, though, particularly when the various equity classes are sharing a relatively small distribution. In some cases preferred stock is treated identically to the common, and in many other cases it receives a modest premium over the common.

Only if the debt holders are paid off more or less in full are you likely to see the preferred receive a much higher return than the common. For example, in the Manville reorganization preferred holders received new securities worth about $27 per share, while the old common stock was exchanged for new common worth only about $1 per share.

Some companies have several different classes of preferred with different levels of seniority and different liquidation preferences. It is difficult to generalize about whether the differences will ultimately be recognized in a reorganization plan — sometimes the different preferreds are treated differently and sometimes they are all treated identically.

The common stock of a troubled company is usually worth considering only if you think the company will be able to avoid filing for bankruptcy. After the company goes into Chapter 11, the stock almost always fares poorly. Although there have been some spectacular gains from bankruptcy stocks in the past, in recent years creditors have been leaving less and less value for the stockholders. The old common usually gets very heavily diluted as new stock is issued to satisfy creditors. In a typical reorganization old stockholders may receive 5 percent or less of the equity in the reorganized company, and it is not uncommon, particularly in smaller bankruptcies, for the stockholders to receive nothing at all.

There has been only a handful of bankruptcies in the last few years where you could have made money by buying the common stock after the company went into bankruptcy (other than perhaps by trading on the sharp, short-term swings that bankruptcy stocks sometimes take). Most of the few bankruptcy stocks that have done well have been "special" bankruptcies such as Texaco and A. H. Robins.

The New Value Theory

In bankruptcy law there is one exception to the absolute priority rule discussed previously, known as the *new value theory,* which is worth noting because it may affect the returns on bankruptcy bonds in the future. This approach says that the bankruptcy court may depart from absolute priority when a party injects new value into the bankrupt company. This infusion of new value, so the theory goes, may entitle the investor to a larger stake in the company than it would otherwise receive.

This concept is presently being used by the stockholders of Revco, a bankrupt drug store chain, to try to maintain a substantial equity holding in the company. Revco was one of the first leveraged buyouts to fail, and when it went into bankruptcy it had nearly $1.5 billion in debts. After creditors proposed a reorganization plan that would have given the old stockholders (principally the LBO group) less than 5 percent of the stock in the new company, the stockholders countered with a proposal to inject $150 million of new money into the company in return for 55 percent of the equity.

At this point the Revco case is still pending, and it is not clear whether the new value theory will allow the Revco shareholders to improve their position. However, the theory is likely to be used in other bankruptcies in attempts by junior securityholders to improve their position.

Timing

After identifying a promising company and deciding what class of security to buy, you must then determine the best time to make your purchase. The various types of securities often follow different trading patterns over the course of a bankruptcy or restructuring proceeding.

Before Bankruptcy Filing

The first timing decision, when looking at a company that appears headed for bankruptcy, is whether to buy before or after it files for Chapter 11. Usually, it pays to wait. Virtually all stocks and most debt securities drop when the bankruptcy filing is announced. The exceptions are companies whose troubles are well recognized and where bankruptcy is viewed as a positive, stabilizing factor. This was the case with Public Service of New Hampshire, and most of its debt securities hit bottom before the Chapter 11 filing.

Many distressed companies try to avoid bankruptcy by offering to exchange new, less onerous securities for outstanding issues. It is difficult to generalize about strategies for dealing with these exchange offers. The success or failure of a particular exchange depends largely on the terms of the offer and the mood of the securityholders. To date, relatively few exchange offers have succeeded. However, many companies are currently attempting or considering exchange offers, and new trends may be developing.

One developing trend worth noting is known as the *prepackaged* Chapter 11 filing. In these cases, a company will present its creditors with a reorganization plan and obtain their approval before filing for Chapter 11. If the company has lined up enough creditor support, the bankruptcy proceedings will be short, serving merely as a formal structure for implementing the plan. A few smaller public companies (such as Anglo Energy and Crystal Oil) have successfully used prepackaged bankruptcies over the last few years, emerging from bankruptcy a few months after filing. The concept is just now being tried by larger companies with more complex capital structures, such as Republic Health and Resorts International, and it remains to be seen how successful they will be.

During Bankruptcy

Once a company files for bankruptcy, there are a number of stages in the proceedings at which an investment can be made. Generally, in the early stages, the uncertainty level is the highest, but so is the gain potential.

As mentioned above, in most cases a company's securities will fall in price immediately after the bankruptcy filing. If the filing is a surprise, they will fall sharply; if the filing is expected, the drop will be modest. Then, it is not unusual to see the prices bounce up somewhat a few days after the filing. This price action may be due to speculators who do not really understand the situation thinking that bankruptcy automatically means bargains. Or it may result, at least in part, from short-sellers covering their positions.

After the initial flurry of activity surrounding the filing, many bankruptcy securities will drift lower for several, sometimes many, months. What happens during this period seems to be largely determined by the company's level of visibility.

Eastern Airlines, which was a well-known company and was in the news almost daily during the early part of its bankruptcy, saw its securities decline for only a few days and then begin to rebound. (A year later, however, the securities finally did fall sharply as the business deteriorated.) Other companies in bankruptcy go for years without issuing a press release or even making a filing with the SEC. (In theory, every public company must continue to make its regular filings with the SEC, but in actual practice many bankrupt companies do not.) The securities of these companies usually have little activity and gradually decline until favorable news begins to come out.

The duration of bankruptcy proceedings varies considerably. A successful prepackaged bankruptcy can take only 2 or 3 months. Most publicly traded bankruptcies take about 18 to 36 months, but some can take much longer. The ten largest companies to emerge from bankruptcy in 1989 spent from 13 to 82 months in bankruptcy. The average length of bankruptcy was 29 months and the median was 26 months. The longest bankruptcies are often those involving complex issues that must be litigated. For example, Manville, with its asbestos liability, remained in Chapter 11 for more than 6 years.

In general, there is no need to rush into a situation following the bankruptcy filing. As the foregoing discussion indicates, it usually takes at least several months for bankruptcy securities to bottom out. The principal exception to this is where the bankrupt company is viewed as an acquisition target.

Over the last few years, a number of major companies have been "put in play" as acquisition candidates while in Chapter 11. For example, A. H. Robins agreed to be acquired by American Home Products as the way to emerge from bankruptcy. Even giant Texaco was the subject of acquisition speculation during its bankruptcy. More recently, Allegheny International, Eastern Airlines, and Public Service of New Hampshire have all been involved in merger negotiations while in Chapter 11.

Acquisition rumors often begin shortly after a bankruptcy filing, and they can send the target's securities sharply upwards. However, as in the nonbankruptcy acquisitions, there is a substantial risk that the acquisition will not take place. (In fact, bankruptcy acquisitions are probably even harder to consummate than nonbankruptcy acquisitions.) When an acquisition proposal falls through, the securities can plummet. Some of Allegheny's bonds went from about $40 shortly after the bankruptcy filing to over $90 a few months later as two competing investment groups bid for the company. Then both potential acquirors backed off, and the bonds went into a decline that eventually took them down to below $20.

Many bankruptcy securities follow a calendar pattern that is worth noting. Particularly when there has been little or no positive news, these securities tend to drop fairly sharply in the last month or two of the year. Apparently, some holders sell to realize their losses for tax purposes, and others are probably trying to "clean up" their portfolios for year-end reports. Then in January these securities often rebound, to varying degrees.

For stocks and some of the lower priced bonds, these year-end swings can be quite significant, at least on a percentage basis. Baldwin-United stock provided a dramatic example of this pattern, first in 1984 and then again in 1985. After a bankruptcy filing in September 1983, Baldwin's stock declined during 1984 from a high of $3\frac{1}{4}$ to a low in late December of $\frac{5}{8}$. Then, in January it jumped to $2\frac{1}{2}$, a gain of 300 percent from the December low. The stock sagged again in late 1985, getting down to 1 in December, but in January 1986 it bounced back up to $3\frac{1}{2}$. From there it declined again to less than 1 when the company emerged from bankruptcy in November 1986.

When a Plan Is Filed

As noted in Chapter 16, the filing of a plan of reorganization usually provides the first real indication of what the company is likely to be worth when it emerges from bankruptcy. At that point, you can use the techniques discussed in Chapter 16 to value the company's various securities. However, there are two additional questions that must be answered before you can rely on the value that you calculate: (1) how close is the plan to being in its final form? and (2) how long will it be until the plan is put into effect?

In some bankruptcies, the company files only one plan that is quickly approved by its creditors and the court; in other cases, plans are filed well before the various parties have reached agreement. For example, at least 12 different reorganization plans have been filed for Allegheny International, and nearly as many for Public Service of New Hampshire.

If it appears that a particular plan does not represent a consensus among the company and its creditors, you must try to predict the direction that future plans will take. Generally, recalcitrant parties must be given more value to persuade them to accept a new plan. Unless new value can be added to the company, value must be taken away from one class of creditors to give to others. There is also a risk that the value of the whole company will deteriorate as the creditors continue to wrangle.

The Allegheny and Public Service of New Hampshire situations provide contrasting examples of how value shifts can occur as a succession of plans are proposed. In Allegheny the value of the whole company has been shrinking as the bankruptcy wears on. As a result, junior bondholders and stockholders have been faring worse and worse with each new plan. In PSNH, by contrast, several competing bidders have been sweetening their offers for the company, and so the positions of the junior securityholders improve with each successive plan.

A delay in implementing a plan can also have a significant effect on returns. For example, Manville's plan of reorganization was approved by the bankruptcy court in December 1986, but a series of appeals, which went all the way up to the U.S. Supreme Court, delayed the effective date of the plan until November 1988. This delay reduced the returns that many holders expected to receive from their Manville securities. And the stock market crash in October 1987 made the wait even more painful for many Manville creditors.

When valuing bankruptcy securities based on a plan of reorganization, it can be useful to look for arbitrage opportunities. Some securities, particularly stocks, are slow to react to the terms of a reorganization plan. For example, when Western Company of North America was emerging from bankruptcy in early 1989, its plan called for some of its old bonds to be exchanged for new stock. Based on the exchange ratio and the market price of the bonds in late February, you could obtain the new stock at a price of $5.67 per share by buying certain bonds. The old stock was also being exchanged for new stock but at a much less favorable ratio. To obtain new stock by buying old stock you would have had to pay $19.76 per share.

Two Final Keys to Any Strategy

As you can see from this chapter, there are a variety of strategies for investing in distressed securities with quite different risk/return characteristics. However, there are two key elements that should be part of any such strategy: diversification and patience.

Diversification is important because virtually every strategy involving distressed securities is fraught with uncertainty. The vagaries that make the analysis of "normal" securities challenging are compounded by the special characteristics of the workout/bankruptcy process. Even the most thorough analysis can be thwarted by a recalcitrant creditor, an unpredictable judge, or many other factors. The only defense against this uncertainty is diversification.

Also, the same factors that make turnarounds particularly uncertain tend to make them particularly slow. This is especially true of bankruptcies. The American judicial system has many great characteristics, but speed is not one of them.

Despite these disadvantages of uncertainty and long duration — or perhaps because of them — distressed securities can be very profitable. To achieve those profits you must discern a company's general prospects for survival, dissect its capital structure to find the security that best fits your goals, and estimate the timetable for the company's recovery.

INDEX